What Readers Are Saying About *Rails Recipes, Rails 3 Edition*

Even the best chefs are loathe to re-create a recipe from scratch if they know a good one already exists. Rails programmers would do well to code like a great chef cooks and have this tome on their shelf.

➤ **David Heinemeier Hansson**
Creator of Ruby on Rails; partner at 37signals; coauthor of *Agile Web Development with Rails*; and blogger

Rails Recipes is a great resource for any Rails programmer. The book is full of hidden gems (no pun intended) that many programmers may not discover in their daily quest to get the job done.

➤ **Gary Sherman**
Principal of GeoApt, LLC; chair of QGIS PSC; and author of *The Geospatial Desktop*

Rails Recipes has always been the definitive guide for aspiring Rails developers. It doesn't just cover how you could build something, but delves into the details and explains all the reasons why you should build it that way. You can be sure that if you follow the tips and tricks in this book, you're on the right path.

➤ **Michael Koziarski**
Software developer, Rails Core team member, and partner, Southgate Labs

Superlative. This readable, engaging book strikes a balance between laying out a practical solution to a problem and teaching the principles and thought processes behind it. You learn how to fix a problem today and gain the insight you need to avoid problems in the future.

➤ **Alex Graven**
  Senior developer, Zeevex, a division of InComm

Rails Recipes is a great book for any Rails developer. There is so much going on in the Rails community these days that I find it hard to keep all of it in context. This book provides the context I need.

➤ **Mike Gehard**
  Lead software engineer, Living Social

Rails Recipes

Rails 3 Edition

Chad Fowler

The Pragmatic Bookshelf

Dallas, Texas • Raleigh, North Carolina

Many of the designations used by manufacturers and sellers to distinguish their products are claimed as trademarks. Where those designations appear in this book, and The Pragmatic Programmers, LLC was aware of a trademark claim, the designations have been printed in initial capital letters or in all capitals. The Pragmatic Starter Kit, The Pragmatic Programmer, Pragmatic Programming, Pragmatic Bookshelf, PragProg and the linking *g* device are trademarks of The Pragmatic Programmers, LLC.

Every precaution was taken in the preparation of this book. However, the publisher assumes no responsibility for errors or omissions, or for damages that may result from the use of information (including program listings) contained herein.

Our Pragmatic courses, workshops, and other products can help you and your team create better software and have more fun. For more information, as well as the latest Pragmatic titles, please visit us at *http://pragprog.com*.

The team that produced this book includes:

John Osborn (editor)
Potomac Indexing, LLC (indexer)
Kim Wimpsett (copyeditor)
David J Kelly (typesetter)
Janet Furlow (producer)
Juliet Benda (rights)
Ellie Callahan (support)

Printed in the United States of America.
ISBN-13: 978-1-93435-677-7
Printed on acid-free paper.
Book version: P1.0—March 2012

Contents

Part III — User Interface Recipes

Part IV — Testing Recipes

Part V — Email Recipes

Part VI — Big-Picture Recipes

Part VII — Extending Rails

Introduction

What Makes a Good Recipe Book?

If I were to buy a *real* recipe book—you know, a book about cooking food—I wouldn't be looking for a book that tells me how to dice vegetables or how to use a skillet. I can find that kind of information in an overview about cooking.

A recipe book is about how to *make* food you might not be able to easily figure out how to make on your own. It's about skipping the trial and error and jumping straight to a solution that works. Sometimes it's even about making food you never imagined you *could* make.

If you want to learn how to make great Indian food, you buy a recipe book by a great Indian chef and follow his or her directions. You're not buying just any old solution. You're buying a solution you can *trust* to be good. That's why famous chefs sell lots and lots of books. People want to make food that tastes good, and these chefs know how to make (and teach *you* how to make) food that tastes good.

Good recipe books *do* teach you techniques. Sometimes they even teach you about new tools. But they teach these skills within the context of and with the end goal of *making something*—not just to teach them.

My goal for *Rails Recipes* is to teach you how to make great stuff with Rails and to do it right on your first try. These recipes and the techniques herein are extractions from my own work and from the "great chefs" of Rails: the Rails core developer team, the leading trainers and authors, and the earliest of early adopters.

I also hope to show you not only *how* to do things but to explain *why* they work the way they do. After reading through the recipes, you should walk away with a new level of Rails understanding to go with a huge list of successfully implemented hot new application features.

Who's It For?

Rails Recipes is for people who understand Rails and now want to see how an experienced Rails developer would attack specific problems. Like with a real recipe book, you should be able to flip through the table of contents, find something you need to *get done*, and get from start to finish in a matter of minutes.

I'm going to assume you know the basics or that you can find them in a tutorial or an online reference. When you're busy trying to *make* something, you don't have spare time to read through introductory material. So if you're still in the beginning stages of learning Rails, be sure to have a copy of *Agile Web Development with Rails* [RTH11] and a bookmark to the Rails API documentation handy.[1]

Rails Version

The examples in this book, except where noted, should work with Rails 3.1 or newer. All of the recipes that were part of the first edition of this book have been updated to Rails version 3.1, and several recipes cover new features that became available with that release.

Resources

The best place to go for Rails information is the Rails website.[2] From there, you can find the mailing lists, IRC channels, and blogs of the Rails community.

Pragmatic Programmers has also set up a forum for *Rails Recipes* readers to discuss the recipes, help each other with problems, expand on the solutions, and even write new recipes. While *Rails Recipes* was in beta, the forum served as such a great resource for ideas that more than one reader-posted recipe made it into the book! The forum is at http://forums.pragprog.com/forums/8.

The book's errata list is at http://books.pragprog.com/titles/rr2/errata. If you submit any problems you find, we'll list them there.

You'll find links to the source code for almost all of the book's examples at http://www.pragmaticprogrammer.com/titles/rr2/code.html.

If you're reading the PDF version of this book, you can report an error on a page by clicking the "erratum" link at the bottom of the page, and you can

---

1.   http://api.rubyonrails.org
2.   http://www.rubyonrails.org

get to the source code of an example by clicking the gray lozenge containing the code's filename that appears before the listing.

Acknowledgments

Thank you for reading this book. Thanks to everyone else who made the book what it is.

Specifically, thanks to the following technical reviewers who read the last drafts and provided valuable input: Akira Matsuda, Mike Gehard, Rick DeNatale, Alex Graven, and Ryan Bates.

Chad Fowler
mailto:chad@chadfowler.com
March 2012

Part I

Database Recipes

The model layer of an MVC application is arguably the most important. It's where your business logic lives. And business logic is the heart of almost any application. Active Record and its libraries are packed with features that allow us to model our domains richly and efficiently. These recipes will show you some of the highlights as well as some of the lesser-known secrets of model development in Rails.

Create Meaningful Many-to-Many Relationships

Problem

Sometimes, a relationship between two models is just a relationship. For example, a person has and belongs to many pets, and you can leave it at that. This kind of relationship is straightforward. The association is all there is to track.

But relationships usually have their own data and their own meaning within a domain. For example, a magazine has (and belongs to) many readers by way of their subscriptions. Subscriptions are interesting entities in their own right that a magazine-related application would probably want to track. A subscription might have a price or an end date. It might even have its own business rules. Thinking about the connections between entities as you model them can create a richer, more fluent domain model.

How can you create meaningful many-to-many relationships between your models?

Solution

To model rich many-to-many relationships in Rails, use join models to leverage Active Record's has_many :through() macro.

When modeling many-to-many relationships in Rails, many newcomers assume they should use the has_and_belongs_to_many() (habtm) macro with its associated join table. For years, application developers have been creating strangely named join tables in order to simply connect two tables. But habtm is best suited to relationships that have no attributes or *meaning* of their own. And, given some thought, almost every relationship in a Rails model deserves its own name to represent its function in the domain being modeled.

For the majority of many-to-many relationships in Rails, we use *join models*. Don't panic: this isn't a whole new type of model you have to learn. You'll still be using and extending ActiveRecord::Base. In fact, join models are more of a technique or design pattern than they are a technology. The idea with join models is that if your many-to-many relationship needs to have some richness in the association, instead of putting a simple, dumb join table in the middle of the relationship, you can put a full table with an associated Active Record model.

Let's look at an example. We'll model a magazine and its readership. Magazines (their owners hope) have many readers, and readers can potentially have many magazines. We might first choose to use habtm to model this relationship. Here's a sample schema to implement this approach:

```
rr2/many_to_many/beginning_schema.rb
create_table :magazines do |t|
  t.string   :title
  t.datetime :created_at
  t.datetime :updated_at
end

create_table :readers do |t|
  t.string   :name
  t.datetime :created_at
  t.datetime :updated_at
end

create_table :magazines_readers, :id => false do |t|
  t.integer :magazine_id
  t.integer :reader_id
end
```

As you see here, the table joining the two sides of the relationship is named after the tables it joins, with the two names appearing in alphabetical order and separated by an underscore. You would then say that the Magazine model has_and_belongs_to_many :readers, and vice versa. This relationship does the trick, enabling you to write code such as this:

```
magazine = Magazine.create(:title => "The Ruby Language Journal")
matz = Reader.find_by_name("Matz")
magazine.readers << matz
matz.magazines.size # => 1
```

Now imagine you need to track not only current readers but everyone who has ever been a regular reader of your magazine. The natural way to do this would be to think in terms of subscriptions. People who have subscriptions are the readers of your magazine. Subscriptions have their own attributes, such as a length and a date of last renewal.

It is possible with Rails to add these attributes to a habtm relationship and to store them in the join table (magazines_readers in this case) along with the foreign keys for the associated Magazine and Reader entities.

However, this technique relegates a *real*, concrete, first-class concept in our domain to what amounts to an afterthought. We'd be taking what should be its own class and making it hang together as a set of attributes hanging from an association. It feels like an afterthought because it is.

This is where join models come in. Using a join model, we can maintain the convenient, directly accessible association between magazines and readers while representing the relationship itself as a first-class object: a Subscription in this case.

Let's put together a new version of our schema, but this time supporting Subscription as a join model. Assuming we already have a migration that set up the previous version, here's the new migration:

`rr2/many_to_many/db/migrate/20101127162741_convert_to_join_model.rb`
```ruby
def self.up
  drop_table :magazines_readers
  create_table :subscriptions do |t|
    t.column :reader_id, :integer
    t.column :magazine_id, :integer
    t.column :last_renewal_on, :date
    t.column :length_in_issues, :integer
  end
end
```

Our new schema uses the existing magazines and readers tables but replaces the magazines_readers join table with a new table called subscriptions. Now we'll also need to generate a Subscription model and modify all three models to set up their associations. Here are all three models:

`rr2/many_to_many/app/models/subscription.rb`
```ruby
class Subscription < ActiveRecord::Base
  belongs_to :reader
  belongs_to :magazine
end
```

`rr2/many_to_many/app/models/reader.rb`
```ruby
class Reader < ActiveRecord::Base
  has_many :subscriptions
  has_many :magazines, :through => :subscriptions
end
```

`rr2/many_to_many/app/models/magazine.rb`
```ruby
class Magazine < ActiveRecord::Base
  has_many :subscriptions
  has_many :readers, :through => :subscriptions
end
```

Subscription has a many-to-one relationship with both Magazine and Reader, making the *implicit* relationship between Magazine and Reader a many-to-many relationship.

We can now specify that a Magazine object has_many() readers *through* their associated subscriptions. This is both a conceptual association and a technical one. Let's load the console to see how it works:

```
$ rails c
>> magazine = Magazine.create(:title => "Ruby Illustrated")
 => #<Magazine id: 1, title: "Ruby Illustrated", ...>
>> reader = Reader.create(:name => "Anthony Braxton")
 => #<Reader id: 1, name: "Anthony Braxton", ... >
>> subscription = Subscription.create(:last_renewal_on => Date.today,
                    :length_in_issues => 6)
 => #<Subscription id: 1,
        reader_id: nil,
        magazine_id: nil,
        last_renewal_on: "2010-11-27",
        length_in_issues: 6>
>> magazine.subscriptions << subscription
 => [#<Subscription id: 1,
        reader_id: nil,
        magazine_id: 1,
        last_renewal_on: "2010-11-27",
        length_in_issues: 6>]
>> reader.subscriptions << subscription
 => [#<Subscription id: 1,
        reader_id: 1,
        magazine_id: 1,
        last_renewal_on: "2010-11-27",
        length_in_issues: 6>]
>> subscription.save
 => true
```

This doesn't contain anything new yet. But now that we have this association set up, look what we can do:

```
>> magazine.reload
>> reader.reload
>> magazine.readers
 => [#<Reader id: 1, name: "Anthony Braxton", ...>]
>> reader.magazines
 => [#<Magazine id: 1, title: "Ruby Illustrated", ...>]
```

Though we never explicitly associated the reader to the magazine, the association is implicit through the :through parameter of the has_many() declarations.

Behind the scenes, Active Record generates a SQL select that joins the tables for us. For example, calling reader.magazines generates the following:

```
SELECT "magazines".* FROM "magazines"
  INNER JOIN "subscriptions" ON "magazines".id = "subscriptions".magazine_id
  WHERE (("subscriptions".reader_id = 1))
```

With a join model relationship, you still have access to all the same has_many options you would normally use.[3] For example, if we wanted an easy accessor for all of a magazine's semiannual subscribers, we could add the following to the Magazine model:

ManyToManyWithAttributesOnTheRelationship/app/models/magazine.rb
```
class Magazine < ActiveRecord::Base
  has_many :subscriptions
  has_many :readers, :through => :subscriptions
  has_many :semiannual_subscribers,
           :through => :subscriptions,
           :source => :reader,
           :conditions => ['length_in_issues = 6']
end
```

We could now access a magazine's semiannual subscribers as follows:

```
$ rails c
>> Magazine.first.semiannual_subscribers
 => [#<Reader id: 1, name: "Anthony Braxton", ... >]
```

Sometimes, the name of a relationship isn't obvious to you. For example, aren't users just *in* groups? Over years of working with join models, I've learned that the step of trying to name the relationships helps flesh out my domain model in a positive way. Indeed, users are in groups, but that relationship is a membership. Are there other missing domain models you can think of?

---

3. One exception to this is the :class_name option. When creating a join model, you should instead use :source, which should be set to the name of the association to use, instead of the class name.

Create Declarative Named Queries

Problem

One of the most obvious advantages of Rails is its emphasis on declarative programming. A Rails application speaks the language of its domain, rather than littering itself with low-level configuration and implementation details. For example, rather than embedding ugly SQL statements in a controller to find the most active users on a site, it's much more expressive to write something like User.most_active, which returns a collection of User objects.

How do we write queries in our models so that we can best take advantage of the declarative style that makes Rails so great?

Solution

Many of us launch into Rails development and blissfully take advantage of the declarative, concise syntax available for features such as one-to-many relationships and controller development, but when it comes time to query a database, we fall back on our old SQL habits. In a Model View Controller application, you only ever want to see SQL code in the model.

Many aspects of Rails development are made simple because Rails supports a declarative style of web application development. In fact, Rails is so declarative that some developers refer to it as a domain-specific language for web development. That's a fancy way of saying that, where possible, Rails lets you code in terms of your application's actual requirements instead of its low-level implementation details.

Active Record's "scope" macro allows you to declare named, composable, class-level queries on your models. But most of us start out writing our queries directly in the controllers, like this:

rr2/declarative_scopes/app/controllers/wombats_controller.rb
```
class WombatsController < ApplicationController
  def search
    @wombats = Wombat.where("bio like ?", "%#{params[:q]}%").
                      order(:age)
    render :index
  end
```

That works, it uses the model, and since Rails as a framework gets out of our way, it actually doesn't look that bad to the eye of a new Rails developer. But we've broken a cardinal rule of Rails development: we put model code in the controller. A reader of this code has to drop down into another level of abstraction to understand what the controller does. Reading this code, we'd have to look not just at what the original author *means* the code to do but also at *how* it does it. A more readable version of this action might look like this:

```
def search
  @wombats = Wombat.with_bio_containing(params[:q])
  render :index
end
```

Now someone reading this code can very easily understand what it does without worrying about how it does it. That's what we want in a controller. We've asked the model to do the work, and we can ignore it unless we need to specifically change how it does its job. In addition, it's now easier to test, since we can completely test this code in a simple unit test. So, how do we make this model code work?

The obvious, naive option would be to write a class-level method such as the following implementation:

```
class Wombat < ActiveRecord::Base
   def self.with_bio_containing(query)
       where("bio like ?", "%#{query}%").
         order(:age)
   end
end
```

That would work. But what we're doing here is not defining some arbitrary behavior on the Wombat class. We're defining a named query. Active Record gives us a way to make that fact explicit: scopes. Active Record scopes allow you to name query fragments that can then be called as class-level methods or chained together and then called. Before revisiting our with_bio_containing() method, let's look at a simple example:

rr2/declarative_scopes/app/models/person.rb
```
class Person < ActiveRecord::Base
  scope :teenagers, where("age < 20 AND age > 12")
  scope :by_name, order(:name)
end
```

In this code, we define two named scopes. The teenagers() scope enables querying for records that have an age in the teens. The by_name() scope sorts queried records by the name column. Let's give these a try:

```
ruby-1.9.3-p0 > Person.count
 => 30
ruby-1.9.3-p0 > Person.teenagers.count
 => 9
ruby-1.9.3-p0 > Person.all[0..4].map &:name
 => ["Josefina Hand",
     "Beau West",
     "Donna Pfeffer",
     "Tremaine Hagenes DDS",
     "Clementine Funk"]
ruby-1.9.3-p0 > Person.by_name[0..4].map &:name
 => ["Andy Stroman",
     "Beau West",
     "Buck Koepp",
     "Chauncey Gleason",
     "Clementine Funk"]
ruby-1.9.3-p0 >
```

As you can see, we use these scopes as if they were class-level methods. What makes scopes even more powerful is that they can be combined:

```
ruby-1.9.3-p0 > Person.teenagers.by_name.map &:name
 => ["Beau West",
     "Chauncey Gleason",
     "Clementine Funk",
     "Donna Pfeffer",
     "Easton Zemlak",
     "Lavada Vandervort",
     "Mariana Tremblay",
     "Soledad Greenholt",
     "Tremaine Hagenes DDS"]
```

You can imagine setting up a library of meaningful, reusable query conditions and then composing complex queries by simply chaining them together.

You probably noticed that neither of these scopes accepts parameters. To demonstrate how to create a scope that does, let's go back to our original example and implement it as a scope:

rr2/declarative_scopes/app/models/wombat.rb
```
class Wombat < ActiveRecord::Base
  scope :with_bio_containing, lambda {|query| where("bio like ?", "%#{query}%").
                                                order(:age) }
end
```

In this revision, we've chained two conditions into one scope (the where() and order() clauses). Since we need to pass the query text into the scope, we define the entire scope definition to be a Ruby Proc object, which we create with the Ruby lambda() method. lambda() takes a block and returns a new Proc instance that encapsulates that block. We can use this Proc in scopes to regenerate the scope whenever it's called. Any parameters passed into the scope will be passed right into the Proc.

Putting this all together, our original controller action now works.

Many people look at chained scopes for the first time and think they're ineffi-cient, because it *looks* like they would generate one query for each chained scope call. Active Record is smarter than that. Though it may look as though a call to a scope returns an Array of queried objects, the scope actually returns a special proxy that performs the query only when absolutely necessary (for example, when you want to display all of the results in the console). Back in the console, we can see this in action:

```
ruby-1.9.3-p0 > Person.teenagers.class
 => ActiveRecord::Relation
ruby-1.9.3-p0 > puts Person.teenagers.to_sql
SELECT     "people".* FROM
     "people"  WHERE     (age < 20 AND age > 12)
 => nil
ruby-1.9.3-p0 > puts Person.teenagers.by_name.to_sql
SELECT     "people".* FROM
     "people"  WHERE     (age < 20 AND age > 12) ORDER BY   name
 => nil
```

You see here that a call to our teenagers() scope actually returns an instance of ActiveRecord::Relation, *not* an Array of Person objects! We can ask an ActiveRecord::Rela-tion to convert itself to SQL with the to_sql() method. If we combine two scopes, you see that the ActiveRecord::Relation objects actually combine to generate one composed query.

So, Active Record scopes are more expressive, are easier to test, and can generate sane, well-performing queries. A well-written Rails application using Active Record will likely make judicious use of scopes. Try them on your current project!

Connect to Multiple Databases

Problem

The simple default Rails convention of connecting to *one* database per application is suitable *most* of the time. That's why its creators made it so easy.

But what if you need to step outside the norm and connect to multiple databases? What if, for example, you need to connect to a commercial application's tables to integrate your nifty new rich web application with a legacy tool that your company has relied on for years? How do you configure and create those multiple connections? How do you cleanly connect to multiple databases in a single Rails application?

Solution

To connect to multiple databases in a Rails application, we'll set up named connections in our application's database configuration, configure our Active Record models to use it, and use inheritance to safely allow multiple models to use the new named connection.

To understand how to connect to multiple databases from your Rails application, the best place to start is to understand how the *default* connections are made. How does an application go from a YAML configuration file to a database connection? How does an Active Record model know which database to use?

When a Rails application boots, it invokes the Rails initialization process. The initialization process has the big job of ensuring that all the components of Rails are properly set up and glued together. In Rails 3 and newer, this process does its work by delegating to each subframework of Rails and asking that subframework to initialize itself. Each of these initializers is called a Railtie. Active Record defines ActiveRecord::Railtie to play the initialization role. One of its jobs is to initialize database connections.

The Active Record Railtie is responsible for calling the method ActiveRecord::Base.establish_connection(). If you call this method with no arguments, it will check the value of the Rails.env variable and will look up that value in the loaded config/database.yml. The default value for Rails.env is development. So, by

How Rails Connects to Databases

By default, on initialization a Rails application discovers which environment it's running under (development, test, or production in a stock Rails app) and finds a database configuration in config/database.yml that is named for the current environment. Here's a simple sample:

```
rr2/multiple_dbs/config/typical-database.yml
development:
  adapter: mysql2
  encoding: utf8
  reconnect: false
  database: multiple_dbs_development
  pool: 5
  username: root
  password:
  socket: /tmp/mysql.sock

test:
  adapter: mysql2
  encoding: utf8
  reconnect: false
  database: multiple_dbs_test
  pool: 5
  username: root
  password:
  socket: /tmp/mysql.sock

production:
  adapter: mysql2
  encoding: utf8
  reconnect: false
  database: multiple_dbs_production
  pool: 5
  username: root
  password:
  socket: /tmp/mysql.sock
```

If you've done *any* database work with Rails, you've already seen (and probably configured) a file that looks like this. The naming conventions make it quite obvious what goes where, so you may find yourself blindly editing this file to achieve the desired effect.

default, if you start a Rails application, it looks up the database configuration section named development in its config/database.yml file and sets up a connection to that database.

Note that an actual connection has not yet been *established*. Active Record doesn't actually make the connection until it needs it, which happens on the first reference to the class's connection() method. So if you're following along and watching open database connections, don't be surprised if you don't see an actual connection made immediately after your application boots.

Having set up a connection to a database solves only part of the puzzle. That connection still has to be referenced by the model classes that need it. Things get interesting here. When the default connections are made by the Railtie, they are made directly from the ActiveRecord::Base class, which is the superclass of all Active Record models. Because the call to establish_connection() is made on ActiveRecord::Base, the connection is associated with the ActiveRecord::Base class and is made available to all of its child classes (your application-specific models).

So, in the default case, all your models get access to this default connection. If you make a connection from one of your model classes (by calling establish_connection()), that connection is available from that class and any of its children but *not* from its superclasses, including ActiveRecord::Base.

When asked for its connection, the behavior of a model is to start with the exact class the request is made from and work its way up the inheritance hierarchy until it finds a connection. This is a key point in working with multiple databases. A model's connection applies to that model and any of its children in the hierarchy unless overridden.

Now that we know how Active Record connections work, let's put our knowledge into action. We'll contrive a couple of example databases with which to demonstrate our solution. The following is our config/database.yml file. We have two databases. One is labeled as development and will be our default database. The other is labeled products and simulates the hypothetical scenario of having an existing, external product database for a new application.

rr2/multiple_dbs/config/database.yml
```
development:
  adapter: mysql2
  encoding: utf8
  reconnect: false
  database: myrailsdatabase_development
  pool: 5
  username: root
  password:
  socket: /tmp/mysql.sock

products:
  adapter: mysql2
  encoding: utf8
  reconnect: false
  database: products
  pool: 5
  username: root
  password:
  socket: /tmp/mysql.sock
```

We'll also create some tables in these databases so we can hook them up to Active Record models. For our default Rails database, we'll create a migration defining tables for users and shopping carts.

```ruby
rr2/multiple_dbs/db/migrate/20101128140540_add_users_and_carts.rb
class AddUsersAndCarts < ActiveRecord::Migration
  def self.up
    create_table :users do |t|
      t.string :name
      t.string :email
    end
    create_table :carts do |t|
      t.integer :user_id
    end
    create_table :selections do |t|
      t.integer :cart_id
      t.integer :product_id
    end
  end
end
```

In a typical scenario like this, the second database would be one that already exists, which you wouldn't want to (or be able to) control via Active Record migrations. As a result, Active Record's migrations feature wasn't designed to manage multiple databases. That's OK. If you have that level of control over your databases and the tables are all related, you're better off putting them all together anyway. For this example, we'll assume that the products database already has a table called products, with a varchar field for the product name and a float for the price. For those following along, the following simple DDL can be used to create this table on a MySQL database:

```sql
rr2/multiple_dbs/products.sql
DROP TABLE IF EXISTS `products`;
CREATE TABLE `products` (
  `id` int(11) NOT NULL auto_increment,
  `name` varchar(255) default NULL,
  `price` float default NULL,
  PRIMARY KEY (`id`)
) ENGINE=InnoDB DEFAULT CHARSET=latin1;
```

Now that we have our databases set up, we'll generate models for User, Cart, and Product. The User model can have an associated Cart, which can have multiple Products in it. The User class is standard Active Record fare:

```ruby
rr2/multiple_dbs/app/models/user.rb
class User < ActiveRecord::Base
  has_one :cart
end
```

Things start to get a little tricky with the Cart class. It associates with User in the usual way. We'd like to use has_many() with a join model to link to :products, but we can't, because our products table is not in the same database. The has_many() method will result in a table join, which we can't do across database connections. Here's the Cart class without any association with the Product class:

rr2/multiple_dbs/app/models/plain_cart.rb
```
class Cart < ActiveRecord::Base
end
```

Before we deal with hooking Carts to Products, let's look at our Product model:

rr2/multiple_dbs/app/models/plain_product.rb
```
class Product < ActiveRecord::Base
  establish_connection :products
end
```

As we learned earlier, Active Record establishes connections in a hierarchical fashion. When attempting to make a database connection, Active Record models look for the connection associated with either themselves or the nearest superclass. So, in the case of the Product class, we've set the connection directly in that class, meaning that when we do database operations with the Product model, they will use the connection to our configured products database.

If we were to load the Rails console now, we could see that we are indeed connecting to different databases depending on the model we're referencing:

```
$ rails console
>> Cart.connection.current_database
=> "myrailsdatabase_development"
>> Product.connection.current_database
=> "products"
```

Great! Now if we were to call, say, Product.find(), we would be performing our select against the products database. So, how do we associate a Cart with Products? We have many different ways to go about doing this, but I tend to favor the laziest solution. To make the connection, we'll create a mapping table in our application's default database (the same one the cart table exists in):

rr2/multiple_dbs/db/migrate/20101128145152_create_product_references.rb
```
class CreateProductReferences < ActiveRecord::Migration
  def self.up
    create_table :product_references do |t|
      t.integer :product_id
      t.timestamps
    end
  end
  def self.down
```

```
      drop_table :product_references
    end
end
```

This table's sole purpose is to provide a local reference to a product. The product's id will be stored in the product reference's product_id field. We then create a model for this new table:

rr2/multiple_dbs/app/models/product_reference.rb
```
class ProductReference < ActiveRecord::Base
  belongs_to :product
  has_many :selections
  has_many :carts, :through => :selections

  def name
    product.name
  end
  def price
    product.price
  end
end
```

We've created the has_many() relationship between our new ProductReference class and the Cart class with a join model called Selection, and we've associated each ProductReference with a Product. Here's the Selection definition:

rr2/multiple_dbs/app/models/selection.rb
```
class Selection < ActiveRecord::Base
  belongs_to :cart
  belongs_to :product, :class_name => "ProductReference"
end
```

Since our Product class is simple, we have also manually delegated calls to name() and price() to the Product, so for read-only purposes, the product *reference* is functionally equivalent to a Product.

All that's left is to associate the Cart with its products:

rr2/multiple_dbs/app/models/cart.rb
```
class Cart < ActiveRecord::Base
  has_many :selections
  has_many :products,
           :through => :selections
end
```

We can now say things such as User.first.cart.products.first.name and get the data we desire. This solution would, of course, require the necessary rows to be created in the product_references table to match any products we have in the alternate database. This could be done either in a batch or automatically at runtime.

Now what if you would like to connect to multiple tables in the same external database? Based on what we've done so far, you'd think you could add calls to establish_connection() in the matching models for each of the new tables. But, what you might not expect is that this will result in a separate connection for every model that references your external database. Given a few tables and a production deployment that load balances across several Rails processes, this can add up pretty quickly.

Thinking back to what we learned about how database connections are selected based on class hierarchy, the solution to this problem is to define a parent class for all the tables that are housed on the same server and then inherit from that parent class for those external models. For example, to reference a table called tax_conversions on the products database, we could create a model called External as follows:

```
rr2/multiple_dbs/app/models/external.rb
class External < ActiveRecord::Base
  self.abstract_class = true
  establish_connection :products
end
```

Then, our Product and TaxConversion models could inherit from External like so:

```
ConnectingToMultipleDatabases/app/models/product.rb
class Product < External
end
```

```
rr2/multiple_dbs/app/models/tax_conversion.rb
class TaxConversion < External
end
```

Note that we've moved the establish_connection() call from Product to External. All subclasses of External will use the same connection. We also set abstract_class to true to tell Active Record that the External class does not have an underlying database table.

You won't be able to instantiate an External, of course, since there is no matching database table. If there *is* a table in your external database called externals, choose a different name for your class to be on the safe side.

Though it's possible to configure multiple database connections, it's preferable to do things "the Rails way" when you can. Given the choice, always house new tables in a given application in the same database. There's no sense in making things harder than they have to be.

If you *have* to continue using an external database, you might consider exposing that data as a REST service, allowing access only via HTTP calls as opposed to direct database access. For read-only feeds of data that need to participate in complex joins, consider replicating the data from its source table to the databases that need to use it.

Credit

Thanks to Dave Thomas for the real-world problem and the inspiration for this solution.

Set Default Criteria for Model Operations

Problem

Do you ever find yourself repeatedly typing the same snippet of SQL every time you query for, or create, a record in a database? I know I do. For example, if you are creating an online store, everywhere you display products you might want to display only those products that are set to available in the store. If you are creating a publishing system, you might want all queries to return by default only those articles whose published column is set to true. How can you make ActiveRecord scope all queries the same way by default?

Solution

We can set default criteria for model operations using Active Record's default_scope() method.

As we learned in Recipe 2, *Create Declarative Named Queries*, on page 7, the problem isn't so bad in Active Record. Sure, you might still suffer from *some* code duplication, but we could, for example, create a scope called available() in our Product model and then use that scope every time we interact with the model. Given a model definition like this:

rr2/default_scopes/app/models/product_first.rb
```
class Product < ActiveRecord::Base
  scope :available, where(:available => true)
end
```

we could interact with that model in the Rails console like so:

```
 > Product.count
=> 6
 > Product.available.count
 => 4
 > Product.available.map(&:name)
 => ["Furbie",
     "Godzilla",
     "Mr. Bill",
     "Cat Lady Action Figure"]
 > Product.available.find_by_name("Godzilla")
 => #<Product id: 2, name: "Godzilla", ...>
```

But what if we wanted to apply this scope to all queries? It turns out that Active Record has just the tool we need to solve this problem: default scopes. Here's another version of our model, using the default_scope() class-level method to declare a default set of criteria for the Product model:

rr2/default_scopes/app/models/product.rb
```ruby
class Product < ActiveRecord::Base
  default_scope :available, where(:available => true)
end
```

Now let's take it for a spin!

```
        > Product.all.map &:available
        => [true, true, true, true, true]
        > Product.connection.execute("select count(*) from products")
        => [{"count(*)"=>11, 0=>11}]
> lb = Product.create(:name => "Liquid Brains",
                                :price => 19.74)
        => #<Product id: 12, ... updated_at: "2010-11-04 23:34:49">
        > lb.available?
        => true
```

That's much better! There's less code, and it works for creating new records, too. Note that it won't automatically set available() to true when you update a record. That's very unlikely to be the behavior you'd expect, since you would have to explicitly set any default-scoped attributes *every* time you update.

What if you need to bypass the default scope? ActiveRecord also makes that easy in Rails 3. Simply wrap your code in a call to the unscoped() method, like so:

```
        > Product.create(:name => "Hideous Harvey",
            :price => 2.99,
            :available => false)
        => #<Product id: 13, name: "Hideous Harvey" ... >
        > Product.find_by_id(13)
        => nil
> Product.unscoped { Product.find_by_id(13) }
        => #<Product id: 13, name: "Hideous Harvey" ...>
```

When we created the Product, this time we passed in an explicit value for the available attribute. The default scope's value doesn't apply if you override it explicitly. On our first attempt to find the record we just created, the query responds as if the record doesn't exist. When we bypass the default scope with the unscoped() method, the record is returned.

Before you go romping through your codebase, applying default scopes to all of your methods, let's temper our newfound enthusiasm with a word of caution. Implicit scoping like this, though convenient, is somewhat obfuscated.

Without reading through your models, another programmer won't know that a default scope is implied. Someone maintaining your code in the future might reasonably expect a call to Product.all() to return *all* of the records in the products table. The decision to use default scopes is a trade-off between convenience and transparency.

Add Behavior to Active Record Associations

Problem

When you access a has_many or has_and_belongs_to_many association on an Active Record model object, it returns an array-like object that provides access to the individual objects that are associated with the object you started with. Most of the time, the stock array-like functionality of these associations is good enough to accomplish what you need to do.

Sometimes, though, you might want to add behavior to the association. Adding behavior to associations can make your code more expressive and easier to understand. For example, you might want to further limit the scope of the orders associated with a user of a shopping site or calculate the combined cost of all the line items in a shopping cart. However, since these associations are generated by Rails, how do you extend them? There isn't an easily accessible class or object to add the behavior to. So, how do you do it?

Solution

The collection returned by an Active Record association isn't actually an Array. It's a collection proxy. Collection proxies are wrappers around the collections, allowing them to be lazily loaded and extended. To add behavior to an Active Record association, you add it to the collection proxy during the call to has_many().

Before we get started, let's create a simple model with which to demonstrate. For this example, we'll create models to represent students and their grades in school. The following are the Active Record migrations to implement the schema:

```
rr2/assoc_proxies/db/migrate/20101221033031_create_students.rb
class CreateStudents < ActiveRecord::Migration
  def self.up
    create_table :students do |t|
      t.string :name
      t.integer :graduating_year
      t.timestamps
    end
  end
```

```ruby
  def self.down
    drop_table :students
  end
end
```

rr2/assoc_proxies/db/migrate/20101221033237_create_grades.rb
```ruby
class CreateGrades < ActiveRecord::Migration
  def self.up
    create_table :grades do |t|
      t.belongs_to :student
      t.integer :score
      t.string :class_name

      t.timestamps
    end
  end

  def self.down
    drop_table :grades
  end
end
```

We'll next create simple Active Record models for these tables. We'll declare the Student class has_many() Grades. Here are the models:

AddingBehaviorToActiveRecordAssociations/app/models/student.rb
```ruby
class Student < ActiveRecord::Base
  has_many :grades
end
```

AddingBehaviorToActiveRecordAssociations/app/models/grade.rb
```ruby
class Grade < ActiveRecord::Base
end
```

Now that we have a working model, let's create some objects:

```
$ rails console
>> me = Student.create(:name => "Chad", :graduating_year => 2020)
=> #<Student:0x26d18d8 @new_record=false, @attributes={"name"=>"Chad",
"id"=>1, "graduating_year"=>2020}>
>> me.grades.create(:score => 1, :class_name => "Algebra")
=> #<Grade:0x269cb10 @new_record=false, @errors={}>, @attributes={"score"=>1,
"class_name"=>"Algebra", "student_id"=>1, "id"=>1}>
```

(I was never very good at math—a 1 is a failing grade.)

If you're paying close attention, you'll notice that this has already gotten interesting. Where does this create() method come from? I don't recall seeing create() defined for the Array class. Maybe these associations don't return arrays after all. Let's find out:

```
>> me.grades.class
=> Array
>> Array.instance_methods.grep /create/
=> []
```

Just *what* is going on here? The association claims to return an Array, but where's the create() method coming from?

Ruby is a very dynamic language. When I encounter something magical like this, I find myself mentally working through all the possible ways it could be implemented and then ruling them out. In this case, I might start by assuming that the association is indeed an instance of Array with one or more singleton methods added.

But, looking at the Rails source code for verification, it turns out I'd be wrong. What's really going on is that the call to grades() returns an instance of ActiveRecord::Associations::CollectionProxy. This sits between your model's client code and the actual objects the model is associated with. It masquerades as an object of the class you expect (Array in this example) and delegates calls to the appropriate application-specific model objects.

So, where does create() come from? It is defined on the association itself, and it delegates to the Grade class to create grades.

If you understand that an association call really returns a proxy, it's easy to see how you could add behaviors to the association. You would just need to add the behavior to the proxy. Since each access to an association can create a new instance of CollectionProxy, we can't just get the association via a call to grades() and add our behaviors to it. Active Record controls the creation and return of these objects, so we'll need to ask Active Record to extend the proxy object for us.

Fortunately, Active Record gives us *two* ways to accomplish this. First, we could define additional methods in a module and then extend the association proxy with that module. We might, for example, create a module for doing custom queries on grades, including the ability to select below-average grades. Such a module might look like the following:

rr2/assoc_proxies/lib/grade_finder.rb
```ruby
module GradeFinder
  def below_average
    where('score < ?', 2)
  end
end
```

This is a simple extension that adds a below_average() method to the grades() association, which will find all grades lower than a C (represented as a 2 on the four-point scale). We could then include that module in our model with the following code:

```
rr2/assoc_proxies/app/models/student.rb
require "grade_finder"
class Student < ActiveRecord::Base
  has_many :grades, :extend => GradeFinder
end
```

The new method is now accessible on the association as follows:

```
$ rails console
>> Student.first.grades.below_average
=> [#<Grade:0x26aecc0 @attributes={"score"=>"1",
"student_id"=>"1", "id"=>"1"}>]
```

Alternatively, we could have defined this method directly by passing a block to the declaration of the has_many() association:

```
rr2/assoc_proxies/app/models/student.rb
class Student < ActiveRecord::Base
  has_many :grades do
    def below_average
      where('score < ?', 2)
    end
  end
end
```

These association proxies have access to all the same methods that would normally be defined on the associations, such as find(), count(), and create().

An interesting point to notice is that inside the scope of one of these extended methods, the special variable self refers to the Array of associated Active Record objects. This means you can index into the array and perform any other operations on self that you could perform on an array.

Understanding association proxies is one of the keys to expressive Active Record development. Try looking in some of your existing Rails application code for opportunities to create more expressive implementations using association proxies.

Create Polymorphic Associations

Problem

Active Record's has_many() and belongs_to() associations work really well when the two sides of the relationship have fixed classes. An Author can have many Books. A Library can have Books.

But sometimes you may want to use one table and model to represent something that can be associated with many types of entities. For example, how do you model an Address that can belong to both people *and* companies? It's clear that both a person and a company can have one or more addresses associated with them. But a has_many() relationship relies on a foreign key, which should uniquely identify the owner of the relationship. If you mix multiple owning tables, you can't rely on the foreign key to be unique across the multiple tables. For instance, there may be a person with id 42 *and* a company with id 42. How do you associate models from one table to records from multiple other tables?

Solution

This is a job for the Active Record *polymorphic associations* feature. Although its name is daunting, it's actually nothing to fear. Polymorphic associations allow you to associate one type of object with objects of *many* types. So, for example, with polymorphic associations, an Address can belong to a Person or a Company or to any other model that wants to declare and use the association.

Let's work through a basic example. We'll create a simple set of models to represent people, companies, and their associated addresses. We'll start with Active Record migrations that look like the following:

```
rr2/polymorphic/db/migrate/20101214163755_create_people.rb
class CreatePeople < ActiveRecord::Migration
  def self.up
    create_table :people do |t|
      t.string :name
      t.timestamps
    end
  end
end
```

```ruby
  def self.down
    drop_table :people
  end
end
```

rr2/polymorphic/db/migrate/20101214163759_create_companies.rb
```ruby
class CreateCompanies < ActiveRecord::Migration
  def self.up
    create_table :companies do |t|
      t.string :name

      t.timestamps
    end
  end

  def self.down
    drop_table :companies
  end
end
```

rr2/polymorphic/db/migrate/20101214163839_create_addresses.rb
```ruby
class CreateAddresses < ActiveRecord::Migration
  def self.up
    create_table :addresses do |t|
      t.string :street_address1
      t.string :street_address2
      t.string :city
      t.string :state
      t.string :country
      t.string :postal_code
      t.integer :addressable_id
      t.string :addressable_type

      t.timestamps
    end
  end

  def self.down
    drop_table :addresses
  end
end
```

You'll immediately notice something unusual about the addresses table. First, the name of the foreign key is neither people_id nor company_id, which is a departure from the usual Active Record convention. It's called addressable_id instead. Second, we've added a column called addressable_type. You'll see in a moment how we're going to use these columns. You get extra credit if you can guess before reading on!

Now that we have a database schema to work with, let's create models using the generator. We'll generate models for Person, Company, and Address. We'll then add has_many() declarations to the Person and Company models, resulting in the following:

rr2/polymorphic/app/models/person.rb
```ruby
class Person < ActiveRecord::Base
  has_many :addresses, :as => :addressable
end
```

rr2/polymorphic/app/models/company.rb
```ruby
class Company < ActiveRecord::Base
  has_many :addresses, :as => :addressable
end
```

As you can see, the has_many() calls in the two models are identical. And now we start to get some insight into the addressable columns in the addresses table. The :as option, part of the new polymorphic associations implementation, tells Active Record that the current model's role in this association is that of an "addressable," as opposed to, say, a "person" or a "company." This is where the term *polymorphic* comes in. Though these models exist as representations of people and companies, in the context of their association with an Address they effectively assume the *form* of an "addressable" thing.

Next we'll modify the generated Address model to say that it belongs_to() addressable things:

rr2/polymorphic/app/models/address.rb
```ruby
class Address < ActiveRecord::Base
  belongs_to :addressable, :polymorphic => true
end
```

If we had omitted the :polymorphic option to belongs_to(), Active Record would have assumed that Addresses belonged to objects of class Addressable and would have managed the foreign keys and lookups in the usual way. However, since we've included the :polymorphic option in our belongs_to() declaration, Active Record knows to perform lookups based on both the foreign key *and* the type. The same is true of the has_many() lookups and their corresponding :as options.

The best way to understand what's going on here is to see it in action. Let's load the Rails console and give our new models a spin:

```
$ rails c
Loading development environment (Rails 3.0.3)
>> person = Person.create(:name => "Egon")
 => #<Person id: 1, name: "Egon", created_at: "2010-12-14 16:44:43",
    updated_at: "2010-12-14 16:44:43">
    >> address = Address.create(
```

```
    :street_address1 => "Wiedner Hauptstrasse 27-29",
    :city => "Vienna", :country => "Austria", :postal_code => "091997")
 => #<Address id: 1, street_address1: "Wiedner Hauptstrasse 27-29", ...,
    addressable_id: nil, addressable_type: nil>
>> address.addressable = person
 => #<Person id: 1, name: "Egon", created_at: "2010-12-14 16:44:43",
    updated_at: "2010-12-14 16:44:43">
>>  address.addressable_id
 => 1
>> address.addressable_type
 => "Person"
```

Aha! Associating a Person with an Address populates both the addressable_id field
and the addressable_type field. Naturally, associating a Company with an Address
will have a similar effect:

```
>> company = Company.create(:name => "Infoether, Inc.")
=> #<Company id: 1, name: "Infoether, Inc.",
    created_at: "2010-12-14 16:47:14",
    updated_at: "2010-12-14 16:47:14">
>> address = Address.create(:street_address1 => "123 Main",
    :city => "Memphis", :country => "US", :postal_code => "38104")
    => #<Address id: 2,
      street_address1: "123 Main",
      street_address2: nil,...,
      addressable_id: nil,
      addressable_type: nil,
      created_at: "2010-12-14 16:47:25">
>> address.addressable = company
=> #<Company id: 1,
    name: "Infoether, Inc.",
    created_at: "2010-12-14 16:47:14",
    updated_at: "2010-12-14 16:47:14">
>> address.addressable_id
 => 1
>> address.addressable_type
 => "Company"
```

Notice that in both examples, the addressable_id values have been set to 1. If
the relationship wasn't declared to be polymorphic, a call to Company.find(1).
addresses would result in the same (incorrect) list that Person.find(1).addresses would
return, because Active Record would have no way of distinguishing between
person 1 and *company* 1.

Instead, a call to Company.find(1).addresses will execute the following SQL:

```
SELECT *
     FROM addresses
     WHERE (addresses.addressable_id = 1 AND
            addresses.addressable_type = 'Company')
```

Though it's easy to configure polymorphic associations, don't forget that sometimes duplication isn't *that* bad. A separate address table for people and companies might be the right design for your application. If you *do* turn to polymorphic associations, be sure to carefully consider the right indexes for your tables, since you'll be performing many queries using both the associated id and type fields.

Version Your Models

Problem

Applications often let users edit the data they enter. But users make mistakes, and when they do, they like to have an "Undo" feature available to correct them, like the ones their spreadsheets and word processors provide. Sometimes users need to be able to compare two versions of a piece of data to see what has changed. In some cases, they might even have a *legal* requirement to keep track of those changes through time.

To handle any one of these scenarios, you must be able to version user data. But how can you version data in an Active Record model?

Solution

Rick Olson's acts_as_versioned plugin provides just the solution we need. Install it by adding the following statement to your project's Gemfile:

```
gem 'acts_as_versioned'
```

Then update your bundle:

```
$ bundle install
```

The acts_as_versioned plugin allows you to easily cause a model to save each version of its data in a special table, complete with a version identifier that can be used to list, retrieve, or roll back to previous, arbitrary versions of that data.

As a demonstration of its power, we'll work on a model for a simple, collaborative book-writing tool. In this application, each Book is divided into Chapters, each with its own stored version history. If one of the authors of a book comes along and wipes out an important plot twist, our users will be able to easily roll back to the previous or even earlier versions of their data to see a history of the chapter's development.

We'll start by defining the model for our version-controlled Chapter objects. Notice that we're doing the model first. You'll see why this is important as we start defining the database tables to support the model.

```
$ rails g model Chapter title:string body:text version:integer book_id:integer
      invoke  active_record
      create      db/migrate/20101215025803_create_chapters.rb
      create      app/models/chapter.rb
      invoke  test_unit
      create        test/unit/chapter_test.rb
      create        test/fixtures/chapters.yml
```

Now we'll edit chapter.rb to declare that our Chapter model should be version controlled. Because we already installed the acts_as_versioned plugin, this is a simple one-liner:

rr2/versioned/app/models/chapter.rb
```
class Chapter < ActiveRecord::Base
  acts_as_versioned
end
```

That single call to acts_as_versioned() is, in the background, defining a bunch of filters that will stand between our code and the actual saving of our Chapter objects. Now that we have defined Chapter to be versioned, the acts_as_versioned plugin takes care of everything else.

With our model defined, we'll edit the migration that will define the tables to support a versioned Chapter model. The migration should look like the following:

rr2/versioned/db/migrate/20101215025803_create_chapters.rb
```
class CreateChapters < ActiveRecord::Migration
  def self.up
    create_table :chapters do |t|
      t.string :title
      t.text :body
      t.integer :version
      t.integer :book_id
      t.timestamps
    end
    Chapter.create_versioned_table
  end
  def self.down
    drop_table :chapters
    Chapter.drop_versioned_table
  end
end
```

Notice the call to Chapter.create_versioned_table() and its inverse, Chapter.drop_versioned_table(). These special methods were added to our model dynamically by the acts_as_versioned plugin. They define what is essentially a copy of the table for a given model. If we hadn't created our model class first, we wouldn't have been able to use these methods in our migration file. Run rake db:migrate now to add these tables.

Now that we have a versioned model and a database schema to support it, let's load rails console and see what this thing can do:

```
$ rails c
Loading development environment (Rails 3.0.3)
>>   chapter = Chapter.create(:title => "Ligeti's Legacy", :body =>
>>                 "Ligeti turned in time to see a look of ...wife's face..")
 => #<Chapter id: 1,
               title: "Ligeti's Legacy",
               body: "Ligeti turned in time to see a look of terror sweep...",
               version: 1,
               book_id: nil,
               created_at: "2010-12-15 03:30:35",
               updated_at: "2010-12-15 03:30:35">
>> chapter.version
 => 1
>> chapter.title = "Ligeti's Legacy of Lunacy"
 => "Ligeti's Legacy of Lunacy"
>> chapter.version
 => 1
>> chapter.save
 => true
>> chapter.version
 => 2
>> chapter.body << "Ligeti didn't know what to think."
 => "Ligeti turned in time to see ...Ligeti didn't know what to think."
>> chapter.save
 => true
>> chapter.version
 => 2
```

In our dialog, we created a Chapter instance, and it was automatically assigned a version of 1. Note that when we changed the title of the chapter, the version didn't get updated until we saved the object. Now we have a Chapter instance with two versions. What can we do with them? We can access all versions of the record. We can locate and find a version and even revert to it. Here's how:

```
>> chapter.versions.size
 => 2
>> chapter.versions.find_by_version(1)
 => #<Chapter::Version id: 1, chapter_id: 1, version: 1, ...
       body: "Ligeti turned in time to see a look of terror sweep...",
       book_id: nil,
       created_at: "2010-12-15 03:30:35",
       updated_at: "2010-12-15 03:30:35">
>> chapter.revert_to(1)
 => true
>> chapter.body
=> "Ligeti turned in time to see a look of
    terror sweep over his wife's face.."
```

```
>> chapter.versions.size
 => 2
>> chapter.title = "Another version's title"
 => "Another version's title"
>> chapter.save
 => true
>> chapter.version
 => 3
```

We can access data from previous versions and even revert the object to a previous version. What if we wanted to change the object without creating a new revision? For this, we can use the save_without_revision() method. We'll start a fresh Chapter object to demonstrate:

```
>> chapter = Chapter.create(:title => "The Next Day",
>>             :body => "Liget woke up with a throbbing headache...")
 => #<Chapter id: 3,
            title: "The Next Day",
            body: "Liget woke up with a throbbing headache...",
            version: 1,
            book_id: nil,
            created_at: "2010-12-15 17:26:40",
            updated_at: "2010-12-15 17:26:40">
>> chapter.title = "different title"
 => "different title"
>> chapter.save
 => true
>> chapter.versions.size
 => 2
>> chapter.title = "The Previous Day"
 => "The Previous Day"
>> chapter.save_without_revision
 => true
>> chapter.versions.size
 => 2
>> chapter.title
 => "The Previous Day"
>>
```

Under the covers, acts_as_versioned manages your model's versions using the additional table it created when you ran your migration. This is done, not surprisingly, using an Active Record model. The model for your version tables is constructed in memory at runtime. You can access it via the method versioned_class(), which acts_as_versioned adds to your model's class. With this class, you can do all the usual stuff you'd expect to be able to do with an Active Record model. So, for example, if you wanted to look at all the versions of every instance of Chapter, you would do something like this:

```
>> Chapter.versioned_class.all.map do |version|
>>     [version.chapter_id, version.title]
>?>  end
 => [[1, "Ligeti's Legacy"], [1, "Ligeti's Legacy of Lunacy"],
 [1, "Another version's title"],
 [2, "The Next Day"],
 [2, "different title"],
 [2, "different title again"],
 [3, "The Next Day"],
 [3, "different title"]]
```

As you can see, with the acts_as_versioned plugin in place, support for versioned data in a Rails project is not only possible but easily provided.

Perform Calculations on Your Model Data

Problem

You want to perform numeric calculations on the data in your database. For example, you want to calculate the average cost of a purchase on a shopping site. You don't want to have to drop into SQL, but your data sets are too big to select all the data and perform the calculations in Ruby.

Solution

The ActiveRecord::Calculations module, included by default into Active Record, is just what we need. It wraps the SQL necessary to perform in-database calculations while also providing a friendly interface that will be comfortably familiar to everyone who already uses Active Record.

ActiveRecord::Calculations provides model-level methods for querying the count, sum, average, maximum, and minimum values of data in a model. For example, if we wanted to find out the number of people older than 21 in our system, we can do this:

```
>> Person.where("age > 21").count
=> 23
```

Under the covers, Active Record generates something like this:

```
SELECT COUNT(*) FROM "people" WHERE (age > 21)
```

To find the average, minimum, and maximum ages of all the people in your system, we can do this:

```
>> Person.average(:age)
=> 22
>> Person.minimum(:age)
=> 1
>> Person.maximum(:age)
=> 49
```

Because ActiveRecord::Calculations methods can be chained onto any Active Relation, its interface allows you to define complex calculations with simple code.

For example, the following code averages the ages of everyone whose name contains the letter *T*:

```
>> Person.where("name like ?", "%T%").average(:age)
=> 25
```

We can also group your calculations by an attribute of the model. For example, to sum the number of donations to a charity for each day in a pledge drive, we can do this:

```
>> Donation.group(:created_at).sum(:amount)
=> {2010-12-19 22:28:35 UTC => 96,
   2010-12-19 23:27:01 UTC => 370,
   2010-12-19 24:08:25 UTC => 86...}
```

We can also use SQL functions in the group() call. To perform the same operation but group by year, we can do this:

```
>> Donation.group("strftime('%Y', created_at)").count
=> {"2006"=>8, "2007"=>25, "2008"=>20, "2009"=>28, "2010"=>19}
```

> **Tip 1** Beware of Raw SQL. If we need our code to be database-agnostic, beware of using SQL directly. Not all databases support the same functions.

We can group by associations, too. If we have a blog with a rating system and want to get the average rating for each post in the system, instead of using the usual group() method, we can do this:

```
>> Rating.average(:value,
     :group => :post).map{|post, rating| [post.title, rating]}
=> [["innovate enterprise e-markets", 3],
   ["disintermediate vertical experiences", 1],
   ["embrace magnetic systems", 2]...etc.
```

Grouping on associations yields an OrderedHash whose key is the full, instantiated associated object. So if we want to get the average of a specific post, given the full list, we can do this:

```
>> Rating.average(:value, :group => :post)[Post.find(1)]
=> 3
```

Finally, performing calculations within a certain scope works the same as the rest of Active Record. For example, to average the rating of posts by a specific person, we can do this:

```
>> Person.find_by_name("Haruki Murakami").ratings.average(:value)
=> 2
```

Although it may be tempting to do things the "easy" way by performing calculations in Ruby, as you can see, Active Record's calculation support is simple and will usually result in snappier application performance.

Use Active Record Outside of Rails

Problem

In a standard Rails application, database connectivity and database configuration are done for you. However, in a complex system, we often need to access the database outside the scope of a Rails application. Batch processing, background workers, and simple scripts need to connect and process data. How do you use Active Record outside of a Rails application?

Solution

The Rails environment is really well configured. It's so well configured that we rarely (if ever) have to concern ourselves with the process of initializing the Rails subframeworks.

In fact, you might not even realize it's *possible*, for example, to use Active Record outside of the context of a Rails application. Not only is it possible, but it's really easy.

Here's a script that uses Active Record to connect to a database and search for pending orders. Once connected, it shells out to an external program that sends those orders to a legacy mainframe system for fulfillment.

rr2/use_active_record_outside_of_rails/process_orders_nightly
```
require 'logger'
require 'active_record'
ActiveRecord::Base.establish_connection(
  :adapter  => "mysql2",
  :host     => "localhost",
  :username => "root",
  :password => "",
  :database => "web_orders"
)

class Order < ActiveRecord::Base
end
ActiveRecord::Base.logger = Logger.new(STDOUT)

Order.all.each do |o|
  puts "Processing order number #{o.id}"
```

```
  p `./sendorder -c #{o.customer_id} \
     -p #{o.product_id} \
     -q #{o.quantity}`
end
```

If you work in an environment that has any non-Rails applications, this kind of lightweight script can really come in handy. You don't need to create an entire Rails application or incur the start-up overhead of the full Rails environment for something this simple.

Connect to Legacy Databases

Problem

You need to connect to a database that doesn't follow the Rails naming conventions. You may have an old legacy system you're replacing piece by piece. Or perhaps you need to integrate with an external, non-Rails application that follows its own naming conventions.

Solution

Active Record offers a number of overrides to its conventional mapping from objects to tables, allowing you to configure table names, primary key names, column name prefixes, and other options.

One of the Rails mantras is "convention over configuration." It's a great idea, but the problem with conventions is that there can be more than one. In this recipe, you'll learn not only how to buck Rails naming conventions but also how to snap your model onto *another*, as we'll demonstrate using the Word-Press[4] database schema.

Let's start by looking at the definition of one of WordPress's more representative tables. Here's the WordPress comments table:

```
CREATE TABLE `wp_comments` (
  `comment_id` bigint(20) unsigned NOT NULL auto_increment,
  `comment_post_id` int(11) NOT NULL default '0',
  `comment_author` tinytext NOT NULL,
  `comment_author_email` varchar(100) NOT NULL default '',
  `comment_author_url` varchar(200) NOT NULL default '',
  `comment_author_IP` varchar(100) NOT NULL default '',
  `comment_date` datetime NOT NULL default '0000-00-00 00:00:00',
  `comment_date_gmt` datetime NOT NULL default '0000-00-00 00:00:00',
  `comment_content` text NOT NULL,
  `comment_karma` int(11) NOT NULL default '0',
  `comment_approved` enum('0','1','spam') NOT NULL default '1',
  `comment_agent` varchar(255) NOT NULL default '',
  `comment_type` varchar(20) NOT NULL default '',
```

---

4. WordPress is a popular, open source blog engine written in PHP and available from http://www.wordpress.org.

```
  `comment_parent` int(11) NOT NULL default '0',
  `user_id` int(11) NOT NULL default '0',
  PRIMARY KEY  (`comment_id`),
  KEY `comment_approved` (`comment_approved`),
  KEY `comment_post_id` (`comment_post_id`)
)
```

The first step of hooking Active Record into this table is to generate a model
for it. By Rails conventions, the model name for this table would have to be
WpComment. That's ugly, so we'll generate a model called Comment and deal with
the incompatibility.

Active Record has a configuration option to set the table name prefix for
models. We can simply call ActiveRecord::Base.table_name_prefix=() to set it. Since
we want that setting to affect our entire application, we'll add it to a new file
in the config/initializers directory:

rr2/legacy_databases/config/initializers/wordpress_db_conventions.rb
```
ActiveRecord::Base.table_name_prefix = "wp_"
```

There is also a _suffix form of this attribute for setting the suffix of table names.

At this point, we can start the console and query the wp_comments table with
our model. If we had already started the console, we would need to restart it
to detect the change. Note that if the table names were really unusual, you
could always call set_table_name() in your model's definition, passing in the name
of the table.

```
>> spam = Comment.first
=> #<Comment comment_id: 449,
             comment_post_id: 11,
             comment_author: "texas holdem",
             comment_author_url: "http://texas-holdem.ebloggy.com"...
             comment_parent: 0,
             user_id: 0>
>> spam.destroy
  NoMethodError: undefined method `eq' for nil:NilClass
from /../lib/active_support/whiny_nil.rb:48:in `method_missing'
from /../lib/active_record/persistence.rb:79:in `destroy'
```

Oops. Something unfortunate happened. Digging through the source of Active
Record (using the provided backtrace), it's clear that the error happens when
we try to do a comparison on the primary key field of the table. Oh! No id field.

```
 >> ActiveRecord::Base.connection.columns("wp_comments").map(&:name).grep(/id/)
=> ["comment_id", "comment_post_id", "comment_author_id", "user_id"]
```

The key is called comment_id. Scanning the other WordPress tables, it looks
like this is a standard convention used throughout (most of) the product.

Fortunately, it's also used widely enough throughout the industry that Rails provides an easy way to accommodate it. Adding the following to the end of the config/initializers/wordpress_db_conventions.rb file we created earlier will cause Active Record to work correctly with this convention:

rr2/legacy_databases/config/initializers/wordpress_db_conventions.rb
```
ActiveRecord::Base.primary_key_prefix_type = :table_name_with_underscore
#
```

If we were working with a schema that used a convention such as commentid, we could have set this parameter to :table_name.

Now we can find and destroy records by their primary keys:

```
<![[CDATA
    >> Comment.find(441)
    => #<Comment comment_id: 441, comment_post_id: 7.. >
    >> Comment.destroy(441)
    => #<Comment comment_id: 441, comment_post_id: 7.. >
]]>
```

Now what if the table had been called wp_comment and all the other tables used singular forms of the name as well? Simply add the following to the initializer file, and you'll be in business:

```
ActiveRecord::Base.pluralize_table_names = false
```

Finally, if your schema were to use an arbitrary (but repeatable) primary key field name throughout, such as identifier, much in the same way Rails uses id, you could set the primary key name using the following:

```
ActiveRecord::Base.primary_key = "identifier"
```

Though Rails allows some configuration to adapt to schemas outside of its usual convention, the path of least resistance (and greatest joy!) with Rails is to stick to its conventions when you can. Use these tips if you have a legacy database to which you must adapt. But if you're creating a new application or migrating an old one, do yourself a favor and just stick to the defaults. You'll save a lot of time and have a lot more fun.

Credit

Thanks to reader Frederick Ros for the ideas he contributed to this recipe.

Make Dumb Data Smart with composed_of()

Problem

Though it makes sense to store simple data in flattened structures in your database tables, sometimes you want a rich, object-oriented representation of the data in your Ruby code.

Imagine we're managing student records for a school. We want to use our students' course histories to determine whether they meet the academic requirements needed to participate in various school-sponsored extracurricular activities. For example, we might say that a student has to have completed Algebra II with a grade of B or better to be part of the math club.

How do you construct intelligent, structured objects from flat data?

Solution

For a long time, Active Record has shipped with a powerful but poorly understood macro called composed_of(), which, it so happens, we can use to map a flat data structure to objects. The basic syntax of the macro looks like this:

```
class SomeModel < ActiveRecord::Base
  composed_of :some_attribute,
              :class_name => 'SomeSpecialClass',
              :mapping => [%w(model_attr_name special_class_attr)]
end
```

The problem here is that it reads like this: "SomeModel is composed of some attribute." That doesn't quite capture the meaning of composed_of(). How it should really read is as follows: "Add some attribute, composed of SomeSpecialClass, and map SomeModel's model_attr_name field to special_class_attr."

Back to our student course histories example, when a student completes a course, we store the letter grade that the student received for the course in the student's record. Letter grades can range from A through F and be modified with a plus or minus sign such as B+. We store the letter grade as a string in the database.

This is a perfect place to use a composed_of() mapping. Our internal field is "dumb": it's just a string with no grade-specific behavior. But we need to ensure that A- is higher than F, regardless of its case. Here's what the relevant code from our CourseRecord class would look like:

rr2/composed_of/app/models/course_record.rb
```
class CourseRecord < ActiveRecord::Base
  composed_of :grade,
              :mapping => %w(letter_grade letter_grade)
end
```

The CourseRecord model has a table attribute called letter_grade that will be mapped to an identically named field in the class, Grade, which will be accessible via CourseRecord's grade() attribute. The class name Grade is determined by the same conventions used to translate model and controller class names to their associated source files.[5] The composed_of() macro assumes that it can instantiate the composing class, passing each of the mapped values into its constructor. So, we'll make sure our Grade class accepts a single argument. Here's the class now:

rr2/composed_of/app/models/grade.rb
```
class Grade
  include Comparable
  attr_accessor :letter_grade
  SORT_ORDER = ["f", "d", "c", "b", "a"].inject({}) {|h, letter|
    h.update "#{letter}-" => h.size
    h.update letter => h.size
    h.update "#{letter}+" => h.size
  }
  def initialize(letter_grade)
    @letter_grade = letter_grade
  end
  def <=>(other)
    SORT_ORDER[letter_grade.downcase] <=>
      SORT_ORDER[other.letter_grade.downcase]
  end
end
```

We've defined the <=> method and included the Comparable module, which is all any Ruby class needs to implement comparison functionality. The <=> method returns 1, 0, or -1 depending on whether the receiving object is semantically greater than, equal to, or less than the supplied argument. The SORT_ORDER hash defines how letter grades should be sorted, including the pluses and minuses.

---

5. You can override the naming convention by passing the :class_name option to the composed_of() method.

Let's take a look at a console session to see how this works:

```
chad> ruby script/console
>> grade = CourseRecord.first.grade
=> #<Grade:0x2241618 @letter_grade="a">
>> grade > Grade.new("a-")
=> true
>> grade > Grade.new("a+")
=> false
```

The value objects that we create in a composed_of() scenario should be treated as immutable. You can modify these objects in place all you want, but the values will never get saved:

```
>> course =  CourseRecord.first
=> #<CourseRecord:0x2237514
    @attributes={"student_id"=>..."letter_grade"=>"a"...>
>> course.grade
=> #<Grade:0x22364c0 @letter_grade="a">
>> course.grade.letter_grade = "f"
=> "f"
>> course.save
=> true
>> course =  CourseRecord.first
=> #<CourseRecord:0x222e900
    @attributes={"student_id"=>..."letter_grade"=>"a"...>
```

To actually modify the value stored in the database, you have to create a new Grade object and assign it to the CourseRecord class:

```
>> course.grade = Grade.new("f")
=> #<Grade:0x222c54c @letter_grade="f">
>> course.save
=> true
>> course =  CourseRecord.find(:first)
=> #<CourseRecord:0x2226d90
    @attributes={"student_id"=>"..."letter_grade"=>"f",...>
```

You can also use the composed_of() macro to make a flat structure look normalized. If for some reason you needed to store structured data, such as an address, in the same table with the entity that data belongs to, you could map multiple fields into a single object. For example:

```
class Person < ActiveRecord::Base
  composed_of :address, :mapping => [ %w(address_street street),
                                      %w(address_city city),
                                      %w(address_state state),
                                      %w(address_country country) ]
end
```

This would map the fields address_street, address_city, address_state, and address_country of the people table to the Address class, allowing you to work with addresses as first-class objects, even though they're stored as flat attributes in the database.

Now your models represent your application's core domain. With composed_of(), your domain can be expressed more fluently.

DRY Up Your YAML Database Configuration File

Problem

DRY. It's Pragmatic Programmer–speak for "Don't Repeat Yourself."[6] Duplication is a waste of your time and a source of bugs and rework.

But can you apply this rule to YAML-formatted Rails database.yml configuration files when multiple databases are involved? For example, suppose you want to use the same host or login information to access a collection of databases used by the same application.

Solution

A database.yml file is so small and simple (by default) that it's easy to forget that it is written in a pretty robust markup language: YAML. YAML has a little-used feature called *merge keys*. A merge key allows you to literally *merge* one Hash into another, and therein lies the solution to our problem.

Guess what the database.yml configuration entries are. That's right: they're hashes. This means you can use YAML merge keys to convert a duplication-ridden file like this one into one that's DRYer:

```
rr2/dry_db/config/database.yml.yuck
development:
  adapter: mysql2
  encoding: utf8
  reconnect: false
  database: dry_db_development
  pool: 5
  username: root
  password:
  socket: /tmp/mysql.sock

test:
  adapter: mysql2
  encoding: utf8
  reconnect: false
  database: dry_db_test
```

---

6.   *The Pragmatic Programmer* [HT00]

```
  pool: 5
  username: root
  password:
  socket: /tmp/mysql.sock

production:
  adapter: mysql2
  encoding: utf8
  reconnect: false
  database: dry_db_production
  pool: 5
  username: root
  password:
  socket: /tmp/mysql.sock
```

Here's the result:

rr2/dry_db/config/database.yml
```
defaults: &defaults
  adapter: mysql2
  encoding: utf8
  reconnect: false
  socket: /tmp/mysql.sock
  pool: 5
  username: root
  password: secret

development:
  database: dry_db_development
  <<: *defaults

test:
  database: dry_db_test
  <<: *defaults

production:
  database: dry_db_production
  <<: *defaults
```

They're functionally equivalent, but the second one is much less likely to cause an embarrassing head-smacking moment down the road.

We didn't go into detail about how merge keys work. YAML is a rich language with many features you might want to take advantage of in your database configuration or your fixtures. Make an afternoon project out of reading through the YAML specification, which is freely available at http://yaml.org/spec/.

Use Models Safely in Migrations

Problem

Migrations are version control for your database schema. At any given point, you should be able to check out the latest version of your code from its source control repository and rebuild your database schema from scratch. Sometimes it's useful to perform model-level operations in your migrations. How do you use models in your migrations without causing version mismatch problems between your historical database schema and your code?

Solution

To ensure your migrations always have compatible versions of any models required, you can create locally namespaced model classes *inside* your migrations.

Active Record migrations are wonderful things in that they support constant evolution of your database schema. Where it used to be painful to rename, add, or drop columns, migrations makes it easy.

But with this flexibility comes the increasing probability that we'll want to not only add, drop, and rename tables and columns but want and need to do the same with our models as well. This can lead to problems. Since you sometimes need to manipulate data during a migration, it's tempting to use your Active Record models in the migrations themselves. After all, Active Record is usually quite a bit easier and less wordy to use than raw SQL.

But what if you rename your models? Early migrations will cease to work, since your file system (and even your source control tool) doesn't have a built-in versioning system that would be compatible with migrations. Your earlier migrations would be relying on models that were either deleted or removed.

The solution? Define your models (even if they already exist in the usual place) *in the migration itself.* For example:

```
class AddPositionToProducts < ActiveRecord::Migration
  class Product < ActiveRecord::Base; end
  class SoftwareProduct < Product; end
  class CourseProduct < Product; end
```

```
def self.up
  add_column :products, :position, :integer
  Product.reset_column_information

  # Set default list orders
  SoftwareProduct.all.each_with_index {|p, i| p.position = i; p.save!) }
  CourseProduct.all.each_with_index {|p, i| p.position = i; p.save! }
end
def self.down
  remove_column :products, :position
end
end
```

Regardless of which models exist on your file system, this migration will *always* work. Take notice that the models it uses are defined *inside* the migration class. This is important, because they are separated by namespace, just in case you need to use different versions of the model classes in other migrations. For example, the Product class is really AddPositionToProducts::Product. This guarantees that among your migrations the model will be unique.

Credit

Thanks to Tim Lucas for inspiring and supplying code for this recipe.

Create Self-referential Many-to-Many Relationships

Problem

You have a model that needs a many-to-many relationship with itself. For example, you might want to keep track of a bunch of people and who their friends are. In Active Record–speak, a Person has many friends (through their friendships), who are also people. But how do you represent a has_many :through relationship when both ends of the relationship are of the same class?

Solution

You can solve this problem by configuring the has_many() relationships beyond Active Record's defaults and by using Active Record callbacks. You can use callbacks to specify actions to take place when records are saved or destroy. These actions can manage the reciprocal property of a many-to-many relationship by automatically associating records with each other and then cleaning up whose associations when a record is destroyed.

Let's start by setting up a simple data model representing people and their friends. To keep things simple, we'll give people the bare minimum of information in our system. The following are the Active Record migrations for creating our data model:

```
rr2/self_ref/db/migrate/20110111152835_create_people.rb
class CreatePeople < ActiveRecord::Migration
  def self.up
    create_table :people do |t|
      t.string :name

      t.timestamps
    end
  end

  def self.down
    drop_table :people
  end
end
```

```
rr2/self_ref/db/migrate/20110111152844_create_friendships.rb
class CreateFriendships < ActiveRecord::Migration
  def self.up
    create_table :friendships do |t|
      t.integer :person_id
      t.integer :friend_id

      t.timestamps
    end
  end

  def self.down
    drop_table :friendships
  end
end
```

We now have a table structure that is capable of storing a dead-simple Person and a link between people and friends. This looks like a typical has_many :through relationship, given the existence of both a Person model *and* a Friend model. Since we want to have Person objects on both ends of the relationship, we'll have to get more explicit than usual as we specify the has_many :through relationship. The following is the Person code:

```
rr2/self_ref/app/models/person.rb
class Person < ActiveRecord::Base
  has_many :friendships
  has_many :friends, :through => :friendships,
                     :source => :friend
end
```

This declaration creates an attribute on Person called friends. Since we're bucking the usual Rails naming conventions, we have to specify the class name of the model that we are relating to—in this case, the class Person. To complete the association, we need to declare the relationships in the join model:

```
rr2/self_ref/app/models/friendship.rb
class Friendship < ActiveRecord::Base
  belongs_to :person
  belongs_to :friend, :class_name => "Person"
end
```

The only unusual thing here is that we need to specify the class name of the friend attribute. If we hadn't specified the class name explicitly, Active Record would expect a relationship to a Friend model, which is not what we want.

Loading the console, we can see that this works as expected:

```
$ rails console
Loading development environment.
>> chad = Person.create(:name => "Chad")
=> #<Person id: 1, name: "Chad", ... updated_at: "2011-01-11 15:33:37">
>> erik = Person.create(:name => "Erik")
=> #<Person id: 2, name: "Erik", ... updated_at: "2011-01-11 15:33:40">
>> chad.friends << erik
=> [#<Person id: 2, name: "Erik", ... updated_at: "2011-01-11 15:33:40">]
>>
```

Great! But now that I think of it, as an idealist, I like to think that if I count someone as being my friend, they reciprocate the feeling....

```
>> erik.friends
   => []
```

That makes me sad, though I'm convinced that the problem is not one of human nature but just a limitation of Active Record's conventions. Because we need one key for the possessor and another key for the possessed party in a join model, there's no way for the relationship to be fully reciprocal on naming convention alone. Thankfully, Active Record gives us the ability to make the world a friendlier place by way of callbacks.

A quick change to our Friendship model gives us the following:

rr2/self_ref/app/models/friendship.rb
```ruby
class Friendship < ActiveRecord::Base
  belongs_to :person
  belongs_to :friend, :class_name => "Person"
  after_create :be_friendly_to_friend
  after_destroy :no_more_mr_nice_guy

  def be_friendly_to_friend
    friend.friends << person unless friend.friends.include?(person)
  end
  def no_more_mr_nice_guy
    friend.friends.delete(person)
  end
end
```

Even though we might never explicitly create a Friendship instance in our application, when Active Record creates relationships via a join model, that model's callbacks get invoked. This is really cool, because it means we can declare callbacks to be triggered when two objects are related. In this code, we declare be_friendly_to_friend() to be executed on a Friendship when it's created and no_more_mr_nice_guy() to be called when a Friendship is destroyed. So, now when we call the following code:

```
person.friends << another_person
```

our code will encourage—OK, *force*—another_person to accept person as his or her friend.

Credit

Thanks to Luke Redpath for the ideas that led to this recipe.

Protect Your Data from Accidental Mass Update

Problem

The way Rails integrates forms with Active Record models is a modern marvel of convention. Form parameter naming conventions inform the Rails form parameter parser to arbitrarily generate Ruby Hashes in your controllers. Active Record models can be instantiated given Ruby Hashes that are used to set their initial values.

Although mass attribute updates like this are a beautiful time-saving feature, Rails does not discriminate when doing these mass Hash-driven assignments. So, how do we protect attributes we *don't* want users to be able to update?

Solution

Active Record ships with two built-in ways to protect attributes from mass assignment, which can be invoked when record is either created or updated: the attr_protected() and attr_accessible() methods. If, for example, our User model contains a flag to identify a user as an administrator, we will want to make sure that users can't flag *themselves* as administrators by modifying the form we provide them to edit their profiles.

For a case like this, we can use the Active Record attr_protected() macro to guard this and other attributes against mass update. attr_protected() accepts a list of zero or more attribute names, which should *not* be mass-updatable. Here's how we would use it for this example:

```
class User < ActiveRecord::Base
  attr_protected :admin
end
```

Now if we were to add the admin attribute to a form and try to update the model, the model would save, and the new value for admin would be silently ignored.

That's fine, but if we were to add another sensitive field, we would need to remember to update this call to attr_protected(). And if we added yet another, we'd have to update it yet again. Sure, this approach doesn't require a lot of typing, but the problem is that we're likely to forget to do it.

So, on models that are likely to contain such sensitive fields, you might choose to focus on what's *allowed* instead of what's *forbidden*. It'll be more verbose, but it's always best to err on the side of safety when in doubt.

If our `User` model had the attributes `name`, `password`, and `admin`, we could accomplish the same thing as our previous example with the following:

```
class User < ActiveRecord::Base
    attr_accessible :name, :password
end
```

Now, the *only* mass-updatable attributes for the `User` model are `name` and `password`. Any new attributes added to the model will not be mass-updatable unless they are added to this list. Safe but slightly inconvenient.

For the paranoid (or cautious) among us, a nice trick with attr_accessible() (and attr_protected()) is that they can be called with no parameters. If you call attr_accessible() with no parameters, *no* attributes will be mass-updatable. As a matter of convention, you might consider making attr_accessible() the default for every new model in your application.

Create a Custom Model Validator

Problem

Rails ships with a nice collection of model validators. You can use them to validate presence, numericality, format, and several other qualities commonly associated with attributes. Most of the time, these validators are enough to meet our needs. But sometimes they're not, such as when an application requires validation specific to a domain that the built-in validators can't handle and that we'd like to reuse elsewhere.

How do we create a clean, reusable custom validator for Rails?

Solution

The solution is to create and reference a subclass of ActiveModel::Validator.

In Rails 3, all of the fancy declarative validators are built on a single, configurable method called validates_with(). Under the covers, Rails uses this single configurable method to set up all validations instead of validation-specific methods such as validates_uniqueness_of(). As a shortcut to simplify the options, the class-level method validates() is provided to our models.

The validates() method allows us to specify multiple validations for a given attribute in one call. It uses naming conventions to locate the validators. The following code, for example, will ensure that instances of Person include a value for age that is an integer:

```
class Person < ActiveRecord::Base
  validates :age, :presence => true, :numericality => {:only_integer => true}
end
```

The validates() method takes one or more attributes and a Hash of validation options. The keys in these options are not hard-coded into Rails. They work from naming conventions. The name :presence is translated and resolved to the class name PresenceValidator. The name :numericality is resolved to the class name NumericalityValidator. The validates() (and its underlying validates_with()) has no knowledge of these specific validators. Let's look at an example of how we can use this to our advantage.

Imagine we had a Product model for which we wanted to validate the format of a stock-keeping unit (SKU) code. Let's say that in our business the SKUs consist of four uppercase ASCII letters, followed by a dash, followed by an eight-digit numeric code. We could declare this validation "manually" with the built-in validates_format_of() and a regular expression. But we're missing the beauty of Ruby and Rails: the ability it gives us to program close to the domain!

So, instead, we'll make a custom validator. This will give us a more declarative, domain-level representation of our validation as well as giving us the added benefit of being able to reuse the validation in other models or on other fields.

We'll start by defining our Product model and the validation for the sku field:

rr2/custom_validator/app/models/product.rb
```
class Product < ActiveRecord::Base
  validates :identifier, :sku => true
end
```

Let's start the console and take a look at the Product model:

```
>> Product
ArgumentError: Unknown validator: 'sku'
        from .../validations/validates.rb:87:in `rescue in block in validates'
        from .../validations/validates.rb:84:in `block in validates'
        from .../validations/validates.rb:83:in `each'
        from .../validations/validates.rb:83:in `validates'
        ....
```

Oops! We haven't created the validator for sku yet. This gives us some insight into how the validators are resolved. During the call to validates(), the validator is located and put in place. So, we need to define a validator that matches the expected naming convention for sku. Let's name this validator SkuValidator. We can define it anywhere as long as Rails loads it. Let's put it in app/models. If we name it using the usual Rails filenaming convention, sku_validator.rb, Rails will automatically find it without having to explicitly require() it. Here's the validator:

rr2/custom_validator/app/models/sku_validator.rb
```
class SkuValidator < ActiveModel::EachValidator
  def validate_each(record, attribute, value)
    record.errors[attribute] << (
      options[:message] || "is not a valid SKU code"
    ) unless
      value =~ /\A([A-Z]{4})-([0-9]{8})\z/i
  end
end
```

Our validator class inherits from ActiveModel::EachValidator, which is what most of the built-in validators inherit from. EachValidator's job is to iterate through the list of given attributes, calling validate_each() for each one. The validate_each() method takes the object being validated, the attribute name currently being validated, and the value assigned to that attribute. To signal a validation error, we simply add a message for the given attribute to the object's error list.

Now we can reload the console and interact with the model:

```
>> shampoo = Product.new(:name => "Glue Shampoo", :identifier => "shampoo!")
 => #<Product id: nil, name: "Glue Shampoo", identifier: "shampoo!">
>> shampoo.valid?
 => false
>> shampoo.errors.full_messages.to_sentence
 => "Identifier is not a valid SKU code"
>> shampoo.identifier = "ABCD-12345678"
 => "ABCD-12345678"
>> shampoo.valid?
 => true
```

Now that we've created the custom validator, we can use it in any class or future application that may need it. Even if we don't reuse it, we've separated validation logic from the rest of the model, making the code easier to understand and maintain.

Nest has_many :through Relationships

Problem

The standard Active Record conventions for many-to-many relationships give us an easy way to query and join models that are two tables away. For example, a user has many groups through its memberships with them. When a user is configured properly, we can easily ask for a user's groups without having to explicitly walk through its memberships. But what if we wanted to get a list of meetings a user was expected to attend based on his or her groups? How do you easily query a relationship that is three steps away from the source?

Solution

Rails 3.1 introduced the ability to do multilevel has_many :through() relationships.

If we had defined the relationships mentioned in the problem statement, the models would traditionally look like these:

rr2/nested_hm_thru/app/models/user.rb
```
class User < ActiveRecord::Base
  has_many :memberships
  has_many :groups, :through => :memberships
end
```

rr2/nested_hm_thru/app/models/membership.rb
```
class Membership < ActiveRecord::Base
  belongs_to :user
  belongs_to :group
end
```

rr2/nested_hm_thru/app/models/group.rb
```
class Group < ActiveRecord::Base
  has_many :memberships
  has_many :users, :through => :memberships
  has_many :meetings
end
```

rr2/nested_hm_thru/app/models/meeting.rb
```
class Meeting < ActiveRecord::Base
end
```

To get access to a given user's meetings, you'd have to query for the user's groups and then loop through querying for the group's meetings. This is both ugly and inefficient. Here's what it would look like in a console session:

```
>> user = User.first
>> groups = user.groups
>> groups.each do |group|
     p group.meetings
   end
=> [#<Meeting id: 1, group_id: 1, created_at ...]
```

As we loop through the groups, querying for meetings, we're making a separate query for each group. That's not good. What if we had hundreds of groups to loop through? Also, this code is just ugly. Why can't we just ask a user for its meetings? In Rails 3.1 and newer, we can. First we need to reconfigure the User model like so:

rr2/nested_hm_thru/app/models/user.rb
```
class User < ActiveRecord::Base
  has_many :memberships
  has_many :groups, :through => :memberships
  has_many :meetings, :through => :groups
end
```

We've added one more line that says we can get to a user's meetings through its groups. That's all it takes! Here's how we could use this new functionality in the console:

```
>> user = User.first
>> user.meetings
```

Not only is it more direct and easier to read, but it's more efficient. The call to the meetings() method results in a single SQL query that would look something like this:

```
SELECT "meetings".* FROM "meetings"
  INNER JOIN "groups" ON "meetings"."group_id" = "groups"."id"
  INNER JOIN "memberships" ON "groups"."id" = "memberships"."group_id"
  WHERE "memberships"."user_id" = 1
```

Keep Your Application in Sync with Your Database Schema

Problem

Active Record migrations are a wonderful, database-independent way to evolve a database schema as your application's code evolves. And as a Ruby programmer, I find the ability to define schemas in a language that I have some chance of remembering is a welcome relief from the inevitable Google searches and head scratching involved whenever I have to go back to SQL DDL.

Unfortunately, many of our Rails applications' schemas either were created before they were moved to Rails or were created by someone not ready to use the migration functionality. So, now it feels like a catch-22. You want to use migrations, but you can't because you're not already using migrations! How do you go from a traditional, SQL-managed schema to an Active Record migrations-managed schema?

Solution

The solution is to dump the schema in Ruby format and use that dump as an initial database migration.

To see a real conversion to migrations in action, let's start with a small set of example tables. The following is the DDL for three simple tables, which back an online cooking recipe database. We'll assume that these tables already exist in our database and that they have data in them.

rr2/migrations/initial_schema.sql
```
CREATE TABLE 'ingredients' (
  'id' INTEGER PRIMARY KEY AUTOINCREMENT NOT NULL,
  'recipe_id' int(11) default NULL,
  'name' varchar(255) default NULL,
  'quantity' int(11) default NULL,
  'unit_of_measurement' varchar(255) default NULL
);
CREATE TABLE 'ratings' (
  'id' INTEGER PRIMARY KEY AUTOINCREMENT NOT NULL,
  'recipe_id' int(11) default NULL,
  'user_id' int(11) default NULL,
  'rating' int(11) default NULL
);
```

```
CREATE TABLE 'recipes' (
  'id' INTEGER PRIMARY KEY AUTOINCREMENT NOT NULL,
  'name' varchar(255) default NULL,
  'spice_level' int(11) default NULL,
  'region' varchar(255) default NULL,
  'instructions' text
);
```

The challenge is to move from this SQL-driven approach of creating and maintaining schema to using Active Record migrations without the loss of any data.

Active Record migrations are managed using a domain-specific language called ActiveRecord::Schema. ActiveRecord::Schema defines a pure-Ruby, database-independent representation of a database schema. Rails ships with a class called ActiveRecord::SchemaDumper whose job is to inspect your databases and print their schema definitions in ActiveRecord::Schema format.

After requireing active_record/schema_dumper (it's not loaded by Rails by default), a call to ActiveRecord::SchemaDumper.dump() will result in your default database's schema being dumped to your console. To see it in action, do the following. (We've split the command across two lines to make it fit.)

```
$ rails runner 'require "active_record/schema_dumper"; \
                          ActiveRecord::SchemaDumper.dump'
```

But the Rails developers have made it even easier than this. Using the supplied Rake task, db:schema:dump, you can dump your schema into the file db/schema.rb at any time. Let's do that with our existing schema:

```
$ rake db:schema:dump
```

Now our existing schema is converted to an ActiveRecord::Schema format in db/schema.rb. Here's what it looks like:

rr2/migrations/db/schema.rb
```
ActiveRecord::Schema.define(:version => 20110115192759) do
  create_table "ingredients", :force => true do |t|
    t.integer "recipe_id",              :limit => 11
    t.string   "name"
    t.integer "quantity",              :limit => 11
    t.string   "unit_of_measurement"
  end

  create_table "ratings", :force => true do |t|
    t.integer "recipe_id", :limit => 11
    t.integer "user_id",   :limit => 11
    t.integer "rating",    :limit => 11
  end
```

```
  create_table "recipes", :force => true do |t|
    t.string  "name"
    t.integer "spice_level",  :limit => 11
    t.string  "region"
    t.text    "instructions"
  end

end
```

That was nice and simple. And, because this format is the same format that migrations use, the create_table() code in this file will be the very code that makes up our first migration! Let's create that migration now:

```
$ rails generate migration InitialSchema
invoke  active_record
create    db/migrate/20110115192759_initial_schema.rb
```

Now we can take the code from db/schema.rb and paste it into our freshly generated migration file, db/migration/20110115192759_initial_schema.rb. Here is what the migration file should look like. (Note: don't jump the gun—read ahead before you run this migration, or you might lose data!)

rr2/migrations/db/migrate/20110115192759_initial_schema.rb
```
class InitialSchema < ActiveRecord::Migration
  def up
    create_table "ingredients", :force => true do |t|
      t.integer "recipe_id",            :limit => 11
      t.string  "name"
      t.integer "quantity",             :limit => 11
      t.string  "unit_of_measurement"
    end

    create_table "ratings", :force => true do |t|
      t.integer "recipe_id", :limit => 11
      t.integer "user_id",   :limit => 11
      t.integer "rating",    :limit => 11
    end

    create_table "recipes", :force => true do |t|
      t.string  "name"
      t.integer "spice_level",  :limit => 11
      t.string  "region"
      t.text    "instructions"
    end
  end

  def down
    drop_table :recipes
    drop_table :ratings
```

```
    drop_table :ingredients
  end
end
```

Notice that we also added drop_table() calls to the migration's down() definition, which tell Active Record to remove those tables if we ever downgrade beyond this version (though that's unlikely to happen given that this is the initial version of the schema). If you use drop_table() calls, remember to drop the tables in such a way that you don't break any foreign key constraints.

At this point, our *application* has been converted to use migrations. On a fresh database, we can run rake migrate to install our schema. We can also start generating subsequent migrations and evolve our database. But we still have a problem. Our migration isn't *quite* ready yet. In its present form, this migration will wipe out our existing data.

```
$ rails runner 'puts Recipe.count'
253
$ rake db:migrate
$ rails runner 'puts Recipe.count'
0
```

Oops! You may have noticed that whenever the create_table() method is called in the schema.rb file, the :force parameter is passed to it with a value of true. This parameter causes Active Record to first *drop* the table if it already exists and then re-create it. And with the loss of the initial table so go all of its rows.

Remove the :force parameter from your migration before you try to run it. It won't get you all the way there, but you should get rid of it nevertheless to avoid losing any data. Here's what happens when we try to run the migration now:

```
chad> rake migrate
(in /Users/chad/src/FR_RR/Book/code/ConvertExistingAppToMigrations)
rake aborted!
Mysql::Error: #42S01Table 'ingredients' already exists:
CREATE TABLE ingredients (`id` int(11) DEFAULT NULL auto_increment PRIMARY KEY,
`recipe_id` int(11), `name` varchar(255), `quantity` int(11),
`unit_of_measurement` varchar(255)) ENGINE=InnoDB
```

This migration can't create the tables, because they already exist. At this point, we have two choices.

The first choice is a brute-force solution. We could dump our existing data as fixtures (see Recipe 44, *Extract Test Fixtures from Live Data*, on page 163 to learn how). This would allow us to drop and re-create our entire database, starting over using migrations from the beginning. After re-creating the database, we would run rake db:migrate and then rake db:fixtures:load to restore the data. Our application would then be ready for any future migrations without any hassle.

The alternative is probably both easier and safer. Active Record was trying to re-create tables that already exist because its method of determining which version of the schema it's on wasn't available. Active Record uses a special table called schema_migrations to keep track of the database's current schema version. This table contains a single column called version. You probably noticed when you generated the migration file that its filename started with a number that looked like a timestamp. It's this number, prepended to every migration's filename, that Active Record uses to determine which files have not yet been applied and in which order they should be applied.

The alternative way to make things work, therefore, is to insert a schema version before the migration runs. Here's a command that will do just that (again, split onto two lines for formatting reasons):

```
$ rails runner 'ActiveRecord::Base.connection.execute(
    "INSERT INTO schema_migrations(version) VALUES(20110115192759);")'
```

Sure enough, after setting the schema version, a call to rake db:migrate works as advertised. Congratulations! You are now one step closer to Rails nirvana. Be careful, though. Migrations will spoil you. Once you've used them, you'll never want to go back.

Also See

For more information about using migrations, see the Rails API documentation.[7]

Also, as mentioned previously, if you want to learn how to extract your existing development data as Active Record fixtures, see Recipe 44, *Extract Test Fixtures from Live Data*, on page 163.

---

7.   http://api.rubyonrails.org/classes/ActiveRecord/Migration.html

Seed Your Database with Starting Data

Problem

Most data-driven applications need some preexisting data the day they're deployed. These might be lists of categories, authorization groups, lookup tables, and other bits of required information. How can you ensure this data will be consistently deployed with each new installation of your application?

Solution

If you want to seed a Rails database with the same data whenever you deploy it, you should automate the process and make it part of your deployment script. Today, the best approach is to run rake db:seed whenever you install a new instance of your application. The rake db:seed task looks for and executes the file named db/seeds.rb after the Rails environment and your application code have been loaded. You can include any Ruby code you want in this file, but typically you'll write Active Record statements such as these:

```
chad = Person.create!(:name => "Chad", :location => "Boulder, CO")
rich = Person.create!(:name => "Rich", :location => "Reston, VA")
chad.pets.create!(:name => "Shrenik")
chad.pets.create!(:name => "Arnie")
chad.pets.create!(:name => "Polkadot")
rich.pets.create!(:name => "Ewok")
```

What we have here is typical Active Record code. The one unusual aspect is that we're using the create!() method instead of the usual create() method. The <!> version of create() (and of save()) raises an exception when the record is invalid.

This is *very* important to remember in seed data if you want to keep your sanity! Forgetting to check the validity of records in the seed data has wasted a lot of time for a lot of people. Don't be one of them!

After having filled in the db/seeds.rb file, simply type rake db:seed to load the data. And that's it!

Keep in mind that this is just Ruby code executing in the context of your Rails application. It's essentially the same as running a script through rails runner.

Therefore, any Ruby code is valid. You can and should clean up your seed data in the same way you clean up your usual Ruby code. Remove duplication, create methods, and generally refactor for readability and maintainability. The previous example might better be expressed as follows:

```
chad = Person.create!(:name => "Chad", :location => "Boulder, CO")
rich = Person.create!(:name => "Rich", :location => "Reston, VA")
%w(Shrenik Arnie Polkadot).each do |pet_name|
  chad.pets.create!(:name => pet_name)
end
rich.pets.create!(:name => "Ewok")
```

When you run the rake db:seed command, the existing database is not automatically wiped out of the database. Sometimes this is what you want. Sometimes it isn't. Rails chooses the safer, ideally less destructive default. If you need to clean out your database and start over, a good way to do it in development is rake db:reset. This task drops and re-creates your database, loads the migrations, and applies the seed data.

Use Helpers in Models

Problem

Rails provides us with a number of useful text- and link-related helpers to use in our views. But sometimes we need to generate links and manipulate other view-related text in our models. How do we do this?

Solution

Fortunately, the helpers we use in our views are implemented using Ruby modules. By default, they are mixed into the views, but if we want to use them in our models as well, we simply need to mix them in.

Imagine we had a Meeting model whose to_s() method should return the subject of the meeting and how many people are planning to attend. We'd like to use the pluralize() helper to generate this text. Here's how to use it:

rr2/using_helpers_in_models/app/models/meeting.rb
```ruby
class Meeting < ActiveRecord::Base
  include ActionView::Helpers::TextHelper

  has_many :attendances
  has_many :attendees,
           :through => :attendances,
           :source => :person
  def to_s
    "#{subject} - #{pluralize(attendees.count, 'person')} attending"
  end
end
```

The following test demonstrates the behavior of our new to_s() method:

rr2/using_helpers_in_models/test/unit/meeting_test.rb
```ruby
test "Generates a help summary" do
  meeting = Meeting.create(:subject => "Plan the plan")
  assert_equal "Plan the plan - 0 people attending", meeting.to_s
  meeting.attendees << Person.create(:name => "Haruki")
  assert_equal "Plan the plan - 1 person attending", meeting.to_s
end
```

At the top of the definition of Meeting, we mix the ActionView::Helpers::TextHelper module into the class. This gives us the capability to invoke any method defined in ActionView::Helpers::TextHelper as an instance method of Meeting.

Also See

How did we know where to find the pluralize() method? We looked in the Rails RDoc documentation. To determine which module defines any given method in the Rails source, locate the method in the Rails API documentation (for example, at http://api.rubyonrails.org), click the method, and then scroll to the top of the page for that method's documentation.

Avoid Dangling Database Dependencies

Problem

By default, when you delete an Active Record with a one-to-many relationship, the child rows of the parent remain in the database. Sometimes this is the behavior you want. Often, it isn't. How do you tell Active Record to delete dependent records when a parent row is deleted?

Solution

Active Record's has_many()—often forgotten and woefully underused—supports a :dependent option that takes care of this problem. You can use this option to tell Active Record what do with child records when a parent is deleted.

You can use it one of three ways, as the following table summarizes::

:dependent value	Behavior
:destroy	Calls destroy() on each child record, invoking callbacks
:delete	Deletes each child record in a single database query
:nullify	Sets the foreign key to null for each child record in a single database query

Most common is :dependent => :destroy. When a parent is deleted, a relationship configured with :dependent => :destroy will cause Active Record to load every dependent record and call the destroy() on each. This allows your application to take advantage of any before_destroy() or after_destroy() hooks on the child objects, so it's a good choice in many cases. Here's an example:

```
class Flight < ActiveRecord::Base
  has_many :seats, :dependent => :destroy
end

class Seat < ActiveRecord::Base
  belongs_to :flight
  after_destroy :cancel_tickets!
  def cancel_tickets!
    # ...
  end
end
```

This example from a fictitious airline reservation system destroys the seats associated with a flight when that flight record is destroyed. This gives each Seat the opportunity to cancel any associated tickets.

This solution might be OK if there were always a limited number of Seat records. But imagine using :dependent => :destroy in an application with millions of child rows. Instantiating all of those objects and running their callbacks might bring the application to its knees. For these situations, we have two options.

If we wanted to delete all of the child records and didn't need to run any callbacks, we could use :dependent => :delete. This option tells Active Record to issue a single SQL delete statement for the parent record's children. For large numbers of child rows, this option performs significantly better than :dependent => :destroy.

What if we didn't want to delete the child rows at all? Sometimes we need to keep the children of a one-to-many relationship but simply clear the foreign key value so it doesn't point to an invalid record. That's where :dependent => :nullify comes in. Using :dependent => :nullify tells Active Record to issue a SQL query to set the foreign key to null for every child row as a parent is destroyed.

In my own work, I frequently encounter Rails applications that don't use the :dependent option. This results in wasteful, messy data. I recommend auditing your current applications and evaluating each has_many() call in terms of whether you're missing the :dependent option.

Part II

Controller Recipes

Controllers are the primary entry point into any Rails application. They typically control what we can do and how we can do it. They're the gateway between the Internet and our application's business logic. In a well-written Rails application, controllers and their actions are succinct but expressive. These recipes offer tips not only on how to make the most of what Rails offers in the controller layer but how to keep your controllers clean and maintainable.

Create Nested Resources

Problem

Often in web applications, a given resource makes sense only in the context of another resource. For example, in an event registration system, it doesn't make sense to create a registration without actually specifying which event the user is registering for. In an e-commerce application, a selection makes no sense outside the context of a shopping cart or order. A group membership is meaningless without the group.

Therefore, it should be easy to express our resources in a way that makes this contextual relationship explicit, while at the same time saving ourselves from repetition and effort. In Rails, this concept is expressed through nested resources.

How do we nest resources in our Rails routes so that we support URLs such as http://example.com/people/123/orders/456?

Solution

To nest resources in our Rails routes, we can make nested calls to the resources() method.

A resource that is nested inside another is created just like any other resource. The controller is named the same way, and the actions and views for the resource follow the usual conventions. The primary difference is in how the resource is routed. Let's look at the example of an event management system and its registrations.

In this system, we want to allow for the ability to register for an event. Staying true to the Rails CRUD conventions, we'll accomplish this using a Registration model. As I mentioned, a registration makes sense only in the context of an event. We'll set up the Registration model with an event_id attribute and declare it to belong to an Event:

rr2/create_nested_resources/app/models/registration.rb
```
class Registration < ActiveRecord::Base
  belongs_to :event
end
```

Then, after creating the EventsController and RegistrationsController, we'll configure our routing like this:

```
rr2/create_nested_resources/config/routes.rb
CreateNestedResources::Application.routes.draw do
  root :to => "events#index"
  resources :events do
    resources :registrations
  end
end
```

By passing a block to the declaration of the event resource, we are able to nest configuration inside that resource. This route configuration declares that we have nested our registration's resources inside our event's resources. You'll notice now that if we dump our routing configuration, all of our registration's routes are hierarchically nested inside of the route to an event:

```
$ CONTROLLER=registrations rake routes
event_registrations GET    /events/:event_id/registrations(.:format) \
  {:action=>"index", :controller=>"registrations"}
event_registrations POST   /events/:event_id/registrations(.:format) \
  {:action=>"create", :controller=>"registrations"}
new_event_registration GET    /events/:event_id/registrations/new(.:format) \
  {:action=>"new", :controller=>"registrations"}
edit_event_registration GET  /events/:event_id/registrations/:id/edit(.:format) \
  {:action=>"edit", :controller=>"registrations"}
event_registration GET    /events/:event_id/registrations/:id(.:format) \
  {:action=>"show", :controller=>"registrations"}
event_registration PUT    /events/:event_id/registrations/:id(.:format) \
  {:action=>"update", :controller=>"registrations"}
event_registration DELETE /events/:event_id/registrations/:id(.:format) \
  {:action=>"destroy", :controller=>"registrations"}
```

Every path to the RegistrationsController requires an event_id for the route to match!

This means that forms for nested resources also need to supply the ID of the object under which the resource is nested. There are many ways you could imagine passing this id attribute around, including hidden form fields and other explicitly coded hacks. Fortunately, Rails makes this easy. Here's an example of how you might set up a form to create a new Registration. First the controller code sets up both the empty registration and the containing event as instance variables:

```
rr2/create_nested_resources/app/controllers/registrations_controller.rb
class RegistrationsController < ApplicationController
  def new
    @event = Event.find(params[:event_id])
    @registration = Registration.new
  end
```

Note that we look up the Event by the supplied event_id parameter. Because we have used a nested route, we can rely on this parameter being filled in. By looking up the event from the database, we also verify that the ID passed in corresponds to a valid event before displaying the form. Here's the view for the new() action:

```
rr2/create_nested_resources/app/views/registrations/new.html.erb
<%= form_for [@event, @registration] do |f| %>
  <p>
        <%= f.label :name %>
        <%= f.text_field :name %>
  </p>
  <p>
        <%= f.label :email %>
        <%= f.text_field :email %>
  </p>

  <%= f.submit "Register! "%>
<% end %>
```

Linking a form to a nested resource couldn't be easier. Instead of passing only the @registration variable to the call to form_for(), we pass both the @event and the @registration as an Array. If the form_for() method is given an Array, it constructs the corrected nested route to the resource automatically. That's all there is to it!

Now back in the controller, to finish the task, we could implement the create() action to look something like this:

```
rr2/create_nested_resources/app/controllers/registrations_controller.rb
def create
  @event = Event.find(params[:event_id])
  @registration = @event.registrations.build(params[:registration])
  if @registration.save
    redirect_to root_url, :notice => "Successfully registered!"
  else
    render :new
  end
end
```

Again, because we're operating in the context of a nested route, we can rely on the event_id being supplied. We first look up the Event, and we then use that Event object to build and save the Registration.

There's only one problem: code duplication. In both actions, we looked up the @event variable using identical code. Since a registration makes sense only in the context of an event, it's easy to imagine this code being duplicated for every action in the controller. Since this is a pattern we'll see over and over again in nested resources, let's clean it up. An idiomatic way to remove this duplication in a Rails controller is to use a before_filter(). This way, we can declare that every action in our controller should have the associated @event populated before the action's code is executed. We could then remove the duplicated code from each action. Here's the before_filter() declaration and implementation:

rr2/create_nested_resources/app/controllers/registrations_controller.rb
```
before_filter :setup_event
def setup_event
  @event = Event.find(params[:event_id])
end
```

Now before any action in the RegistrationsController is executed, the @event will be retrieved from the database. If an invalid event ID is passed in, Rails will automatically abort the request with a 404 Not Found HTTP status code, displaying the application's 404 page.

This recipe presents a common pattern in the use of nested resources. If you're like me and many of the Rails developers I've worked with, your first foray into nested resources might lead you to go overboard. Don't get too caught up in creating deep hierarchies in your routes. If you find yourself setting up more than one level of nesting, take a step back and consider whether you're making the application easier or harder to maintain.

Create a Custom Action in a REST Controller

Problem

By default, when we create a new REST controller, the resource-oriented routing configuration constrains us to the standard set of seven actions: create, update, edit, new, index, show, and destroy. How can we add custom actions to controllers whose routes we have constrained using the resources() method in our routing configuration?

Solution

To add a custom action to a REST controller, create a new controller method and view and then add the action as either a member or a :collection route to the routing configuration.

When you create a controller and configure its routing to go through the resources or resource macro, Rails gives you a number of routes for free. Because they're automatically programmed, you don't have to type in each of the possible routes for the various create, read, update, and delete functions of a resource controller. But at the same time, viewing a controller as a resource manager is constraining.

If you want to do anything other than the standard seven CRUD actions, there is no default way to route to those actions. This limitation is intentional. At David Heinemeier Hansson's 2006 RailsConf keynote, he used the phrase "freedom through constraints" to describe this limitation, arguing that being forced to think of all operations as CRUD actions leads to better designs. In my own work, I've come to agree strongly with this idea. But sometimes you really do need a custom, non-CRUD action in your REST controllers.

Suppose you have a simple application you use to track your music collection. Manually adding albums to the list might become a chore. It would be nice if you could copy information about similar album, one by the same artist, say, instead of being forced to type the same information about him for each album repeatedly. For example, if you were adding a stack of vintage David Bowie albums to your collection, you could populate your database by copying information from the album on the top of the pile to all of the other records.

That way, all you need to change for each entry is its title, tracks, and other specifics, while preserving information about the artist copied from the first album. Here's what the model method to accomplish this might look like:

rr2/custom_rest_action/app/models/album.rb
```
class Album < ActiveRecord::Base
  def copy
    self.class.new.tap do |new_album|
      attributes.each do |key, value|
        new_album.send("#{key}=", value) unless key == "id"
      end
      new_album.save
    end
  end
end
```

The copy method creates a new Album object, copies all of the original album's attributes into it except for the id(), and saves it. Next we would want to be able to call this method from our controller, so in the AlbumsController used to manage the Album resource, we could add an action like this one:

rr2/custom_rest_action/app/controllers/albums_controller.rb
```
def copy
  original_album = Album.find(params[:id])
  @album =  original_album.copy
  redirect_to edit_album_path(@album),
            :notice => "This is a copy of #{original_album.title}"
end
```

We would like to be able to post to this action, given the original album's id(), and then get redirected to the form with which we can edit and save our new record. The problem we run into is that there are no default REST routes that respond to an HTTP POST given an ID. So, we need to configure the resource in our config/routes.rb file. Here's an example configuration:

rr2/custom_rest_action/config/routes.rb
```
CustomRestAction::Application.routes.draw do
  resources :albums do
    member do
      post :copy
    end
  end
end
```

In a routing configuration, the resources() accepts an optional block. Inside this block, as we saw in Recipe 22, *Create Nested Resources*, on page 76, you can nest resources and set up custom routes. The first thing we do inside the configuration of our album resource is to call the member() method, passing yet another block. Inside the member() block, we declare that our controller accepts a POST to the copy() action. That all makes sense, but what does member() mean?

There are two types of entry points in any REST resource: member and collection routes. Member routes operate on a specific member of the set of resources this controller is managing. So if albums are our resource, a member route would operate on a specific album. This means member routes require the id() of the resource they operate on. Collection routes point to actions that operate on the full set of resources. The index() action is an example of a collection route. You don't pass an id() to the index() action, because it wouldn't have any meaning.

Now that we can route to our new action, all that's left to do is to create a way to get to it from the application's user interface. Let's add a "copy" button in the Album's show() action:

rr2/custom_rest_action/app/views/albums/show.html.erb
```
<%= button_to 'Copy', copy_album_path(@album) %>
```

Here we've created a button that posts to the named route called copy_album_path(). Remember, this named route is a member route, so we have to pass in the id() of the album we're copying. As a shortcut, we can pass in the @album object, and Rails will obtain its id() for us. In this case, we didn't use a link, opting for a button instead. There are two good reasons for this. The first, and less technical, reason is that a link doesn't as clearly tell the user that when the link is clicked, something is going to change. As users of web browsers, we've been trained over the years to expect buttons to perform actions and links to take us to new pages. The second reason we chose a button instead of a link is that buttons, unlike links, create an HTTP POST by default, which is what is required for our route to match. A normal link would generate an HTTP GET, which would result in a routing error. If you *really* wanted a link to this copy() action, you could generate it using the :method option to the link_to() helper like this:

```
<% link_to "Copy", copy_album_path(@album), :method => :post %>
```

I've found that when something is hard(er) to do in Rails, it's usually for good reason. So, opt for buttons for generating POSTs, and think long and hard before using this :method() option.

Create a Helper Method to Use in Both Controllers and Views

Problem

If you want to create a method you can use throughout a controller, you can simply define it as an instance method and call it from your actions. If you want to create a method you can use in your views, you can put the method in one of your view helper modules. Sometimes you want to use exactly the same logic from both your controllers and your views. How would you accomplish this?

Solution

Because we're using Ruby, there are many possible answers to this question. But Rails gives us an easy, consistent way to do it using the built-in helper_method() declaration. Define an instance method in your controller—in this case, we'll do it in ApplicationController so it will be available to all of the controllers in our application—and then declare that method to be a helper method: [8]

```
rr2/helper_in_controller_and_views/app/controllers/application_controller.rb
class ApplicationController < ActionController::Base
  protect_from_forgery
  helper_method :impressive_assertion
  def impressive_assertion
    [Faker::Company.catch_phrase, Faker::Company.bs].join(" will ")
  end
end
```

We use the built-in class-level helper_method() to declare that any named methods should be made available to the views for this controller and its subclasses. That's all there is to it. Now, from a view, we can simply call this method:

```
rr2/helper_in_controller_and_views/app/views/marketing/index.html.erb
<h1>Welcome to Fancy Corp</h1>
<%= impressive_assertion %>!
```

---

8. This code uses the fabulous Faker gem to generate random catchphrases, installable via gem install faker.

Now we can use our impressive_assertion() method in any controller or view in our application. There's no need to duplicate logic between the controller and view layers, and changes made in our ApplicationController will be reflected application-wide.

Trim Your REST Resources

Problem

Imagine you are creating a service in which users can send messages to each other. In this service, you want users to be able to create messages, but you don't want to let them edit the messages once they've been sent. Changing the content of a message that other users might have already viewed would be a confusing way to communicate.

How can we remove unimplemented references from our REST routes?

Solution

The resources() method in a routing configuration accepts options allowing us to limit the routes it builds for a given resource.

As we know, REST controllers wrap CRUD operations for resources in a Rails application. CRUD stands for "create, read, update, and delete." While Rails provides support for all four of these operations on a resource, not every REST controller *needs* them. Because the Rails scaffold makes it so easy to generate the full range of CRUD actions and because the resources() router method automates the mapping of those actions to HTTP requests, it can be tempting to just create the full set of CRUD actions and routes every time we make a resource.

But unused code is forgotten code. And forgotten code is bad code. Forgotten code can develop confusing inconsistencies with the rest of its codebase. It can confuse maintainers who don't realize it is unused. Worse than these concerns, however, is that forgotten code doesn't get updated with security fixes. Unused code can easily lead to accidental back doors into a system.

So, the best rule of thumb is to always delete code you don't need. Never leave code in your codebase just because you think you *might* one day need it. This applies to CRUD controllers and their routes. So, how do we trim them down?

Back to the specific example problem of removing unwanted actions from our REST resources, the first thing to do, of course, is to simply delete the actions and views for edit() and update() from the application. However, once those are removed, you'll still see the following routing configuration:

```
$ rake routes
(in /Users/chad/src/rr2/Book/code/rr2/trim_down_your_rest_resources)
    messages GET     /messages(.:format) \
      {:action=>"index", :controller=>"messages"}
    messages POST    /messages(.:format) \
      {:action=>"create", :controller=>"messages"}
    new_message GET     /messages/new(.:format) \
      {:action=>"new", :controller=>"messages"}
    edit_message GET    /messages/:id/edit(.:format) \
      {:action=>"edit", :controller=>"messages"}
    message GET    /messages/:id(.:format) \
      {:action=>"show", :controller=>"messages"}
    message PUT    /messages/:id(.:format) \
      {:action=>"update", :controller=>"messages"}
    message DELETE /messages/:id(.:format) \
      {:action=>"destroy", :controller=>"messages"}
```

Those extra routes for edit() and update() take memory, so they cause each request to be processed just a little more slowly. It might not be a big deal for a small application, but a huge application with many routes should be freed of any unneeded routes.

To remove the unneeded routes, we can pass one of two options in the call to the resources() (or resource()) method. To exclude certain routes, use the :except option, passing an Array of action names *not* to generate routes for. Alternatively, you can use the :only option to explicitly name every action to generate a route for.

In our code, we'll use :except to exclude route generation for the :edit() and update() actions.

rr2/trim_down_your_rest_resources/config/routes.rb
```
TrimDownYourRestResources::Application.routes.draw do
  resources :messages, :except => [:edit, :update]
end
```

After applying this change, we'll see the new trimmed-down configuration reflected in our routing configuration:

```
$ rake routes
(in /Users/chad/src/rr2/Book/code/rr2/trim_down_your_rest_resources)
    messages GET     /messages(.:format) \
      {:action=>"index", :controller=>"messages"}
    messages POST    /messages(.:format) \
      {:action=>"create", :controller=>"messages"}
    new_message GET     /messages/new(.:format) \
      {:action=>"new", :controller=>"messages"}
```

```
message GET    /messages/:id(.:format) \
  {:action=>"show", :controller=>"messages"}
message DELETE /messages/:id(.:format) \
  {:action=>"destroy", :controller=>"messages"}
```

Now our application is (slightly) faster and less susceptible to accidentally executable code.

Constrain Routes by Subdomain (and Other Conditions)

Problem

Sometimes you want to route to certain paths in your application only if the application is accessed via a specific subdomain. For example, for convenience, you might want to route to the administrative index page of your "example.com" application when accessed via the URL http://admin.example.com." Though it would be possible to do this in a before_filter() in your controllers, how can you take advantage of the more declarative routing syntax to do per-subdomain routes?

Solution

The arrival of Rails 3 introduced a flexible constraint-matching system to its routing engine in the form of a :constraints key, which is the perfect solution to this problem. By passing a :constraints key to any route, you can constrain how Rails chooses to match that routing rule. Since subdomain-based constraints are common, Rails includes a :subdomain key for this purpose right out of the box.

The following simple routing configuration maps the root of an application to the AdminController's index() action, but only if it is accessed with the "admin" subdomain:

```
rr2/route_based_on_subdomain/config/routes.rb
RouteBasedOnSubdomain::Application.routes.draw do
  root :to => "admin#index", :constraints => {:subdomain => "admin"}
  root :to => "home#index"
end
```

Since route recognition occurs in a top-down order, if you were to access this application via http://admin.example.com, the first route would match because the request was made for the root of the application, and the subdomain constraint would match. If, however, you accessed the application through any other subdomain, such as http://www.example.com, the first rule would fail to match the constraint, and the routing engine would continue to the next rule in the configuration, which would match, rendering the HomeController's index() action. That's all there is to it!

The special :subdomain constraint is a specific instance of a more general framework. Routes can be matched based on arbitrary constraints. For more flexible constraint matching, the routing engine gives you two more choices. The first choice is to pass a Proc in as the value for the :constraint key in the routing rule:

rr2/route_based_on_subdomain/config/routes.rb
```
RouteBasedOnSubdomain::Application.routes.draw do
  root :to => "phone#index",
       :constraints => lambda{ |req|
                         req.params.keys.grep(/iphone/i).any?
                       }
  root :to => "home#index"
end
```

This rule matches any parameter key whose name contains "iphone" case-insensitively. You might use a flexible rule like this to handle legacy URLs when porting an older site to Rails. In this case, our routing configuration would match a URL such as http://www.example.com?iphone=1 and route to the special phone index page. If you need to implement a constraint with more complex logic, you can create your own class or object that responds to the method matches?(). Here's a more flexible version of the rule we just implemented using a custom class. First, here's the matcher class itself:

rr2/route_based_on_subdomain/config/routes.rb
```
class LegacyParameterMatcher
  def initialize(regular_expression)
    @regular_expression = regular_expression
  end

  def matches?(request)
    request.params.keys.grep(@regular_expression).any?
  end
end
```

We could then use this class like this:

rr2/route_based_on_subdomain/config/routes.rb
```
RouteBasedOnSubdomain::Application.routes.draw do
  root :to => "phone#index",
       :constraints => LegacyParameterMatcher.new(/iphone/i)
end
```

This constraint system is extremely flexible and opens up a world of creative routing possibilities. If you're like me and have been using Rails since the early days, you may need to train yourself to turn to the routing configuration for more dynamic solutions than were available in the past.

Add Web Services to Your Actions

Problem

You need to access the same business logic whether it's via a web browser as posts or it's via an XML or JSON service. How do you cleanly support multiple sets of view logic within the same action?

Solution

Web services can be easily added to your actions by taking advantage of the Rails parameter parsers, using respond_to() to detect what format the client is communicating with, and supplying additional options to the built-in render() method, causing it to generate the appropriate output format and headers.

The following simple action creates a new Contact row in the database. It follows the fairly typical pattern of saving the contact and then redirecting to the page for that contact.

```
rr2/simple_web_services/app/controllers/contacts_controller.rb
def create
  @contact = Contact.new(params[:contact])
  if @contact.save
    redirect_to @contact, :notice => 'Contact was successfully created.'
  else
    render :new
  end
end
```

What if the client were posting XML instead of the usual encoded data? And now what if we wanted to change the output based on the kind of client accessing the action?

We'll start with the first question, because it's the easiest. How could we modify this action to accept XML? What if we had, say, the following Java program making a post from a legacy system to a new Rails application?

```
rr2/simple_web_services/CommandLinePost.java
import java.io.BufferedReader;
import java.net.URLConnection;
import java.net.URL;
import java.io.InputStreamReader;
```

```java
import java.io.OutputStreamWriter;
public class CommandLinePost {

  private static void usage()
  {
    System.err.println("usage: java CommandLinePost <url>");
    System.exit(1);
  }

  public static void main(String args[])
  {
    if(args.length > 2)
        usage();
    String endPoint = args[0];
    try {
        String data = "<contact>" +
                      "<name>Kurt Weill</name>" +
                      "<phone>501-555-2222</phone>" +
                      "</contact>";

        URL url = new URL(endPoint);
        URLConnection conn = url.openConnection();
        conn.setRequestProperty("Content-Type", "application/xml");
        conn.setDoOutput(true);
        OutputStreamWriter wr =
                new OutputStreamWriter(conn.getOutputStream());
        wr.write(data);
        wr.flush();

        BufferedReader rd =
            new BufferedReader(new InputStreamReader(conn.getInputStream()));
        String line;
        while ((line = rd.readLine()) != null) {
            // Imagine this was putting the data back into a legacy
            // Java system.  For simplicity's sake, we'll just print
            // it here.
            System.out.println(line);
        }
        wr.close();
        rd.close();
    } catch (Exception e) {
        e.printStackTrace();
    }
  }
}
```

How do we modify our action to accept XML input like this and parse it into a form that we can work with? We don't.

By default, any POST made with a content type of application/xml will be parsed by the Rails built-in XML parser and converted into a familiar hash of parameters that will be available, as always, via the params method in your controller. Rails uses simple but effective rules for translating the XML into a hash. If your root element is (as it is in this case) <contact>, a parameter will be available via params[:contact]. If the <contact> tag contains a set of children, it will be converted into an array in the params list. Otherwise, as in this case, it will be converted into a hash with its child element names as keys.

So, if you construct your XML the way Rails expects it to be constructed, the parameters will be populated exactly as if they had been submitted via an HTML form.

Let's move on to the second question we started with: how do we render a response that depends on the kind of client that is accessing our action? We could hack something together where different clients pass a special parameter. Or we could inspect the HTTP USER_AGENT field if it's set. We could make our judgment based on the content type of the input to our action.

But there's a cleaner way. The HTTP specification supports a header field called *Accept*. In this field, a client can list all of the MIME types (technically called *media ranges* in this context) it is capable of accepting. So, to cook up a simple example, a browser might pass something like text/html,text/plain to indicate that either of these formats is OK.

Clients can also pass wildcards such as text/* or even */*. The server should then deliver content of the *most specific* type requested (that the server is capable of returning). It's also possible for clients to include a parameter, q, appended to each content type and connected by a semicolon. This is called the *quality* parameter and can be used to further specify an order of preference for the media ranges reported.

The advantage of this approach is that it uses the HTTP standard in the way it was intended. Many HTTP clients support this behavior, and it's easy to code an Accept header into your web service clients. The disadvantage is that with so many standards to choose from, the logic to implement this would be far more complex than our initial simple hack ideas.

Thankfully, however, this logic is already integrated into Rails. Via the method respond_to(), it's trivial to set up a single action to respond to various media ranges and, therefore, client types. Here's a revised version of our create() action from earlier:

rr2/simple_web_services/app/controllers/contacts_controller.rb

```ruby
def create
  @contact = Contact.new(params[:contact])

  respond_to do |format|
    if @contact.save
      format.html do
        redirect_to(@contact,
                    :notice => 'Contact was successfully created.')
      end
      format.xml  do
        render :xml => @contact,
               :status => :created,
               :location => @contact
      end
    else
      format.html { render :new }
      format.xml  do
        render :xml => @contact.errors,
               :status => :unprocessable_entity
      end
    end
  end
end
```

The new version of our action behaves similarly to the last one if the client expects HTML. However, if the client expects XML, it sets the HTTP status code to 201 (using the shortcut, :created) and then uses the to_xml() method on our model to render XML to the client. The to_xml() method renders XML that follows the same basic convention that the XML input mechanism expects. Since we used the :xml option when we called render(), the content type of the response is automatically set to application/xml for us.

Note that for this behavior to be enabled for our client, we'd have to add the Accept header to our client program. Here's the Java code to set the client from our earlier example to accept XML:

```java
conn.setRequestProperty("Accept", "application/xml");
```

That's it! If we recompile our Java code and run it against our create() action, we should receive a nice, usable XML response.

Write Macros

Problem

You notice a recurring pattern in your application. You're writing code for the same actions over and over again in your controllers.

Looking at the declarative style of many of the Rails helpers such as respond_to() and before_filter(), you want your own code to be expressed as succinctly.

How does Rails implement these so-called macros—code that writes code for you? And how can you create your own?

Solution

To write our own Rails macros, we can take advantage of Ruby's metaprogramming capabilities. In this recipe, we'll use define_method() to dynamically define named methods to our controllers, which will be available as actions.

Ruby is an extremely dynamic language. We are all exposed to its dynamic typing system daily, but the dynamism doesn't end there.

Ruby, like Lisp and Smalltalk before it, allows programmers to easily write code that writes and loads code at runtime. This is a really deep topic, and we're not going to attempt to dig too far into it here. Instead, we'll focus on the details necessary to implement our own Action Controller macros.

Let's imagine we have a complex application with a large domain model for which we have many actions that implement a simple search. We have standardized the look and feel of this search across the application so that users have a consistent interface. In fact, we've made the look and feel so consistent that we are able to reuse the same view for all the search actions and would like to create a macro to do the work.

A typical instance of one of these actions might look like the following, a simple search through contacts in a contact database:

`rr2/metaprogramming/app/controllers/contacts_controller.rb`
```
def search
  @title = "Your Contacts"
  @results = Contact.where("name like ?", "%#{params[:term]}%")
```

```
  @display_as = :name
  @display_path = :contact_path
  render 'shared/search_results'
end
```

Over the life of our application, because we have refactored separate actions into being able to use a single view, we ended up with this "configure by instance variable" style. We set several variables in this action that influence the behavior of the shared view. Let's look at the shared view now:

```
rr2/metaprogramming/app/views/shared/search_results.html.erb
<h2 class='search_header'>
  <%= @title %>
</h2>
<ul>
  <% @results.each do |result| %>
  <li>
    <%= link_to result.send(@display_as),
                send(@display_path, result)
    %>
  </li>
  <% end %>
</ul>
```

We see here that the view of search results is structurally the same across all search actions and uses the instance variables set in the search action to decide what heading to use, which named route to link each result to, and which attribute of the returned item to use as the display value for the link. We can now easily use this same view to display search results for practically any Active Record model, provided we create a search action that follows the expected protocol.

The problem here is that although the view has been nicely cleaned of duplication, we still have a ton of duplicated code in our controllers. In a big application, this kind of pattern might propagate itself tens of times. If we needed to change the behavior of the search results view, we would have to edit each action that references it. Bad news.

What would be *great* is if we could simply do something like the following in our controllers whenever we wanted a search action:

```
search_action_for :contacts, :title => "Your Contacts"
```

In idiomatic Rails style, this would create a search action for the Contact model with a sensible set of defaults that could be overridden by an options Hash passed in as the second parameter to the method. Let's convert our existing search() action to a macro-driven implementation.

The quickest and easiest way to make this macro available from any controller in the application is to define it in ApplicationController. Here's our ApplicationController with the macro defined:

```
rr2/metaprogramming/app/controllers/application_controller.rb
Line 1  class ApplicationController < ActionController::Base
          def self.search_action_for(table, options = {})
            table = table.to_s
            model_class = table.classify.constantize
     5      define_method(:search) do
              @title = options[:title] || "Your #{table.humanize}"
              search_column = options[:search_column] || 'name'
              @display_as = options[:display_as] || :name
              @display_path = options[:display_path] || "#{table.singularize}_path"
    10        @results = model_class.where("#{search_column} like ?", "%#{params[:term]}%")
              render 'shared/search_results'
            end
            #FIXME: do routing configuration here

    15    end
        end
```

Walking through the code, you'll see that search_action_for() is defined using self.search_action_for(). This is because we're defining the method to be called on the controller class itself, not on *instances* of that class. When we call a method inside a class definition, it gets called on that class. This method uses the Rails built-in constantize() to dynamically look up a constant by name. In Ruby, classes are constants, so in this case we're actually looking up the class using its name.

Rails actions are simply methods defined on controllers. So, to write code that writes Rails actions for us, we need to be able to define methods dynamically. We can do this with Ruby's define_method() method. We name the method search(), because we want the action to be called search(). Although we're defining this code in ApplicationController, it will be run in the context of the controller from which it is called. So, if we call it inside ContactsController, it will define a method called search() in that controller, not in ApplicationController.

Next we pass a block of code to define_method(). This is the code that makes up the search() action's real logic. The first step of the search code's logic is setting up our configuration. We support a set of sensible defaults, which users can optionally override using the options parameter. In addition to the variables we set in our contact-specific version of search(), we're also providing the ability to override which column the query will use in its WHERE condition, which we've named search_column in the options parameter.

Now that we have all of the configuration taken care of, on line 10 we actually do the query. Notice that we're calling where() on the where variable. This was set *outside the scope of our dynamic method definition* to the model class for which we're creating a search action. That class, by virtue of Ruby's support for closures, gets embedded in the action and won't be looked up again when the action is invoked.

Finally, we need to add a route for this search action.

So, now we have a search() action maker that we can use in any controller we want and with any model. If we had a controller for managing status updates and wanted to support searching them, all we'd have to do is add something like the following to our appointments controller:

```
search_action_for :appointments,
                  :title => "Upcoming appointments",
                  :search_column => 'description',
                  :display_as => :subject
```

This is a great way to use less code for the same features, remove duplication, and make life easier. We've gone through a simple example here, but these basic building blocks can be applied to a diverse set of problems. Now that you've seen it once, let your imagination take over, and you're sure to find many ways this technique could help you on your own projects.

You can confront reuse in many ways. The two most prevalent ways are either to generate code or to create a runtime framework. This recipe combines those two. We generate code at runtime.

This kind of runtime code generation can be powerful. But it comes at a price. Creating powerful abstractions such as these requires code that is sometimes complex and uses the most advanced features of Ruby. During development, it can be difficult to debug problems with generated code.

Typically, though, generated code done *well* creates an expressive, productive environment. It's a balancing act and a decision you shouldn't take lightly.

And as an experiment, see how much of what you've learned in this recipe could be applied to creating macros for Active Record models. You'll be surprised by how much you can already do!

Also See

If you create something reusable in this manner, you might consider packaging it as a gem. See Recipe 57, *Create Your Own Ruby Gem*, on page 221 for more information.

Manage a Static HTML Site with Rails

Problem

How can we take advantage of the Rails layout and templating systems while building a static HTML website?

Solution

Rails caching provides the tools that we need to solve this problem, and we can use them to produce a static website on the fly with Rails.

After spending enough time in Rails, I find myself getting used to the Rails layout mechanism and seriously missing it when I'm building static sites. Sure, other systems are specifically geared toward creating static sites. But I use Ruby and Rails, and I'd rather not learn another system that I have to use in static-site situations. On top of that, many static sites start out being static but quickly need database-driven content. Starting with a simple Rails site makes it easier to grow it into a dynamic site later.

Given that Rails has a simple and robust caching mechanism, we can use Rails as a static-site management tool. Just set up a controller under which to store your static content (I called mine *pages*), and add the following line inside the controller's class definition:

```
after_filter { |c| c.cache_page }
```

This tells the controller to cache every action as it is accessed. It's possible to declaratively cache actions by name, but if we want to cache *all* of the actions in a controller, this after_filter() method is the way to do it. Now, when you access this page via your browser, Rails will create a static, cached version of it that will be served directly by the web server on subsequent requests.

The generated pages will include any layouts that would normally be applied, or even partials that have been rendered within your views. This is a great way to componentize your static content. If your site displays the same contact list in several places, for example, you can create a partial view with that information and render it where appropriate.

Keep in mind that if you use this method on a page that requires authentication, the page that is cached will be the version that the first user saw. So, if this page showed sensitive account information, that user's information would show up for *every* user who accessed the site. Use this technique only with content that is the same for all users!

Syndicate Your Site with RSS

Problem

RSS and Atom feeds are ubiquitous. Although they were originally created to track news stories, it's now common for an application to offer a feed for just about anything that might update over time. Applications offer RSS and Atom feeds to allow their users to track comments, new product releases, version control commits, and pretty much anything you can imagine.

With syndication becoming more and more common, your users will expect you to provide it as well. All of the major browsers support syndicated feeds out of the box. How do you add syndication to your Rails applications?

Solution

To add syndicated feeds, we'll do the following:

- Create a new controller to serve the feeds
- Configure our routes
- Use respond_to() to respond with the appropriate type of feed when requested
- Create an XML Builder template to generate the feed's view

Two major syndication formats[9] are in play today: RSS (Really Simple Syndication) and Atom. Although there are some technical differences between these formats, the end-user experience is the same: RSS and Atom provide the ability to syndicate chronologically sensitive site updates via XML feeds.

Plenty of web resources are available[10] that detail these formats and how they work architecturally, so we won't belabor the points here. Suffice to say that RSS and Atom both involve the production of an XML file by a server of some sort and the consumption and display of the XML file contents (usually in reverse chronological order) by one or more clients called news *aggregators*.

---

9. Actually, RSS is the subject of a huge amount of political tension on the Web, so it has splintered into at least three separate flavors. Save yourself a headache, and don't worry about any of those flavors except for RSS 2.0.

10. http://en.wikipedia.org/wiki/Web_feed

These aggregators allow a simple, unified view of what has changed across a potentially large number of websites.

So, if you want your site to produce a feed that one of these aggregators is capable of displaying, you need to publish with the aggregator in mind. All the major news aggregators these days support both RSS and Atom, so for this recipe we'll focus on just one of the formats: RSS. The concepts involved in producing an RSS feed are nearly identical to those of producing an Atom feed, so with a little research, you can easily produce either. So, let's stop talking and start cooking up a feed!

As an example, we'll create a feed to syndicate new recipes added to an online cookbook application. Whenever a recipe is added or updated, users should be able to receive updates in their news aggregators. Let's create a simple set of models to represent users and recipes in the cookbook, starting with the models:

rr2/syndication/app/models/recipe.rb
```
class Recipe < ActiveRecord::Base
  has_many :ingredients
  belongs_to :author, :foreign_key => 'author_id', :class_name => 'User'
end
```

rr2/syndication/app/models/ingredient.rb
```
class Ingredient < ActiveRecord::Base
  belongs_to :recipe
end
```

rr2/syndication/app/models/user.rb
```
class User < ActiveRecord::Base
  has_many :recipes, :foreign_key => 'author_id'
end
```

The basic story with our schema is that we have users who author many recipes, and the recipes have zero or more ingredients. It's a simplistic schema, but it works. Here's a dump of the actual database schema:

rr2/syndication/db/schema_preserved.rb
```
create_table "ingredients", :force => true do |t|
  t.integer  "recipe_id"
  t.string   "name"
  t.string   "unit"
  t.decimal  "amount"
  t.datetime "created_at"
  t.datetime "updated_at"
end

create_table "recipes", :force => true do |t|
  t.string   "title"
```

```
    t.text      "instructions"
    t.integer   "author_id"
    t.datetime  "created_at"
    t.datetime  "updated_at"
  end

  create_table "users", :force => true do |t|
    t.string    "name"
    t.string    "password"
    t.datetime  "created_at"
    t.datetime  "updated_at"
  end
```

What do we want to accomplish with our RSS feed? If the core functionality of the application is to allow users to share recipes, we would like to add a feed to the application that will enable our users to subscribe to the running stream of new and updated recipes. With information overload plaguing so many of us these days, the ability to let the system keep track of what's new for you can make a huge difference.

We'll start by creating a separate controller for the feed. You don't *have* to serve feeds through a separate controller, but you'll frequently find that in a complex application, even given the ability to use respond_to() to render different formats for a single action, the behavior of the typical action doesn't apply to an RSS feed. For example, you won't want to apply the same authentication or authorization rules to an RSS feed (more on this later). You won't want to run an RSS feed through the same kinds of filters that you might run an HTML action through. It just tends to be cleaner and easier to keep things separate.

This being a food-related website, we'll give the controller a name with two meanings, FeedsController:

```
$ rails g controller Feeds
      create  app/controllers/feeds_controller.rb
      invoke  erb
      create    app/views/feeds
      ...
```

Let's create a simple action that grabs the fifteen latest recipes from the database. We'll call it recipes(). This leaves the FeedsController open to serve other feeds, should we eventually have the need.

rr2/syndication/app/controllers/feeds_controller.rb
```
def recipes
  @recipes = Recipe.order("updated_at, created_at").limit(15)
end
```

Next we'll need to add a route to the action:

rr2/syndication/config/routes.rb
```
match "feeds/recipes(.:format)" => "feeds#recipes"
```

Notice we've left the :format parameter configurable even though we're going to support only RSS for now. That leaves us open to easily add alternate formats later without having to deprecate the URLs our users have been using for their feeds.

Now we've done the easy part. Our FeedsController has selected the latest recipes to be added to the feed. It's time to generate the feed itself. And now we have a decision to make: how should we create the feed's XML?

We have three fairly good ways to create the feed file. We could use Ruby's built-in RSS library. This library provides a nice, clean API for both generating and consuming RSS. Alternatively, we could create an ERb template that is preformatted as an RSS feed and uses dynamically inserted Ruby snippets to generate the recipe's content. Finally, we could use the XML Builder library to generate the RSS feed via a .builder template.

Each possible approach has its merits. Since we want to keep this recipe as feed format–agnostic as possible, we'll rule out using Ruby's built-in RSS library. That leaves us with either ERb or XML Builder. This being an XML feed, we're likely to have a cleaner experience with XML Builder, so we'll go with that.

Just as with ERb templates, XML Builder templates should be named after the actions they provide a view for. As usual, the middle part of the filename specifies the format this template is created to render (RSS in this case). Here's what our recipes.rss.builder template looks like:

rr2/syndication/app/views/feeds/recipes.rss.builder
```
xml.instruct!
xml.rss "version" => "2.0",
        "xmlns:dc" => "http://purl.org/dc/elements/1.1/" do
  xml.channel do
    xml.title 'Freshly Added Recipes'
    xml.link recipes_url
    xml.pubDate CGI.rfc1123_date(@recipes.first.updated_at)
    xml.description h("Cook Book Freshly Added Recipes.")
    @recipes.each do |recipe|
      xml.item do
        xml.title recipe.title
        xml.link recipe_url(recipe)
        xml.description recipe.instructions
        xml.pubDate CGI.rfc1123_date(recipe.updated_at)
        xml.guid recipe_url(recipe)
```

```
        xml.author recipe.author.name
      end
    end
  end
end
```

In case you've never seen an XML Builder template before, here's XML Builder in the shell of a really, really small nut: all those method calls on the implicitly available object, xml, end up generating XML tags of the same name. The tags get whatever value you pass into the method calls, and if you pass in a block, all the nested calls create nested tags.

XML Builder templates are Ruby code, and they run as Rails views, which means you can call all those wonderful helpers you normally use in your .erb files. In this example, we use the Action View named route helpers. We could have just as easily used any other built-in Rails helpers or even custom helpers defined in our application.

We won't go into too much detail on the RSS specification and what each element in this feed means. You can read the full RSS 2.0 specification at http://cyber.law.harvard.edu/rss/rss.html if you're into that kind of thing. This is the high-level overview.

RSS feeds have channels. Channels are named and have URLs, titles, and descriptions. More important, channels have items in them that also have URLs, titles, and descriptions as well as authors and the timestamp of when they were created. In our case, as you can see, these items are going to be recipes.

With this overview of XML Builder and RSS, the workings of recipes.rss.builder become self-apparent. The one little critical nugget you may not have noticed is the use of the _url forms of the named route helpers (for example, recipes_url()). This is easy to forget, because it's seldom necessary in everyday Rails views. It tells Rails to generate a URL with the full protocol and host name as opposed to just the relative path to the URL. Since these feeds will be consumed outside our application, a relative path won't do.

Here's an abbreviated example of the RSS feed we generate:

rr2/syndication/sample.xml
```
<?xml version="1.0" encoding="UTF-8"?>
<rss version="2.0" xmlns:dc="http://purl.org/dc/elements/1.1/">
  <channel>
    <title>Freshly Added Recipes</title>
    <link>http://localhost:3000/recipes</link>
    <pubDate>Tue, 04 Jan 2011 18:13:19 GMT</pubDate>
    <description>Cook Book Freshly Added Recipes.</description>
```

```
  <item>
    <title>Blood Sausage</title>
    <link>http://localhost:3000/recipes/1</link>
    <description></description>
    <pubDate>Tue, 04 Jan 2011 18:13:19 GMT</pubDate>
    <guid>http://localhost:3000/recipes/1</guid>
    <author>hank</author>
  </item>
  <item>
    <title>Natto Omlet</title>
    <link>http://localhost:3000/recipes/2</link>
    <description></description>
    <pubDate>Tue, 04 Jan 2011 18:13:20 GMT</pubDate>
    <guid>http://localhost:3000/recipes/2</guid>
    <author>forrest</author>
  </item>
  </channel>
</rss>
```

And here's what a full feed would look like in an RSS aggregator:

Now that we have a feed available, we naturally want the world to know about it. Of course, there's always the tried-and-true method of putting a big RSS button on your website with a link to the feed. But there's also a trick for helping web browsers and aggregators automatically discover available feeds.

Although it's not a published, official standard, a de facto standard for RSS autodiscovery has emerged using the HTML <link> tag. The tag goes in your page's <head> element and looks like this (from my website):

```
<link href="http://feeds.feedburner.com/Chadfowlercom"
    rel="alternate"
    title="RSS"
    type="application/rss+xml" />
```

Browsers and aggregators know how to extract these tags from web pages to find the feed links. This is a really good thing to put in your layouts. It's much easier for your users to remember mycooldomain.com when they're trying to subscribe to your feed than some technical URL. Thankfully, Rails makes adding an autodiscovery link trivial. Inside the <head> of your page template, insert the following:

```
<%= auto_discovery_link_tag(:rss,
                            :controller => 'feeds',
                            :action => 'recipes') %>
```

If you had created an Atom feed, you could replace :rss with :atom. Rails will generate the <link> code for you, so you don't have to remember the syntax.

Finally, as an optimization measure, since we've put our RSS code in a separate controller, we can add the following to the top of the feed controller, just after the class definition:

```
session :off
```

RSS requests are stateless, so there's no need to generate a session for every request. Since aggregators generally won't send any cookies with their requests, leaving session enabled for a feed could translate into hundreds of thousands of sessions needlessly created in a short span of time, which would be a bad thing if you were storing your session data in a database or memcached service.

RSS feeds are a great way to keep track of a large amount of time-sensitive data. They're good for tracking public sites, but they're also good for keeping track of your private information. For example, an RSS aggregator is a powerful tool for managing a software project when attached to a bug tracker, source control repository, and discussion forum.

The problem is that this kind of data is private and usually requires authentication. RSS aggregators are hit-or-miss when it comes to supporting authentication schemes, so it will probably be necessary to work around the problem. One way to do that is by using obfuscated, resource-specific URLs.

You can read more about how to do that in Recipe 55, *Create Secret URLs*, on page 212.

Also See

Recipe 55, *Create Secret URLs*, on page 212

Set Your Application's Home Page

Problem

By default, in a freshly generated Rails application, the root URL displays the Rails Welcome Aboard page. But you'd like your root URL to point to a meaningful action in your application, such as http://example.com/. When your users access the root URL of your application, how can you configure Rails to route them to the controller and the action of your choice?

Solution

The Rails routing method root() is the tool to use when you want to set a home page for your application. In addition to providing a new route to our preferred root, we also have to delete the existing index file of our application. If we are building a recipe-sharing application, for example, and we want the root of the application to point to a recipe index, we can configure the root to route there like this:

```
rr2/set_home_page/config/routes.rb
SetHomePage::Application.routes.draw do
  root :to => "recipes#index"
  resources :recipes
end
```

Although we have configured the root route, we're not finished. Here's the problem. If you access the root URL of the application now, you will still see that old familiar Rails welcome page. Why? Because it's being served not by Rails but by the web server!

Look at the contents of public/index.html. You'll find that this file contains the source for the Rails welcome page. The public directory is where the Rails web server configuration conventionally finds static pages and assets. Images in public/images, for example, are accessible via http://example.com/images/. That means the public/index.html file is accessible via http://example.com/index.html. For most web server configurations, the filename index.html is special. If a browser requests a directory path on the web server and an index.html file is present, the web server will serve it up.

The web server running your Rails application is configured to serve static files that match the request path when they exist and to delegate to Rails only when there's no static file available. So, to disable the welcome page and allow Rails to route to your intended root action, simply remove the public/index.html file!

Now that you're routing to the action of your choice, don't be fooled by the simplicity of the root() method. You're not limited to simply pointing the root URL to a specific controller and action. You have the same power available here as you do with other routes. You could, for example, set arbitrary parameters or apply constraints to the root mapping.

Perhaps you want to use the Recipe index both as an application home page and as an regular index view for CRUD operations. The only difference between these two modes of access is the sort order of the displayed recipes. You could then configure the root mapping like this:

```
root :to => "recipes#index", :sort_style => "home"
```

Now, when the recipe index is accessed via the root URL, the sort_style parameter is set to home.

Part III

User Interface Recipes

No matter how well organized and efficient your business logic, your views are what your users experience in your application. Important as they are, many developers treat them as an afterthought. Keeping your views clean and maintainable is as important as keeping your business logic clean. These recipes will give you techniques not only for creating solid, maintainable views but for adding extra touches to your application's interface, making it easier and more appealing to use.

Create a Custom Form Builder

Problem

Your application uses particular form elements and styles repeatedly. You want to create a helper you can call whenever you need to build forms in the same style. Suppose, for example, that you like to label every field of the form you create with a name or alternate the color of each row in a grid.

Solution

To create a custom form builder, first define a custom FormBuilder subclass to implement the result you want. Add it to the lib directory of your application. Use the form_for :builder option to tell the framework to use your new FormBuilder subclass instead of the default Rails FormBuilder. For example, to create a form with labels for each of its fields, first define a LabeledFormBuilder class in your application's lib directory. Here's its definition:

```
rr2/custom_form_builder/lib/labeled_form_builder.rb
class LabeledFormBuilder < ActionView::Helpers::FormBuilder
  (field_helpers -
    %w(check_box radio_button hidden_field label)).each do |selector|
    src = <<-END_SRC
      def #{selector}(field, options = {})
        @template.content_tag("p", label(field) + ": " + super)
      end
    END_SRC
    class_eval src, __FILE__, __LINE__
  end
end
```

Now use the build option of the form_for helper to call LabeledFormBuilder, as shown in the following code snippet:

```
<%= form_for :contact, :builder => LabeledFormBuilder do |f| %>
<%= f.text_field :street_address %>
<%= f.text_field :postal_code %>
<%= f.text_field :neighborhood %>
<%= f.text_field :price %>
<%= f.text_area :notes %>
<%= f.submit %>
<% end %>
```

The form_for() family of Rails helpers provides a form builder option that you can use to customize your forms. Code for creating a vanilla Rails form to gather data for a house variable might look like this:

```
<%= form_for @house do |f| %>
<%= f.text_field :street_address %>
<%= f.text_field :postal_code %>
<%= f.text_field :neighborhood %>
<%= f.text_field :price %>
<%= f.text_area :notes %>
<%= f.submit %>
<% end %>
```

This code generates a form for the variable @house and five of its fields. While its syntax is clear, this code generates the same HTML form we'd get with a stock Rails application. The solution gets more exciting when you take advantage of form_for()'s :builder option. The builder is the object that is yielded to form_for()'s block. Because you call the helpers on that object, it's the builder that actually generates the HTML for the form and its tags.

Suppose we always want every field in our forms to have a label. The form_for() call would look something like this:

```
<%= form_for :contact, :builder => LabeledFormBuilder do |f| %>
<%= f.text_field :street_address %>
<%= f.text_field :postal_code %>
<%= f.text_field :neighborhood %>
<%= f.text_field :price %>
<%= f.text_area :notes %>
<%= f.submit %>
<% end %>
```

Then we would define the LabeledFormBuilder in our application's lib directory. Here's its definition:

rr2/custom_form_builder/lib/labeled_form_builder.rb
```
class LabeledFormBuilder < ActionView::Helpers::FormBuilder
  (field_helpers -
  %w(check_box radio_button hidden_field label)).each do |selector|
    src = <<-END_SRC
      def #{selector}(field, options = {})
        @template.content_tag("p", label(field) + ": " + super)
      end
    END_SRC
    class_eval src, __FILE__, __LINE__
  end
end
```

If you haven't done a lot of metaprogramming in Ruby, this class might be a
little jarring at first. It's OK to take this dynamically generated code on faith,
so don't let it bog you down. You can use the LabeledFormBuilder class as a template for creating your own builders. The code loops through all the helpers
defined on FormBuilder and overrides them with our own autogenerated method
definitions. If you turn your head to the side and squint at the code for
LabeledFormBuilder, you can see that, in the loop, the class defines a method with
the same name as each helper (such as text_field() and text_area()). Each method
sets up a paragraph with a label after which the output of the original helper
from FormBuilder is placed.

Our modified form_for() now generates HTML that looks like the following
markup (some newlines were added to make this listing fit the width of the
page):

```
<p>
  <label for="house_street_address">Street address</label>:
  <input id="house_street_address"
         name="house[street_address]" size="30" type="text" />
</p>
<p>
  <label for="house_postal_code">Postal code</label>:
  <input id="house_postal_code"
         name="house[postal_code]" size="30" type="text" />
</p>
```

At last, we're getting somewhere! Now, because our forms are generated using
a builder that we can control, we can tweak this markup to our heart's content
and create the perfect form wherever we need it. In fact, it's so great to be
able to customize and standardize controls like this on a per-application basis
that it would be convenient if we didn't need to include the :builder option on
each and every form. No problem! To do that, we just need to set Action View's
default form builder at Rails startup. A good place to put code to execute at
startup is in the config/initializers directory. Any Ruby file in that directory will
be loaded and evaluated during the configuration phase of boot process.
Here's our file that sets the default form builder for the entire application:

rr2/custom_form_builder/config/initializers/custom_form_builder.rb
```
require 'labeled_form_builder'
ActionView::Base.default_form_builder = LabeledFormBuilder
```

We simply require the file that defines our labeled form builder and set it as
the default on ActionView::Base. Now, unless specifically overridden using the
:builder option, all form_for() calls in our application will use the LabeledFormBuilder
to generate HTML.

Now that you have that working, you can't help but ask yourself what *other* elements you constantly find yourself putting into forms. How about alternating the color of each row in a form? Here's a form builder that does that:

```
rr2/custom_form_builder/lib/alternating_colors_form_builder.rb
class AlternatingColorsFormBuilder < ActionView::Helpers::FormBuilder
  (field_helpers -
   %w(check_box radio_button hidden_field label)).each do |selector|
    src = <<-END_SRC
      def #{selector}(field, options = {})
        @template.content_tag("p",
                              label(field) + ": " + super,
                              :class => @template.cycle("", "alt-row"))
      end
    END_SRC
    class_eval src, __FILE__, __LINE__
  end
end
```

This builder uses the built-in helper method cycle() to toggle the CSS class name with each field's paragraph tag. Adding a CSS snippet like the following to your application's style sheet will give you a nice, readable alternating table row effect:

```
.alt-row { background: #fab444; }
```

Consider creating one or more custom form builders for each of your applications. As you can see here, custom form builders can create consistency in your user interface and help make your code more maintainable and succinct.

Credit

Thanks to Mike Clark and Bruce Williams for their contributions to this recipe.

Pluralize Words on the Fly (or Not)

Problem

One annoying little problem that we have all had to deal with from time to time occurs when you need to choose between the plural or singular version of a word depending on how many items are returned from a database. How many messages does a user have in his or her inbox? How many failed transactions does a financial operations team need to resolve? Wouldn't it be great if the choice to display singular or plural could be automated?

Solution

Rails comes with a wonderful tool called the Inflector, which is the utility that (among doing other tasks) figures out what a table name should be called based on the name of its associated model. Its logic involves a great deal of smarts, which has thankfully been exposed for use anywhere in a Rails application. In fact, a handy wrapper method called pluralize() in Action View was made to handle the most common pluralization scenarios. Here's how you use the pluralize method:

rr2/pluralization/app/views/recipes/index.html.erb
```
Hi <%= @user.name %>.
You have <%= pluralize @recipes.size, "unread recipe" %>  in your inbox.
```

For example, what if your application isn't in English or you want to support the (horrible) geek-culture tendency to refer to server boxes as *boxen*? Casting aside good taste, you can write your own language rules by customizing the Inflector's pluralization rules. A freshly generated Rails app even has a file, config/initializers/inflections.rb, with commented examples. Let's uncomment and modify some of the file's lines:

rr2/pluralization/config/initializers/inflections.rb
```
ActiveSupport::Inflector.inflections do |inflect|
  inflect.plural /(ox)$/i, '\1en'
  inflect.singular /(ox)en/i, '\1'
end
```

Now, the plural form of *box* is *boxen*, and vice versa.

You can also use the Inflector's uncountable() method to mark words that have no plural and the irregular() method to configure words whose pluralization rules don't follow a pattern:

```
inflect.uncountable "fish", "information", "money"
inflect.irregular "person", "people"
```

If you're curious about which rules have already been configured, you can query the configured rules like so:

```
>> ActiveSupport::Inflector.inflections.plurals
 => [[/(ox)$/i, "\\1en"], [/k(?i)ine$/, "kine"], [/K(?i)ine$/, "Kine"]...etc.
>> ActiveSupport::Inflector.inflections.uncountable
 => ["equipment", "information", "rice", "money", "species"...]
```

Noun inflection is a place where the consistency built into Rails really shines. Take advantage of it where you can to avoid manual, often error-prone, pluralization rules in your own code.

Insert Action-Specific Content in a Layout

Problem

Layouts are a great way to keep the view code of your application free of duplication while maintaining a consistent structure in its pages. But suppose you want to add dynamic, action-specific content to a page without dirtying the layout.

Solution

The best way to add dynamic content to a standard Rails page without disrupting its appearance is to use the content_for() view method that ships with the Action Pack. content_for() is used to queue up content for use later. The method takes a Symbol parameter, which is used to name the content (think of it as a view-specific variable name) and a block whose contents get stored and associated with that Symbol. Here's how to make it work.

Imagine we have a simple layout with a sidebar. We want to insert action-specific content into the sidebar displaying "recent items" in a context-specific way. Suppose the application is one that manages recipes. When we view the recipe list, we want to show the most recently added recipes in the sidebar. In our recipe index view, we might include something like this:

rr2/per_action_content/app/views/recipes/index.html.erb
```erb
<% content_for :recent do %>
<h1>Recent Recipes</h1>
    <ul>
    <% @recent_recipes.each do |recipe| %>
      <li><%= link_to recipe.name, recipe %></li>
    <% end %>
    </ul>
<% end %>
```

We define a block of view code that we're storing in the view and naming "recent." This code can appear *anywhere* in the index view. The location doesn't matter, because this code won't be rendered into the view when we call content_for(). It's only processed and stored for later.

Now to use this snippet of view code, we do the following in our layout:

```
rr2/per_action_content/app/views/layouts/application.html.erb
<div id='sidebar'>
        Things that go in the sidebar!
        <% if content_for?(:recent) %>
        <p class='recent'>
          <%= yield :recent %>
        </p>

        <% end %>
</div>
```

This code defines a sidebar in which the static, site-wide sidebar contents would go. Then we use the content_for?() method to conditionally render a paragraph tag in which we'll put our per-action content. If content_for?() returns true, we define the paragraph and then call yield :recent to embed the results of the content_for() call in the action's view code.

The key to understanding the solution is the order in which Rails processes each step of your request. When a request comes in, here's a simplified list of the steps Rails takes to satisfy it:

1. The routing engine uses the incoming HTTP verb and URI to map to a controller and action.

2. The controller is instantiated with Request and Response objects encapsulating input and output.

3. The action method is executed.

4. The view for the action is rendered.

5. Unless otherwise directed, the layout is rendered.

If you're like me, you'll be surprised by the order in which these steps are executed. Given that an action's content is added to the layout by a call to yield() in the layout, you might have expected step 4 to come *after* step 5. But, no. The action's view is rendered first and then simply inserted into the layout using yield().

Thus, the problem at hand is a view-layer problem. So, if you want to prepare action-specific view content, the right place to do it is not in the controller but in the *view*. Since the action's view is rendered before the layout, we can prepare action-specific view content for the layout while in the action's view!

Add Unobtrusive Ajax with jQuery

Problem

You want to issue Ajax-style asynchronous HTTP requests to post and retrieve data from a Rails service without reloading the user's browser page. But you want to keep your HTML as clean and free of code as possible. For example, suppose you want to asynchronously switch between views of a personnel file, one that shows only administrators and one that shows everyone without reloading the entire page?

Solution

The answer is to use the new built-in support for unobtrusive JavaScript that ships with Rails 3. Rails 3 also makes it easier for you to plug in your favorite JavaScript framework, eliminating prior versions' tight coupling with Prototype.js. In fact, because the jQuery framework has become so popular, Rails 3.1 goes one step further and installs jQuery as its default framework.

If you're implementing your site with a version of Rails that precedes version 3.1, you'll need to first install jQuery 3 before you can use it. (See *Installing jQuery for Rails 3*, on page 121.)

With jQuery in place, let's make sure we have the necessary headers in our layout. By default, they will be in app/views/layouts/application.html.erb. We need to ensure the following two lines appear in the head section of our layout:

```
<%= javascript_include_tag "application" %>
<%= csrf_meta_tags %>
```

If we were to forget either of these lines, we might later find ourselves staring at a lifeless HTML page with no sign of error, which as you can imagine would be both frustrating and demotivating.

Now that we're set up and ready to go, for the sake of reproducibility we'll start with a scaffolded controller:

```
$ rails g scaffold Person name:string admin:boolean
      invoke  active_record
      create    db/migrate/20110219192623_create_people.rb
      create    app/models/person.rb
```

Installing jQuery for Rails 3

To install jQuery for your pre–Rails 3.1 project, you'll first need to update the project's Gemfile to include the following declaration:

```
gem 'jquery-rails'
```

To install the jquery-rails gem (and any other dependencies not yet installed for our project), run the following command from the root of our Rails application:

```
$ bundle install
```

With your gems up-to-date, you should find yourself with a new generator that, when you run it, will copy the necessary JavaScript files into your project for jQuery.

```
$ rails generate jquery:install
      remove  public/javascripts/controls.js
      remove  public/javascripts/dragdrop.js
      remove  public/javascripts/effects.js
      remove  public/javascripts/prototype.js
    fetching  jQuery (1.5)
      create  public/javascripts/jquery.js
      create  public/javascripts/jquery.min.js
    fetching  jQuery UJS adapter (github HEAD)
    conflict  public/javascripts/rails.js
Overwrite public/javascripts/rails.js? (enter "h" for help) [Ynaqdh] Y
       force  public/javascripts/rails.js
```

This generator removes Prototype.js and other supporting JavaScript files, replacing them with jQuery. Also, notice we've allowed it to overwrite the file rails.js. This file is where much of the magic of the Rails unobtrusive JavaScript support comes from.

Now you're ready to put jQuery to work.!

```
    invoke    test_unit
    create      test/unit/person_test.rb
    create      test/fixtures/people.yml
     route  resources :people
...
```

We have a collection of people, some of whom are administrators. We want to modify the generated index view to allow us to asynchronously filter only administrators and to toggle back and forth between the filtered and unfiltered views.

We'll start by modifying the app/views/people/index.html.erb view. We need a link to toggle the filtering functionality, but we don't want this to be a normal link, resulting in a browser page reload. We want it to make an Ajax request back to the server without updating the page.

Here's how we do that:

```
rr2/ajax_with_jquery/app/views/people/index.html.erb
<%= link_to "Showing all (toggle)",
    people_path(:admin => true),
    :remote => true,
    :id => 'toggle' %>
```

We're creating a link back to the index() action of the PeopleController, passing in a parameter called admin to signal to the server that we want the filtered list. The part that makes this call special is the option :remote, which we've set to true. This tells Rails to generate an Ajax-enabled link. How does it do this?

Here's where the unobtrusive part comes into play. In the old days, Rails might have generated inline JavaScript that would have overridden the onClick() event for the link. In Rails 3, it does something better. Look at the generated HTML from our link_to() call:

```
<a href="/people?admin=true"
   data-remote="true"
   id="toggle">Showing all (toggle)</a>
```

Hey, that's pretty clean! No JavaScript in sight! So, how does this become an Ajax link? The answer is in the combination of the data-remote attribute we see here and the contents of the public/javascripts/rails.js file we saw earlier. Here's the relevant snippet from that file:

```
$('a[data-confirm], a[data-method], a[data-remote]').live('click.rails',
    function(e) {
                var link = $(this);
                if (!allowAction(link)) return false;

                if (link.attr('data-remote') != undefined) {
                    handleRemote(link);
                    return false;
                } else if (link.attr('data-method')) {
                    handleMethod(link);
                    return false;
                }
        });
```

This code uses jQuery to hook the onClick() event of any anchor tag with the "data-confirm," "data-method," or "data-remote" attribute set. If the "data-remote" attribute is set, as is the case with our generated link, a click is handled by the handleRemote() function. The handleRemote() function is also defined in rails.js. It creates and processes an Ajax request.

So, now that we have a working Ajax link, the next step is to implement the functionality on the server to respond to the request appropriately. Our link points to the route for the index() action of the PeopleController. Here's the new implementation of that action:

```
rr2/ajax_with_jquery/app/controllers/people_controller.rb
def index
  @people = params[:admin] ? Person.where(:admin => true) : Person.all

  respond_to do |format|
    format.html # index.html.erb
    format.xml  { render :xml => @people }
    format.js # renders index.js.erb
  end
end
```

Now, rather than always return all of the people in the database, we conditionally return administrators based only on the presence of the :admin parameter. Finally, to respond properly to Ajax requests, we added the format.js line to the respond_to() block. This signals that we can respond to requests with JavaScript and that the default rendering action will take place, which in our case will be the rendering of the file app/views/people/index.js.erb:

```
rr2/ajax_with_jquery/app/views/people/index.js.erb
<% link_text = params[:admin] ? "Admins" : "All" %>
<% href = params[:admin] ?
               people_path : people_path(:admin => true) %>
$("#toggle").html("Showing <%= link_text %> (toggle)");
$("#toggle").attr("href", "<%= href %>");
$("#people").html('<%= escape_javascript(render @people) %>');
```

This is the final piece of the puzzle. To fully understand how it works, we'll need to look at the structure of our normal index view, app/views/people/index.html.erb. Here's the part that renders our people list:

```
rr2/ajax_with_jquery/app/views/people/index.html.erb
<ul id='people'>
      <%= render @people %>
</ul>
```

Notice we have an unordered list with the id "people." For the list items, we simply render a collection of @people, which implicitly calls app/views/people/_person.erb in a loop. Here's that partial:

```
rr2/ajax_with_jquery/app/views/people/_person.erb
<li><%= link_to person.name, person %></li>
```

So, looking back to our index.js.erb file, you can see that the job of this file is to render JavaScript code back to the browser. Since the filename ends with erb, Rails will run this JavaScript code through the ERB templating system, allowing us to insert dynamic server-generated code. The first five lines replace the toggle link from our view so that it properly indicates whether we're viewing everyone or just administrators and conditionally includes the admin parameter for the next click.

The final line of the template generates JavaScript to replace the contents of the element with the ID "people" (our unordered list), with the contents of rendering the _person.erb partial for each item in the @people list.

Upon rendering this template and returning it to the browser, the calling jQuery code will evaluate the JavaScript in the scope of the already loaded page. So, our .js.erb view enables us to write JavaScript on the server that runs locally in the already loaded page of a browser client. Powerful stuff!

Here we've seen how to generate an Ajax link. The same can be done using the form_for(), form_tag(), and button_to() helpers. In each case, an option called :remote results in the "data-remote" being set and the rails.js file hooking in appropriately.

Now that you see how easy it is to create Ajax effects for your application, avoid the temptation to apply it everywhere. Sometimes the simplest user interface is just a plain old page refresh.

Create One Form for Many Models

Problem

In a well-designed database, tables are partitioned according to their meanings in the application domain and the most efficient methods of access. As database programmers, we spend a lot of time and energy making sure our databases are well-designed. Unfortunately, this design doesn't always translate well into our user interfaces. What's good for a relational database management system may not be good for a human trying to do data entry. Go figure.

The mismatch between design and UI is a particular problem when we want to create a form for entering or editing data that belongs to two or more models. With the form_for() helper that ships with Rails, we can only create forms that wrap *one* ActiveModel object. So, how can we create a form we can use to interact with data from multiple, associated models?

Solution

The keys to creating multimodel forms in Rails are Active Record's accepts_nested_attributes_for() method and Action View's fields_for() method.

Imagine we have a Recipe model with a has_many() association to ingredients. The model code might look like this:

rr2/nested_forms/app/models/recipe.rb
```
class Recipe < ActiveRecord::Base
  has_many :ingredients
end
```

rr2/nested_forms/app/models/ingredient.rb
```
class Ingredient < ActiveRecord::Base
  belongs_to :recipe
end
```

A recipe has a name and a long text field of instructions. An ingredient belongs to a recipe and has a name and a quantity. Recipes can have many ingredients.

When users create a recipe entry in the site's user interface, they aren't going to think of each ingredient as a separate record, even though that's how we've chosen to model them in the database. They're going to want to create a recipe and its ingredients on a single form. We can enable this using the built-in view helper fields_for().

When we create a form with form_for(), it yields an ActionView::Helpers::FormBuilder to the block in our view. Rails developers usually call this local variable f. The FormBuilder is responsible for wrapping the object for which the form is being built, binding to any existing data in that object, and forming the necessary parameter names to match the Rails parameter conventions also used by our controllers.

If we call the fields_for() helper on the FormBuilder, Rails constructs a new FormBuilder instance for us, but this time it wraps an *associated* record or set of records rather than the primary subject of the form. Here's an example that wraps our Recipe and Ingredient models:

rr2/nested_forms/app/views/recipes/new.html.erb
```erb
<h1>Add a Recipe</h1>
<%= form_for @recipe do |f| %>
  <p>
  <%= f.label :name %>
  <%= f.text_field :name %>
  </p>

  <p>
  <%= f.label :instructions %>
  <%= f.text_area :instructions %>
  </p>
  <h2>Ingredients</h2>
  <p>
  <%= f.fields_for(:ingredients) do |ingredients_form| %>
    <%= ingredients_form.label :name %>
    <%= ingredients_form.text_field :name %>
    <%= ingredients_form.label :quantity %>
    <%= ingredients_form.text_field :quantity %>
  <% end %>
  </p>
  <%= f.submit %>
<% end %>
```

To signal to the model that we're going to be pulling in all of these associated attributes from the form, we'll add the following declaration to our Recipe model:

rr2/nested_forms/app/models/recipe.rb
```ruby
accepts_nested_attributes_for :ingredients
```

Combined, these examples create a single form that posts, by convention, to the RecipesController's create() action. However, in addition to the usual fields for the @recipe object, it also wraps fields for a new Ingredient. This seems great so far, but if we were to load this page in our browser, we'd be greeted with an empty list of Ingredients and no way to add one. This is because the fields_for() method generates fields for an *existing* object. If we want to add new Ingredients, we need to first create empty Ingredient objects and associate them with the Recipe.

One way to do that would be to add a new Ingredient to the @recipe when we instantiate it in the new() action in the controller. That might look something like this:

rr2/nested_forms/app/controllers/recipes_controller.rb
```ruby
def new
  @recipe = Recipe.new(:ingredients => [Ingredient.new])
end
```

With this in place, we should see one empty slot for an Ingredient when we view the new Recipe form. Let's look at the generated HTML for the part of the form that wraps associated Ingredients:

```html
<h2>Ingredients</h2>
  <p>

    <label for="recipe_ingredients_attributes_0_name">
      Name
    </label>
    <input id="recipe_ingredients_attributes_0_name"
           name="recipe[ingredients_attributes][0][name]"
           size="30"
           type="text" />
    <label for="recipe_ingredients_attributes_0_quantity">
      Quantity
    </label>
    <input id="recipe_ingredients_attributes_0_quantity"
           name="recipe[ingredients_attributes][0][quantity]"
           size="30"
           type="text" />
  </p>
```

From this generated HTML source we can start to get a feeling for how Rails will parse and process this form for our controller. If we submit this form with no values, we'll see the following param structure on the server:

```
{"utf8"=>"✓",
 "authenticity_token"=>"dUdoPRMb9EFdX0oCF6wJ0yhK7R2PAUQ9Dkz3epC0EdM=",
 "recipe"=>{
   "name"=>"",
```

```
    "instructions"=>"",
    "ingredients_attributes"=>{"0"=>{"name"=>"", "quantity"=>""}}},
    "commit"=>"Create Recipe"
}
```

Notice that the ingredients_attributes key is nested in the main recipe Hash, which means as per Rails convention, the method ingredients_attributes=() will be invoked when a new Recipe is instantiated with this data. Guess what the accepts_nested_attributes_for() macro does? That's right! It metaprograms a method onto Recipe, which defines ingredients_attributes=().

If all we need to do is add one ingredient to a Recipe when we create it, we're done. But this still leaves a little to be desired. For example, every recipe is likely to need more than one ingredient, so providing for only a single addition isn't so great. Also, when we're editing an existing recipe, it might be nice to be able to delete associated ingredients. Let's tackle those two problems.

There are many ways to allow users to add ingredients. The simplest way is to simply preallocate a number of empty ingredients whenever the form is loaded. Rather than hard-code this allocation into the controller as we saw in the previous example, let's make a nice model-level method to do it for us. We'll add a new instance method to the Recipe class:

rr2/nested_forms/app/models/recipe.rb
```ruby
def with_blank_ingredients(n = 5)
  n.times do
    ingredients.build
  end
  self
end
```

Now in our call to form_for(), we can add a reference to this method. Because with_blank_ingredients() returns self, its return value can be passed directly into form_for():

rr2/nested_forms/app/views/recipes/new_prealloc.html.erb
```erb
<%= form_for @recipe.with_blank_ingredients do |f| %>
```

Now five blank ingredients will appear on the form. If we fill out the form, those ingredients will be saved. If we were to use this form for our edit() action, the existing ingredients would appear as well as five blank ingredient fields. Preallocating a set number of blank form elements is a little ugly, but it works. The one major problem with this implementation is that when we save the form, the blank ingredients that we did *not* fill in will also be saved. We can fix that by adding an option to our accepts_nested_attributes_for() call, as shown in the following code:

```
accepts_nested_attributes_for :ingredients,
  :reject_if => lambda { |attrs|
                  attrs.all? { |key, value| value.blank? }
                }
```

This tells the ingredients_attributes=() not to save any Ingredient records whose passed form values are blank.

Finally, let's look at how to remove existing child records in a nested form. One option is, of course, to simply create a button next to each Ingredient row on the form that calls the destroy() action in the IngredientsController. But, our goal here is to allow our users to do as much as possible on this one form, and sending them on round-trips with page refreshes defeats the purpose. So, instead, we can take advantage of yet another Rails convention.

If in our nested form fields we create an attribute called _destroy, we can use it to ask accepts_nested_attributes_for() to automatically destroy nested records for us. Here's what we would have to add to our view:

```
<%= unless ingredients_form.object.new_record?
           ingredients_form.check_box('_destroy') +
             ingredients_form.label('_destroy', 'Remove')
end %>
```

So, if we're working with an Ingredient that has yet to be saved, it doesn't make sense to ask to destroy it. If the record has been saved, we generate a checkbox with the special attribute name _destroy. All that's left to do now is to tell accepts_nested_attributes_for() that it's OK to destroy records. We do that with the :allow_destroy option:

```
accepts_nested_attributes_for :ingredients,
  :reject_if => lambda { |attrs|
                  attrs.all? { |key, value| value.blank? }
                },
  :allow_destroy => true
```

And, now, if we pass down a value for the _destroy attribute associated with an Ingredient, Active Record will destroy that record for us!

Rather than preallocate an arbitrary number of new records for a nested form, it's common practice to use JavaScript to generate those rows. Using your favorite JavaScript library, it can be trivial to templatize and dynamically add elements to the browser's document object model. The trick is in understanding the structure necessary for those new elements. If we look at the generated HTML for one of the Ingredient elements in our solution, we'll see something like this:

```
<input id="recipe_ingredients_attributes_0_name"
       name="recipe[ingredients_attributes][0][name]"
       size="30"
       type="text" />
```

The secret here is that the literal "0" doesn't have to be a number! It just has
to be unique in the set of values we pass from the browser. So, when using
JavaScript to dynamically generate nested form elements, you can use any
trick for generating a per-form unique value. A good choice, for example,
might be to use the current timestamp.

An important point to note about nested forms is that although Rails makes
it *relatively* painless to implement them, big forms can clutter the view and
make life harder for your users. Before turning to a complex nested form on
your next application, ask yourself whether it would be better for the user to
break the form into multiple steps.

Cache Local Data with HTML5 Data Attributes

Problem

Before the introduction of HTML5, if you were creating a rich, JavaScript-driven HTML user interface and wanted to store data in the browser for use by elements on the page, you were on your own. You could certainly store data in a JavaScript structure and access it by element id. Or you could create a custom XHTML namespace. But any solution required some manual work, and anyone who followed you on the project had to learn your way of doing things.

HTML5 introduces a standard solution to this problem with its new data-* attributes. How can we best use these from Rails applications?

Solution

You can create tags that store local data with the new Rails 3.1+ :data option. This gives us a convenient mechanism for generating HTML5 tags with data-* attributes, a feature available with HTML 5. In this recipe, we'll generate a page with data-* and then show how to read those options using CoffeeScript.

The first step is to generate an HTML template containing data attributes. As an example, we'll create a simple contact management app. We want to generate a sparse list of contact names but show more detailed information about the contact when a user hovers over the name with a mouse. We'll start with the default scaffolded index() action and a basic Contact model containing fields for name, city, state, and country.

Here's code to list the Contact records like this:

```
rr2/html5-data/app/views/contacts/index.html.erb
<h1>Listing contacts</h1>
<ul>
<% @contacts.each do |contact| %>
  <%= content_tag_for(:li,
                      contact,
                      :data => {
                        :city => contact.city,
                        :name => contact.name,
```

```
                              :country => contact.country}) do %>
    <%= contact.name %> from <%= contact.city %>
  <% end %>
<% end %>
</ul>

<br />

<%= link_to 'New Contact', new_contact_path %>
<div id='tip' style='display:none'>
</div>
```

There isn't much new here. Except for one feature, it's all the same view code Rails developers have been writing for years. The exception is that when we generate the <li> elements, we use content_tag_for()'s :data option to specify a Hash of data elements we want embedded in the generated element. So, though our <li> element shows only the contact's name, the element itself has more information embedded. An example contact list's source might look like this:

```
<li class="contact" data-city="New Orleans"
  data-country="USA" data-name="Chad Fowler" id="contact_1">
    Chad Fowler from New Orleans
</li>
<li class="contact" data-city="Oak Park" data-country="USA"
  data-name="Donald Shimoda" id="contact_2">
    Donald Shimoda from Oak Park
</li>
<li class="contact" data-city="Tokyo" data-country="Japan"
  data-name="Toru Okada" id="contact_3">
    Toru Okada from Tokyo
</li>
```

Now that we've successfully embedded data into the list elements, we'll write some CoffeeScript to display it. We have prepared an empty, hidden <div> at the bottom of our index() view with the id set to <tip>. Our CoffeeScript code will fill this element with additional contact information when a user hovers over the corresponding list element. Here's our CoffeeScript file, which we've put in app/assets/javascripts/contacts.js.coffee:

rr2/html5-data/app/assets/javascripts/contacts.js.coffee

```
$ ->
  $('.contact').bind 'mouseenter', (event) =>
    contact = event.target
    $('#tip').html text_summary_for(contact)
    $('#tip').show()
    $('.contact').bind 'mouseleave', (event) =>
      $('#tip').hide()
```

Automatic CoffeeScript Compilation

As of Rails 3.1, Rails will automatically compile CoffeeScript files into JavaScript in development mode. Simply edit CoffeeScript files in your app/assets/javascripts directory, and Rails will compile them into JavaScript and serve them as requests are made.

Here we're using jQuery's ability to run code when the document is ready. The code binds the <mouseenter> event to set the tip element's HTML to a text summary of the contact record and show it. Then on a <mouseleave>, we re-hide the tip. The text_summary_for() function simply concatenates a string of text to be rendered into the tip element:

rr2/html5-data/app/assets/javascripts/contacts.js.coffee
```
text_summary_for = (contact) =>
  contact.dataset['name'] +
    " lives in " +
    contact.dataset['city'] +
    " in " +
    contact.dataset['country']
```

That's all there is to it! As you can see, HTML5 data attributes make in-element data storage simple, and the addition of the :data option in Rails 3.1 makes it even cleaner.

Also See

- For more information on new features of HTML5, see Brian Hogan's *HTML5 and CSS3: Develop with Tomorrow's Standards Today* [Hog10].

- To learn more about CoffeeScript, check out the CoffeeScript website at http://jashkenas.github.com/coffee-script/. Another alternative, Trevor Burnham's *CoffeeScript: Accelerated JavaScript Development* [Bur11], is an excellent guide to the language.

Part IV

Testing Recipes

Rails is an "opinionated" application framework. It pushes its opinions on you through conventions and automation. In a vanilla Rails workflow, the shortest command possible causes all of your application's automated tests to run. This is Rails telling you something: testing is important, and you should do it all the time! These recipes show you how to test your models, controllers, views, and emails using both the built-in features of Rails and a collection of the leading-edge testing techniques and third-party tools.

Automate Tests for Your Models

Problem

A well-written Rails application captures all of its business logic in its models. Controllers and views let the outside world interact with those models. So, it stands to reason that most of your work as a Rails developer is going to happen implementing business rules in the model layer of the MVC framework.

If you're spending most of your time writing business rules in model files, it would be really convenient to test them without the interruption of having to wire the application's controllers and views to the models, start up the local development server, and then click links and fill out forms by hand. If you're the lone developer and the only one who knows *how* to performs those manual checks, you'll be left with a system that's hard to maintain and harder to test. Chances are you'll forget the details your application over time, and you're unlikely to take the time to step through the entire application each time you make a change.

An automated test is clearly the answer. How can we automate the testing of the business logic of our application?

Solution

The way to automate your business logic tests is to implement them as Rails unit tests, making use of the unit test and test fixture files that Rails generates, as well as its test() and assert() methods. The test files are automatically generated whenever you create a new model and are stored in the test/units/ directory of your application.

If you haven't started down the path of automated testing yet, you should have at least noticed that every time you generate a model (or really anything) in Rails, a set of tests is generated along with it. Let's look at an example:

```
$ rails g model Song title:string album_id:integer duration_in_seconds:integer
invoke active_record
create db/migrate/20101101225558_create_songs.rb
create app/models/song.rb
invoke test_unit
create test/unit/song_test.rb create test/fixtures/songs.yml
```

In the preceding snippet, we generated a simple Song model, and with it, without us asking for it, Rails generated two extra files: a unit test and a test fixture file. For now let's focus on the unit test in test/unit/song_test.rb. Here's what we get by default:

```
rr2/testing_your_models/test/unit/song_test.rb
require 'test_helper'

class SongTest < ActiveSupport::TestCase
  # Replace this with your real tests.
  test "the truth" do
    assert true
  end
end
```

There isn't much there yet, but it's a great start. With this code in place, after applying the migration Rails generated, we can already execute the test for a satisfying result. Let's give it a go.

```
rake test:units
(in /testing_your_models) Loaded suite
rake-0.8.7/lib/rake/rake_test_loader
Started .
Finished in 0.028537 seconds.
1 tests, 1 assertions, 0 failures, 0 errors, 0 skips
Test run options: --seed 244
```

Success! The important line is the one that shows how many tests, assertions, failures, errors, and skips were encountered during the test run. I'm working in a fresh application here, so this SongTest is the only test in the system. And as you can see, that test passed. What did we test?

Let's look at the code in test/unit/song_test.rb again. The first line loads the Rails testing framework. This is a superset of Ruby's built-in Test::Unit framework, adding Rails-specific features and some syntax sugar. Then we define a class, SongTest, which is a subclass of ActiveSupport::TestCase. That's where all of the magic comes from. Think of a TestCase as a group of related tests. In this case, this is where we'll put all tests for our new Song model.

This brings us to the real heart of the matter: the actual test. In Rails test cases, tests are defined by calling the test() method, passing in a name for the test and then a block of code that implements the test. The essence of each test is its *assertions*. An assertion is defined as a statement of refutable truth. For example, I can assert that my name is Chad. This is true, so the assertion passes. I could assert that I weigh forty pounds. This is not true, so that assertion would fail.

The most basic assertion available in the Test::Unit framework is assert(), which we see in this autogenerated test. You pass a boolean value to assert() along with an optional message to be displayed if the assertion fails. Any boolean false value will cause the assertion to fail. Otherwise, the assertion passes. So, this test, given the literal true, will always pass. If we were to change the true to false or nil, the assertion would fail as follows:

```
$ rake test:units
(in /Users/chad/src/rr2/Book/code/rr2/testing_your_models)
Loaded suite rake-0.8.7/lib/rake/rake_test_loader
Started
F
Finished in 0.030958 seconds.

  1) Failure:
test_the_truth(SongTest) [test/unit/song_test.rb:7]:
Failed assertion, no message given.

1 tests, 1 assertions, 1 failures, 0 errors, 0 skips

Test run options: --seed 22019
rake aborted!
Command failed with status (1): [/bin/...]

(See full trace by running task with --trace)
```

We can see that an assertion failed on line 7 of song_test.rb and that we had one failure altogether. The autogenerated test is clearly useful only as a placeholder, but it's a good placeholder in that it actually runs. To write our own first test, we simply need to change the name of the test and then make real assertions about real code. Let's replace the autogenerated test with:

rr2/testing_your_models/test/unit/song_test.rb
```
class SongTest < ActiveSupport::TestCase
  test "should be findable by title" do
    song = Song.create(:title => "Bat Chain Puller")
    assert_equal song, Song.find_by_title("Bat Chain Puller")
  end
end
```

If we run this code, we'll find once again we have a passing single test. In this test, we used the assert_equal() method, into which we pass an expected value followed by an actual value. assert_equal() compares the two values and fails if they aren't equal. This is probably the most useful of all of Test::Unit's assertions. You can go a long way with just these two if you're just getting started.

So far, we've only tested ActiveRecord itself, which isn't ultimately a very useful exercise for anything other than learning. Also, we're writing tests for code that already exists. If we continued this way, you might imagine spending a great deal of time coding your business logic and then coming back afterwards and writing test after test for that business logic. Please don't do it that way.

As much as we developers like to pretend we are OK with doing it, testing is boring. If I have a huge pile of code and I'm asked to write tests for it, I'm going to be unproductive and demotivated. However, I do like to *specify* how I want my code to look just before I write it. When I have to write a new feature, I ask myself, "If there were a perfect way to do this already in the system, what would it look like?" Then I write that code. My typical day of programming involves repeatedly imagining the "perfect" solution, implementing it, and repeating that process.

Here's the cool part: we can do this in tests. This process is called Test-Driven Development, or TDD for short. When done right, some people also call it Behavior-Driven Development, or BDD. It doesn't really matter what we call it. It's a productive process, it generates repeatable automated tests, and it's *fun*. Let's try adding a feature to our model this way.

I'd like to introduce the concept of an Album to the system. I want Songs to belong to Albums, so I'm going to use a has_many() relationship from Album to Song. Once that's done, I'd like to be able to ask an Album for its duration, which it should get by calculating the duration of the songs. First I'll generate the model and declare the relationships:

```
$ rails g model Album title:string artist:string
invoke active_record
create db/migrate/20101102002840_create_albums.rb
create app/models/album.rb
invoke test_unit
create test/unit/album_test.rb
create test/fixtures/albums.yml
$ rake db:migrate
(in /rr2/testing_your_models)
== CreateAlbums: migrating
...
== CreateAlbums: migrated (0.0013s)
```

The Album model itself will look like this for now:

rr2/testing_your_models/app/models/album_has_many.rb
```
class Album < ActiveRecord::Base
  has_many :songs
end
```

Now let's go into our new AlbumTest and think about how we want this feature to work. I often start by creating a new test and just writing the assertion I'm attempting to make. That gives me a clear goal. So, I might start with something like this:

```
test "should be able to report duration based on \
    the combined duration of its songs" do
  assert_equal 15, album.duration
end
```

We haven't even specified what album is assigned to yet, so this isn't enough code. But we can guess that we're going to have some instance of Album on which we'll be able to call a method called duration(). Also, notice how descriptive the test name is. We're specifying a *behavior* we expect from the system, not just naming a piece of code we're running. Readers of this code later will be able to read the test name and understand what the code does. Let's code the rest of the test:

rr2/testing_your_models/test/unit/album_test.rb
```
test "should be able to report duration based \
    on the combined duration of its songs" do
  album = Album.create
  3.times do
    album.songs.create(:duration_in_seconds => 5)
  end
  assert_equal 15, album.duration
end
```

If we run our tests now, we see an error complaining that the duration() method doesn't exist on Album. That's what we expected. We wrote a test for it and then ran the test to make sure it wasn't already there. Now it's time to write that method in the Album class.

rr2/testing_your_models/app/models/album.rb
```
def duration
  songs.sum(&:duration_in_seconds)
end
```

One little test and one little method to make it pass. Nice and simple. That's the rhythm of Test-Driven Development.

Testing is a deep topic, and there are many tools and tricks surrounding it. If you're new to testing, my advice is to keep it simple. Stick with the built-in tools and rely heavily on assert() and assert_equal(). Don't be intimidated by the many choices available. Testing is better than not testing.

Test Your Controllers

Problem

Testing web applications is difficult. Setting up a server and database and connecting to a running web application can be brittle and hard to automate completely. And despite advances in web browser automation, testing with a browser that crawls a site is both slow and error prone.

Still, though, testing just your models is not enough. You need automated tests for your controller code. How can you create controller tests that are dependable and fast enough to be consistently used?

Solution

Whenever you generate a controller, Rails also generates a placeholder test for that controller. The tests for controllers are placed in the test/functional directory. These tests give you a harness for in-memory testing of your controllers.

If you have a testing background, you may have some preconceived notions about what "functional" testing means. Abandon them now. In Rails, the tests in test/functional are for testing a single controller. If you want to test the behavior of, say, your RecipesController, you can put your tests in test/functional/recipes_controller_test.rb. If we generate an empty controller, Rails will create a test file for us that looks something like this:

```
require 'test_helper'

class RecipesControllerTest < ActionController::TestCase
  # Replace this with your real tests.
  test "the truth" do
    assert true
  end
end
```

To run all of our controller tests, we can use the following command:

```
$ rake test:functionals
(in /code/rr2/controller_tests)
Loaded suite rake-0.8.7/rake_test_loader
```

```
Started

.
Finished in 0.027007 seconds.

1 tests, 1 assertions, 0 failures, 0 errors, 0 skips

Test run options: --seed 58489
```

Now that we have a working test, let's replace the stubbed code with something real. Imagine our recipe index page has been written to display the most recently added recipes so users visiting the site can quickly see the freshest activity. We implement this with the standard index action, but we want to test to make sure the recipes returned are limited to those already published and do not include any scheduled for future publication. This allows site administrators to prepopulate content for the site for phased releases to the site's visitors.

The first thing we'll want to do is to set up some test data. Using the techniques described in Recipe 45, *Create Dynamic Test Fixtures*, on page 168, we can quickly create fixtures, such as the following, with which to test:

rr2/controller_tests/test/fixtures/recipes.yml
```
# Read about fixtures at http://ar.rubyonrails.org/classes/Fixtures.html
<% 10.times do |n| %>
recipe_<%= n %>:
  name: Recipe Number <%= n %>
  ingredients: Eggs, flour, onion
  difficulty: 1
  published_at: <%= 3.days.ago %>
<% end %>


for_tomorrow:
  name: The recipe we'll publish tomorrow
  ingredients: Beef, tofu, greek yogurt, cilantro
  difficulty: 2
  published_at: <%= 1.day.from_now %>
```

Now let's write a test that executes the index action and checks its output:

rr2/controller_tests/test/functional/recipes_controller_test.rb
```
test "index only shows recipes which are already published" do
  recipe_in_the_future =  recipes(:for_tomorrow)
  get :index
  assert_response :success
  assert_not_nil assigns(:recipes)
  assert !assigns(:recipes).include?(recipe_in_the_future),
          "Should not have returned recipes that are not yet published"
  assert_select "tr.recipe", :count => assigns(:recipes).size
end
```

First, we reference the recipe from our fixture that has *not* yet been published. We save this in the variable recipe_in_the_future and then use the get() method to exercise the index() action. Rails functional tests provide five methods for *simulating* HTTP traffic to an application: get(), put(), post(), delete(), and head(). Each of the five methods sets up test request and response objects and then executes our controller code in memory. This means our tests run very quickly, since we don't have to run a server or make HTTP connections, while our application code executes exactly as if we were running full web requests.

The call to get :index runs our index() action and its associated view. After this, we can use the built-in assertion methods to check that the application code behaved as expected.

The first one we use here, assert_response(), checks the actual HTTP response code of the action. The assert_response() method accepts either a literal code number (e.g., 200) or a symbol representing a range of responses. In this example, we check that the server action responds with a success condition (HTTP status code 200) as opposed to a :redirect, :missing, or general :error.

Next, we use a special controller test method called assigns() to look at the value of the instance variable called @recipes. It's unusual in testing to access an object's instance variables, but in the case of Rails controllers, instance variables are used to communicate values to their views. So, it makes sense to reference these variables in our tests. The assigns() method takes a symbol that should be the variable name from the controller *without* the @ sign. In this case, we first check that this value has been set to something non-nil after which we verify that the recipe with a future published_at time is not in the list of returned recipes.

Finally, we call the assert_select() method, which allows us to make assertions about the structure of the rendered view. In this case, we pass in the CSS selector "tr.recipe," which selects HTML table rows with the class recipe. The :count option states that we expect the same number of table rows as we have results in our @recipes instance variable.

We've successfully tested an action! But this was a pretty simple call to the action. We didn't pass any parameters. Fortunately, the functional test HTTP simulation methods make it very easy to pass parameters into the calls to our actions.

Here's an HTTP POST operation that passes a structured form like the ones we typically use when we create Active Record objects:

```
post :create, :recipe => {
                :name => "Haggis Cupcake",
                :ingredients => "Haggis, Flour, Sugar"
            }
```

The second, optional parameter to post() (and get() and the other HTTP simulation methods) is a Hash, which will be passed directly in as the params() of the
request. Simple! And, the convenient argument list doesn't stop there.

Here's a call to the show() action, which not only passes a parameter but also
sets a value in session using the third optional argument to get():

```
get :show, {:id => @recipe.id}, :user_id => 123
assert_response :success
```

Anything you pass into Hash in the third parameter to an action invocation
will be accessible in session() in your action. This is a great way to simulate
user authentication for a test request. Speaking of session(), if you need to
check the values in session() as part of your test, you can do so using the session()
method, which returns the Hash of what was put in session during the execution of your action. Here's an example:

```
test "can authenticate with user and password" do
  post :create, :username => "kurt", :password => "m0th3r-n1ght"
  assert_equal users(:kurt).id, session[:user_id]
end
```

Be careful how detailed your view-level tests become. Once you've seen the
beauty of assert_select(), it's tempting to check every aspect of the view. But if
your tests dig too deeply into the look and feel of your application, they're
going to be brittle and make change more difficult. Use assert_select() to check
the *semantic* structure of your documents, and leave the look-and-feel testing
to a human.

Also See

Recipe 45, *Create Dynamic Test Fixtures*, on page 168

Test Your Helpers

Problem

You have been extracting your view logic into nice, clean helpers. Since these helpers are used throughout your application, you want to make sure they're well tested. But how do you write unit tests for your helpers?

Solution

Rails provides a special type of test case for helper testing called ActionView::Test-Case. Whenever we generate a controller, Rails generates a test case for the controller's associated helper. These generated test cases have access to everything they need to execute helper methods as if being called from a view.

Let's say we have created a set of helper methods that build a navigation bar for the recipe section of our site. The helpers might look like this:

```
rr2/helper_tests/app/helpers/recipes_helper.rb
module RecipesHelper

  def tabs(current_tab)
    content_tag(:div,
                links(current_tab),
                :id => "tabs"
                )
  end

  def links(current_tab)
    nav_items.map do |tab_name, path|
      args = tab_name, path
      if tab_name == current_tab
        args << {:class => 'current'}
      end
      link_to *args
    end.join(separator).html_safe
  end

  def nav_items
    {
    "New" => new_recipe_path,
    "List" => recipes_path,
```

```
    "Home" => root_path
    }
  end

  def separator
    content_tag(:span, "|", :class => "separator").html_safe
  end
end
```

The RecipesHelper class calls its tabs() method, passing in the name of the currently selected tab. The tabs() helper then generates the HTML-formatted tab list, which we can then display in a header or sidebar. Since we've separated this helper into a number of smaller methods, we can start with a simple test. Let's first make sure our separator() method behaves as expected.

In this case, we're testing the RecipesHelper, so we'll put our tests in the generated test/unit/helpers/recipe_helper_test.rb file. Now that we know where our test case is, testing the separator() method is easy. We simply call it and check its output, using code like the following:

rr2/helper_tests/test/unit/helpers/recipes_helper_test.rb
```
class RecipesHelperTest < ActionView::TestCase
  test "can generate a separator" do
    assert_equal %q{<span class="separator">|</span>}, separator
  end
end
```

Since we're in RecipesHelperTest, the test case automatically loads and includes the RecipesHelper for us. Not bad! Let's take it a little further and test the actual tabs() method.

The tabs() method is a greater challenge because its output is more complex. Checking its return value with the assert_equal() would be brittle and require us to tie our tests too closely to the output on the page. It would be easier to check the structure of the resulting HTML. To do that, we'll use assert_select(). But the assert_select() assumes that a view has already been rendered. So, how do we render something in our helper test so that we can use assert_select() to validate it? The answer is to use the built-in render() method.

Here's a simple test that renders the tabs() method and then validates that a <div> with the ID of "tabs" appears in the resulting document:

rr2/helper_tests/test/unit/helpers/recipes_helper_test.rb
```
test "generates a list of links" do
  render :text => tabs("New")
  assert_select "div[id='tabs']"
end
```

We use the render() method's :text option to provide an easy way to call our helper, preparing its output for inspection by assert_select(). Then assert_select() uses the CSS selector to ensure that at least one matching <div> exists.

Finally, we can test the helper's ability to properly set which tab is the current tab:

rr2/helper_tests/test/unit/helpers/recipes_helper_test.rb
```ruby
test "highlights current tab correctly" do
  render :text => tabs("New")
  assert_select "a[class='current']" do |anchors|
    anchors.each do |anchor|
      assert_equal new_recipe_path, anchor.attributes['href']
    end
  end
end
```

We see now that helpers are easy to test independently. For clean, testable views, use helpers whenever possible. Using helpers allows you to keep Ruby code out of your views and makes your view logic easier to write automated tests for.

Test Your Outgoing Mailers

Problem

Action Mailer objects are the right place to put your mail-related logic. We all know that controllers should be lightweight, delegating logic to models and other objects as necessary. When that logic is mail-related, it belongs in a mailer.

Where there's logic, there's a need to write automated tests for that logic! How do we test our outgoing mail functionality?

Solution

When you generate a new Action Mailer, Rails automatically generates a test case. This test is very much like any other Rails test. We instantiate the object we want to check, and then we make assertions about it.

Conveniently, calling any mailer method returns a reference to that generated mail message. This reference is returned in the form of a Mail::Message object. A Mail::Message encapsulates all of the important information you'd expect to find about an email, including the subject of the message, the destination email addresses, and the body of the message.

```
$ rails g mailer ReceiptMailer receipt
create  app/mailers/receipt_mailer.rb
invoke  erb
create    app/views/receipt_mailer
create    app/views/receipt_mailer/receipt.text.erb
invoke  test_unit
create    test/functional/receipt_mailer_test.rb
```

Similar to controller tests, Action Mailer ships with a special Test::Unit::TestCase called ActionMailer::TestCase that automates various aspects of mailer testing. It also generates an example test for each mailer method listed on the command line during generation. Here's what the full generated test case looks like for the mailer we just created:

rr2/email_tests/test/functional/receipt_mailer_test_pristine.rb
```ruby
require 'test_helper'

class ReceiptMailerTest < ActionMailer::TestCase
  test "receipt" do
    mail = ReceiptMailer.receipt
    assert_equal "Receipt", mail.subject
    assert_equal ["to@example.org"], mail.to
    assert_equal ["from@example.com"], mail.from
    assert_match "Hi", mail.body.encoded
  end

end
```

So, as the example demonstrates, after we've run our custom mailer method, we can check that it generated the correct values for each of these important message fields using assertions. What if we want to actually check that an attempt was made to deliver a message? Easy! We can assert that the mail was sent with a built-in helper, assert_emails(), and its opposite, assert_no_emails(). Here's an example, testing customer mailer functionality that sends a receipt for online transactions only to customers who have indicated that they want email receipts:

rr2/email_tests/test/functional/receipt_mailer_test.rb
```ruby
test "only sends receipts to customers who opt in for notifications" do
  customer = Customer.create!(:email_opt_in => false)
  order = customer.orders.create!(:product => products(:rails_studio_ticket))
  assert_no_emails do
    ReceiptMailer.send_receipt_if_opted_in(order)
  end

  order.customer.update_attribute(:email_opt_in, true)
  assert_emails 1 do
    ReceiptMailer.send_receipt_if_opted_in(order)
  end

end
```

And, here's the simple class-level method we're calling from our test:

rr2/email_tests/app/mailers/receipt_mailer.rb
```ruby
class ReceiptMailer < ActionMailer::Base
  class << self
    def send_receipt_if_opted_in(order)
      if order.customer && order.customer.email_opt_in?
        receipt(order).deliver
      end
    end
  end
```

We can see from the test that in the case of a customer set to *not* receive emails, we use assert_no_emails(), which ensures that the code passed in the associated block does not result in an email being sent. When we set the Customer to opt into email notifications, we use assert_emails() to assert that exactly one email is sent during the execution of its associated block.

Believe me when I say you *don't* want real emails sent from your automated tests. As the recipient of my share of unit test spam, I'm pleased to inform you that Action Mailer automatically stubs out the delivery of email in your tests. This is done by setting the attribute ActionMailer::Base.delivery_method() to :test. With the delivery method set to :test, Action Mailer pushes each message into a list of delivered messages that you can access via the attribute Action-Mailer::Base.deliveries(). ActionMailer::TestCase sets the delivery method for you, so you don't have to worry about forgetting it.

Internally, assert_emails() and assert_no_emails() both use ActionMailer::Base.deliveries() to perform their validations. If you ever need to validate the contents of delivered messages—not just count them—you'll find that the ActionMailer::Base.deliveries() contains an Array of Mail::Message objects that you can inspect.

These simple ingredients account for almost anything you'd need in daily mailer testing. Given how easy mailer tests are to write, don't let your emails go untested. Remember that once an email is sent, there's no way to take it back. If email is an important part of your application's business, automated tests are a must!

Test Across Multiple Controllers

Problem

We saw in Recipe 39, *Test Your Controllers*, on page 141 how easy it is to test a single controller, but sometimes that's not enough. How do you test an entire purchase flow on an e-commerce site? How about the process of signing up for a site, confirming the registration, and then logging in? To test these scenarios, we need to write tests for a multistep process that spans multiple controllers.

Solution

Integration tests are the feature of Rails that take testing your applications to a high level. They are the next logical progression in the existing series of available tests:

Unit tests
> Unit tests are narrowly focused on testing a single model.

Functional tests
> Functional tests are focused on testing a single controller and the interactions between the models it employs.

Integration tests
> Integration tests are broad, user story–level tests that verify the interactions between the various actions supported by the application, across all controllers.

This makes it easier to duplicate session management and routing bugs in your tests. What if you had a bug that was triggered by certain cruft accumulating in a user's session? It's hard to mimic that with functional tests. For an example, consider a fictional financial application. We have a set of "stories" describing how the application should function:

- Bob wants to sign up for access. He goes to the login page, clicks the Sign Up link, and fills out the form. After submitting the form, a new ledger is created for him, and he is automatically logged in and taken to the overview page.

- Jim, an experienced user, has received a new credit card and wants to set up a new account for it. He logs in, selects the ledger he wants to add the account to, and adds the account. He is then forwarded to the register for that account.

- Stacey is a disgruntled user who has decided to cancel her account. Logging in, she goes to the "account preferences" page and cancels her account. Her data is all deleted, and she is forwarded to a "sorry to see you go" page.

Starting with the first story, we might write something like the following. We'll create the file stories_test.rb in the test/integration directory.

rr2/integration_testing/test/integration/stories_test.rb
```
class StoriesTest < ActionDispatch::IntegrationTest

  test "signup new person" do
    get "/login"
    assert_response :success
    assert_template "login/index"

    get "/signup"
    assert_response :success
    assert_template "signup/index"

    post "/signup", :name => "Bob", :username => "bob", :password => "secret"
    assert_response :redirect
    follow_redirect!
    assert_response :success
    assert_template "ledger/index"
  end
end
```

Run this by invoking the file directly via Ruby or by typing the following:

```
$ rake test:integration
```

The code is pretty straightforward. First, we get the /login URL and assert that the response is what we expect. Then, we get the /signup URL, post the data to it, and follow the redirect through to the ledger.

However, one of the best parts of the integration framework is the ability to extract a testing DSL[11] from your actions, making it really easy to tell stories like this. At the simplest, we can do that by adding some helper methods to the test. Here's a revised version of our test method and its new helpers:

---

11. Domain-specific language

rr2/integration_testing/test/integration/stories_test.rb
```ruby
test "signup new person" do
  go_to_login
  go_to_signup
  signup :name => "Bob", :username => "bob", :password => "secret"
end

private
def go_to_login
  get "/login"
  assert_response :success
  assert_template "login/index"
end

def go_to_signup
  get "/signup"
  assert_response :success
  assert_template "signup/index"
end

def signup(options)
  post "/signup", options
  assert_response :redirect
  follow_redirect!
  assert_response :success
  assert_template "ledger/index"
end
```

Now you can reuse those actions in other tests, making your tests very readable and easy to build. But it can be even neater! Taking advantage of ActionController::IntegrationTest's open_session() method, you can create your own session instances and decorate them with custom methods. Think of a session as a single user's experience with your site. Consider this example:

rr2/integration_testing/test/integration/stories_test.rb
```ruby
class StoriesTest < ActionDispatch::IntegrationTest

  test "signup new person" do
    new_session do |bob|
      bob.goes_to_login
      bob.goes_to_signup
      bob.signs_up_with :name => "Bob", :username => "bob", :password => "secret"
    end
  end

  private

  module MyTestingDSL
    def goes_to_login
      get "/login"
```

```
        assert_response :success
        assert_template "sessions/new"
    end

    def goes_to_signup
      get "/signup"
      assert_response :success
      assert_template "users/new"
    end

    def signs_up_with(options)
      post "/users", options
      assert_response :redirect
      follow_redirect!
      assert_response :success
      assert_template "ledgers/index"
    end
  end

  def new_session
    open_session do |sess|
      sess.extend(MyTestingDSL)
      yield sess if block_given?
    end
  end
end
```

The new_session() method at the bottom simply uses open_session() to create a new session and decorate it by mixing in our DSL module. By adding more methods to the MyTestingDSL module, you build up your DSL and make your tests richer and more expressive. You can even use named routes in your tests to ensure consistency between what your application is expecting and what your tests are asserting! Here's an example:

```
def goes_to_login
  get login_url
  ...
end
```

Note that the new_session() method will actually return the new session as well. This means you could define a test that mimicked the behavior of two or more users interacting with your system at the same time:

```
rr2/integration_testing/test/integration/stories_test.rb
class StoriesTest < ActionDispatch::IntegrationTest

    test "multiple users" do
      jim = new_session_as(:jim)
      bob = new_session_as(:bob)
      stacey = new_session_as(:stacey)
```

```
      jim.selects_ledger(:jims)
      jim.adds_account(:name => "checking")
      bob.goes_to_preferences
      stacey.cancels_account
    end

  private

  module MyTestingDSL
    attr_reader :person
    def logs_in_as(person)
      @person = people(person)
      post session_url,
          :username => @person.username,
          :password => @person.password
      is_redirected_to "ledgers/index"
    end
    def goes_to_preferences
      # ...
    end
    def cancels_account
      # ...
    end
  end

  def new_session_as(person)
    new_session do |sess|
      sess.goes_to_login
      sess.logs_in_as(person)
      yield sess if block_given?
    end
  end
end
```

To further demonstrate how these DSLs can be built, let's implement the
second of the three stories described at the beginning of this article: Jim
adding a credit-card account:

rr2/integration_testing/test/integration/stories_test.rb
```
test "add new account" do
  new_session_as(:jim) do |jim|
    jim.selects_ledger(:jims)
    jim.adds_account(:name => "credit card")
  end
end
private
module MyTestingDSL
  attr_accessor :ledger
```

```ruby
  def is_redirected_to(template)
    assert_response :redirect
    follow_redirect!
    assert_response :success
    assert_template(template)
  end

  def selects_ledger(ledger)
    @ledger = ledgers(ledger)
    get ledger_url(:id => @ledger.id)
    assert_response :success
    assert_template "ledgers/index"
  end

  def adds_account(options)
    post accounts_url(:id => @ledger.id), options
    is_redirected_to "ledgers/index"
  end
end
```

Integration tests with DSLs make your code more readable and make testing more fun. And, if testing is fun, you're more likely to do it.

You may notice that individual integration tests run slower than individual unit or functional tests. That's because they test so much more. Each of the tests shown in this recipe tests multiple requests. Most functional tests test only one. Also, integration tests run through the entire stack—from the dispatcher, through the routes, into the controller, and back. Functional tests skip straight to the controller.

Credit

Rails core alumni member Jamis Buck wrote this recipe.

Focus Your Tests with Mocking and Stubbing

Problem

In complex systems, testing can get difficult. Complex systems are riddled with dependencies, some of which are impossible for us to control as developers. As the IT world gets more distributed, more and more of our applications will depend on one or many external services. Sometimes these are services created and maintained within your organization. Sometimes they are completely separate, as is the case with payment gateways, email service providers, and social networks. Automated tests that depend on systems whose state isn't guaranteed to be controllable or consistent become brittle very quickly.

In the face of complex applications with both internal and external dependencies, how do you focus your tests strictly on specific parts of your code? Additionally, how can you ensure that your code interacts appropriately with its dependencies?

Solution

You can use mocking and stubbing to temporarily override the behavior of your code's dependencies for a test, eliminating the coupling of a test to the implementation of its code's dependencies. In this recipe, we'll use the Mocha framework to replace the behavior of dependencies as well as set expectations of how those dependencies should be interacted with by the code under test. We'll see how to use Mocha to simplify and decouple tests for both an external dependency as well as to more clearly focus our tests even when there are no dependencies.

The first step in setting up Mocha in your application is to add it to your application's Gemfile and run bundle install. The Gemfile entry is trivial:

rr2/mocking/Gemfile
```
gem 'mocha', :require => false
```

Now that we have Mocha set up, let's look at a real example. Imagine we have created a diary application that posts to a social activity stream. Any time a user posts a diary entry on our site, we want it to post a notice to the external social activity stream via a supplied Ruby gem. We accomplish this using an after_create() hook in our DiaryEntry model. Here's the DiaryEntry class:

rr2/mocking/app/models/diary_entry.rb
```
require 'social_activity_stream'
class DiaryEntry < ActiveRecord::Base
  belongs_to :user
  after_create :post_notice_to_social_stream
  def post_notice_to_social_stream
    SocialActivityStream.notice(:user => user.social_stream_id,
                                :body => %{A new diary entry called
                                #{title} has been created. Check it out!})
  end
end
```

This is simple enough. After we create any DiaryEntry instance, our ActiveRecord hook will automatically use the SocialActivityStream class, passing in a locally stored copy of the user's id on the remote site, to create a new notice in the stream. The implementation details of that class are beyond our control. All we know about it is that it makes an HTTP call to a web service, pushing in the data we provide. It being Ruby, we could go read the code, but we don't need to, and we don't maintain the code.

The after_create() hook works fine until we start running our tests. But, as we run our application's unit tests many times per hour, we discover that a test user's social activity stream is filling up with test content! Every time a new DiaryEntry is created in our unit tests, its body is posted to the remote site. Oops. How do we turn this off while testing?

This is where *stubbing* comes in. Stubbing a method means to override its implementation, providing a default implementation on which the calling code can rely. We can use this to override the behavior of the SocialActivityStream.notice() so it does nothing while in our tests. Here's a unit test that stubs the SocialActivityStream.notice() method:

rr2/mocking/test/unit/diary_entry_test.rb
```
test "can create a diary entry" do
  SocialActivityStream.stubs(:notice).returns nil
  assert_difference "DiaryEntry.count" do
    DiaryEntry.create!(title: "Hallo Wherld",
                       body: "Kaint spale sahree",
                       user: users("chad"))
  end
end
```

For the purpose of the assertion in this test, it doesn't matter whether our code posts to the social activity stream. That's not what we're testing. So, we simply "stub out" the SocialActivityStream.notice() method to tell it to do nothing. We do this using the stubs(), which Mocha conveniently adds to every object in the system. The stubs() method accepts a method name and returns a configuration object on which you can specify other options such as the return value of the stubbed method. Here, we've asked Mocha to cause the notice() method to return nil whenever invoked.

We now have a way for our tests to ignore calls to the SocialActivityStream.notice(). But how do we test that the notice method is being properly called? The fact that we're calling it is a real part of our application's requirements, so we can't just ignore it simply because it's hard to test. That's where *mocking* comes in. With mocking, not only can we stub a method's behavior, but we can set the expectation that it will be called and with a set of expected parameters.

In the following test, we use Mocha's expects() method to indicate that during the execution of this test, we *expect* the code that's under test to invoke the SocialActivityStream.notice() method with a given set of parameters:

rr2/mocking/test/unit/diary_entry_test.rb
```
test "post a notice to the social activity stream on creation" do
  title = "Ode to a House DJ"
  SocialActivityStream.expects(:notice).
    with(user: users("chad").social_stream_id,
        body: %{A new diary entry called #{title}
          has been created. Check it out!}).
                                    returns(nil)
  DiaryEntry.create!(title: title,
                  body: "Thump thump thump thump",
                  user: users("chad"))
end
```

Like the stubs() method, Mocha adds the expects() method to all objects in the system. Its behavior is similar to stubs(), in that the expects() method overrides the existing implementation of the named method and can be configured to return a predetermined value. Additionally, the configuration object returned by expects() supports the method with(), which allows us not only to specify that we expect this method to be called but to declare which parameters should be passed in for the expectation to pass.

In turn, Mocha effectively sets up an assertion as part of the test. Let's experiment with this and show what would happen if we didn't meet the expectation. We'll temporarily comment out the call to SocialActivityStream.notice() in our DiaryEntry class and rerun the test. Here's the relevant part of the output:

```
$ rake
LOADED SUITE test,test/performance,test/unit
...
DiaryEntryTest
    test_can_create_a_diary_entry                                    PASS
    test_post_a_notice_to_the_social_activity_stream_on_creation     FAIL
      not all expectations were satisfied
    unsatisfied expectations:
    - expected exactly once, not yet invoked: SocialActivityStream.notice(
    :user => 1123,
    :body => 'A new diary entry to a House DJ created...it out!')
    ============================================================
    pass: 1,  fail: 1,  error: 0
    total: 2 tests with 2 assertions in 0.186694 seconds
    ============================================================
```

As you can see, mocks act as implicit assertions. We *expect* our mocked method to be called in a certain way. If it's not called in that way, Mocha considers the test to have failed.

Let's look at one last example of how Mocha can help us focus our tests. This time, we'll look at a scaffold-generated controller and its test. Here's the create() action for our DiaryEntriesController:

rr2/mocking/app/controllers/diary_entries_controller.rb
```
def create
  @diary_entry = DiaryEntry.new(params[:diary_entry])

  respond_to do |format|
    if @diary_entry.save
      format.html { redirect_to @diary_entry,
                    :notice => 'Diary entry was successfully created.' }
      format.json { render :json => @diary_entry,
                    :status => :created,
                    :location => @diary_entry }
    else
      format.html { render :action => "new" }
      format.json { render :json => @diary_entry.errors,
                    :status => :unprocessable_entity }
    end
  end
end
```

This is the default code generated by the Rails scaffold generator. To say this is code is *hard* to test is a bit of a stretch, but there is one wrinkle that makes it messy. There are two branches of execution. When a diary entry saves properly, we go down the happy path. When the validations fail, we go down the other path and show validation error messages. The reason this is messy to test is that the most obvious way to get both paths executed is to present both valid and invalid form data to the create() action.

It seems reasonable at first, but as soon as you have to make one change to your validation rules, you'll see why this is no good. Every validation change in your model will result in you being forced to go into your controller's test and make a change. You would then be testing both the model's validation logic *and* the controller's logic in the same test. That's not what a functional test is for! With stubbing, we can get around that problem:

rr2/mocking/test/functional/diary_entries_controller_test.rb
```ruby
require 'test_helper'

class DiaryEntriesControllerTest < ActionController::TestCase
  setup do
    @diary_entry = diary_entries(:one)
    SocialActivityStream.stubs(:notice)
  end

  test "should redirect to diary_entry page after create" do
    DiaryEntry.stubs(:new).returns(@diary_entry)
    @diary_entry.expects(:save).returns true
    post :create, :diary_entry => @diary_entry.attributes
    assert_redirected_to diary_entry_path(@diary_entry)
  end

  test "should redisplay the form on invalid create" do
    DiaryEntry.stubs(:new).returns(@diary_entry)
    @diary_entry.expects(:save).returns false
    post :create, :diary_entry => @diary_entry.attributes
    assert_template 'new'
  end
end
```

Rather than being forced to construct valid and invalid attribute sets for a DiaryEntry, our tests are free to exercise the branches in the controller by telling the @diary_entry's save() method to return true or false at will, simulating the valid and invalid states of a DiaryEntry. Our functional test isn't concerned with what makes a DiaryEntry valid. That's not its job. The functional test's job is to ensure that the controller behaves as expected in both valid and invalid DiaryEntry states.

Also See

- While we've covered most of what you need to know to be productive with Mocha, there's a lot more to learn when you start to dig in. See Mocha's website at http://mocha.rubyforge.org for complete documentation.

- Since you typically need Mocha only when testing, consider using Bundler groups as detailed in Recipe 58, *Use Bundler Groups to Manage Per-Environment Dependencies*, on page 224.

Extract Test Fixtures from Live Data

Problem

You want to take advantage of the unit testing features in Rails, but your data model is complex, and manually creating all those fixtures sounds like a real drag. You've implemented enough of your application that you're able to populate its database via the application's interface—a far better interface than plain-text YAML files! Now you have a rich set of data that would be great for unit testing. How do you create fixtures from that existing data?

Solution

Active Record gives us all the ingredients we need to generate fixtures from our existing data. The basic steps are as follows:

1. Establish a connection to the database.
2. Query the database for the names of its tables.
3. Select the data for each table in turn, and convert it into YAML.
4. Generate a unique name for the data in the row.
5. Write the results to a file named after the table name.

Let's use a simple database model to demonstrate. We'll create a model to represent people and the clubs they are members of. First we'll create the models. We might normally create the table definitions first, but we're going to use the models to create sample data during our migration.

rr2/fixture_dump/app/models/person.rb
```
class Person < ActiveRecord::Base
  has_many :memberships
  has_many :clubs, :through => :memberships
end
```

rr2/fixture_dump/app/models/club.rb
```
class Club < ActiveRecord::Base
  has_many :memberships
  has_many :people, :through => :memberships
end
```

rr2/fixture_dump/app/models/membership.rb
```
class Membership < ActiveRecord::Base
  belongs_to :club
  belongs_to :person
end
```

People can belong to many clubs, and clubs can have many members. The Active Record migration files should look like the following:

rr2/fixture_dump/db/migrate/20101219180605_create_people.rb
```
class CreatePeople < ActiveRecord::Migration
  def self.up
    create_table :people do |t|
      t.string :name
      t.timestamps
    end
  end

  def self.down
    drop_table :people
  end
end
```

rr2/fixture_dump/db/migrate/20101219180600_create_clubs.rb
```
class CreateClubs < ActiveRecord::Migration
  def self.up
    create_table :clubs do |t|
      t.string :name
      t.timestamps
    end
  end

  def self.down
    drop_table :clubs
  end
end
```

rr2/fixture_dump/db/migrate/20101219180616_create_memberships.rb
```
class CreateMemberships < ActiveRecord::Migration
  def self.up
    create_table :memberships do |t|
      t.integer :person_id
      t.integer :club_id
      t.timestamps
    end
  end

  def self.down
    drop_table :memberships
  end
end
```

Then, for the sake of demonstration, we'll generate some sample data in our db/seeds.rb file. In the real world, we would probably set up a simple set of scaffolds for data entry, and we could easily create a lot more sample data.

```
rr2/fixture_dump/db/seeds.rb
chad = Person.create(:name => "Chad")
kelly = Person.create(:name => "Kelly")
james = Person.create(:name => "James")

hindi_club = Club.create(:name => "Hindi Study Group")
snow_boarders = Club.create(:name => "Snowboarding Newbies")

chad.clubs.concat [hindi_club, snow_boarders]
kelly.clubs.concat [hindi_club, snow_boarders]
james.clubs.concat [snow_boarders]

[chad, kelly, james].each {|person| person.save}
```

After we've run the migrations and seed file, we should have two Club objects and three Person objects in our database. Now let's load the Rails console and take some of the steps toward accomplishing our end goal of creating fixtures from this data:

```
$ rails console
    Loading development environment.
    >> ActiveRecord::Base.connection.tables
    => ["clubs", "clubs_people", "people", "schema_info"]
```

Based on the set of steps we laid out at the beginning of this recipe, we're almost halfway there! But there's one table in the list that we don't want to create fixtures for. The special schema_info table is used by Active Record to manage migrations, so we wouldn't want to create fixtures for that. Make a mental note, and let's continue through our checklist. We need to issue a query for each table's data and convert each row to YAML. We'll start with a single table:

```
>> ActiveRecord::Base.connection.select_all("select * from people")
=> [{"name"=>"Chad", "id"=>"1"}, {"name"=>"Kelly", "id"=>"2"},
    {"name"=>"James", "id"=>"3"}]
```

The Active Record connection adapter's select_all() method returns an array of hash objects, each containing key/value pairs of column name and value for its respective row. Not coincidentally, it's trivial to translate these hash objects into the required YAML format for a fixture:

```
>> conn = ActiveRecord::Base.connection
>> puts(conn.select_all("select * from people").map do |row|
      row.to_yaml
    end)
```

```
name: Chad
id: "1"
name: Kelly
id: "2"
name: James
id: "3"
=> nil
```

We're almost there! At this point, we've tackled all the hard stuff that needs to be done, so it makes sense to put this code together in a script that we can keep handy to run when needed. Since most Rails automation tasks are handled using Rake, we'll throw together a quick Rake task. You can refer to Recipe 61, *Automate Work with Your Own Rake Tasks*, on page 230 for a full description of how to create one. We'll create a file called lib/tasks/extract_fix-tures.rake and populate it with the fruits of our exploration:

rr2/fixture_dump/lib/tasks/extract_fixtures.rake
```ruby
desc 'Create YAML test fixtures from data in an existing database.
Defaults to development database.  Set RAILS_ENV to override.'

task :extract_fixtures => :environment do
  sql  = "SELECT * FROM %s"
  skip_tables = ["schema_info"]
  ActiveRecord::Base.establish_connection
  (ActiveRecord::Base.connection.tables - skip_tables).each do |table_name|
    i = "000"
    File.open("#{Rails.root}/test/fixtures/#{table_name}.yml", 'w') do |file|
      data = ActiveRecord::Base.connection.select_all(sql % table_name)
      file.write data.inject({}) { |hash, record|
        hash["#{table_name}_#{i.succ!}"] = record
        hash
      }.to_yaml
    end
  end
end
```

We can now invoke this task by typing rake extract_fixtures in the root directory of our application. The task uses the Rails environment, so by default it will dump the fixtures from your development database. To extract the fixtures from your production database, you would set the RAILS_ENV environment variable to "production".

Note that this task will overwrite any existing fixtures you may have, so be sure to back up your files before running it.

Running the new Rake task results in fixture files being created under the test/fixtures/ directory of our application as in the following people.yml file:

```
rr2/fixture_dump/test/fixtures/people.yml
---
people_001:
  id: 1
  name: Chad
  created_at: 2010-12-19 18:07:42.187541
  updated_at: 2010-12-19 18:07:42.187541
people_002:
  id: 2
  name: Kelly
  created_at: 2010-12-19 18:07:42.246756
  updated_at: 2010-12-19 18:07:42.246756
people_003:
  id: 3
  name: James
  created_at: 2010-12-19 18:07:42.249354
  updated_at: 2010-12-19 18:07:42.249354
```

Also See

Though Rails ships with support for test fixtures, the Factory approach to test data has gained traction and may be a cleaner approach. For information on factories, see Recipe 47, *Create Test Data with Factories*, on page 176.

Credit

Thanks to Rails core developer Jeremy Kemper for the code on which this recipe is based.

Create Dynamic Test Fixtures

Problem

The Rails framework has done us all a service by building in the ability to manage test data through fixture files. These files can be either comma-separated text files or, more commonly, YAML files. You place sample data in fixtures that are then loaded before your tests run, giving you test subjects on which to ensure that your code behaves as you expect.

But even though testing is much easier in the Rails world, creating fixture data can become tedious when you're working on a big application with a rich domain. You want to make sure you have samples that represent normal application usage scenarios as well as edge cases, and creating all that data —especially when many of the attributes are often inconsequential to the test you're creating them for—can be tiring and time-consuming.

Rails development is supposed to be fun! How can we take away the tedium of creating large quantities of test fixtures?

Solution

An often-overlooked feature of the way Rails deals with fixture files is that before passing them into the YAML parser, it runs them through ERb. ERb is the same templating engine that powers our default view templates. It allows you to embed arbitrary Ruby expressions into otherwise static text.

When used in YAML test fixtures, this approach can be extremely powerful. Consider the following example. This fixture data is a sample of a larger file used for testing posts to a message board application. A Post in this application can be a reply to an existing Post, which is specified by the parent_id field. Imagine how bored you'd get (and how many errors you'd probably commit) if you had to create dozens more of such posts to test various edge conditions.

rr2/dynamic_fixtures/test/fixtures/posts.yml

```
first_post:
  title: First post!
  body: I got the first post!  I rule!
  created_at: 2011-01-29 20:03:56
  updated_at: 2011-01-29 21:00:00
```

```
    user: kelly
reply_to_first_post:
  title: Very insightful
  body: It's people like you that make participation in
        this message board worthwhile.  Thank you.
  parent: first_post
  created_at: 2011-01-30 08:03:56
  updated_at: 2011-01-30 08:03:56
  user: barney
third_level_nested_child_post:
  title: This post is buried deep in the comments
  body: The content isn't really important.  We just want to test
        the application's threading logic.
  created_at: 2011-01-30 08:03:56
  updated_at: 2011-01-30 08:03:56
  parent: reply_to_first_post
  user: kelly
```

As I was entering this data into the posts.yml file, by the time I reached the third entry I was annoyed and starting to copy and paste data without much thought. For example, the third entry's purpose in our fictional application is to provide sample data for testing nested comments. We might need to be able to show the total nested child count of replies to a post to get a high-level idea of the activity going on in that part of the discussion.

If that were the case, the only field in the third fixture with any real meaning is the parent field (which dynamically sets the parent_id field based on fixture name). That's the one that associates this post with the child of the root post. I don't care about the post's title or body, and I don't care who posted it. I just need a post to be there and be counted.

Since fixtures are preprocessed through ERb, we can use embedded Ruby snippets to generate fixture data. Assuming we want to test a greater number of posts than three, let's generate a block of posts, randomly disbursed under the existing thread:

rr2/dynamic_fixtures/test/fixtures/posts.yml
```
<% 1.upto(50) do |number| %>
child_post_<%= number %>:
  title: This is auto-generated reply number <%= number %>
  body: We're on number <%= number %>
  created_at: 2011-01-30 08:03:56
  updated_at: 2011-01-30 08:03:56
  <%# Randomly choose a parent from a post we've already generated -%>
  parent: child_post_<%= rand(number - 1) + 1 %>
  user: <%= %w(kelly barney).shuffle.first %>
<% end %>
```

Now, if we load our fixtures, we can see that we have fifty-three Posts in our database:

```
$ rake db:fixtures:load
(in /Users/chad/src/rr2/Book/code/rr2/dynamic_fixtures)
$ rails runner 'puts Post.count'
53
```

Wonderful! Now what if we wanted to do something smart with the dates? For example, we might want to test that when a post is updated, it is moved back to the top of the list and redisplayed as if new. Of course, we could do that by copying and pasting dates and then hand-editing them, but who wants to spend their time that way? We can save ourselves some time, some pain, and probably a few self-inflicted bugs by delegating to some helper methods.

Here's how we'd do that:

rr2/dynamic_fixtures/test/fixtures/posts.yml
```
<%
  def today
    Time.now.to_s(:db)
  end
  def next_week
    1.week.from_now.to_s(:db)
  end
  def last_week
    1.week.ago.to_s(:db)
  end
%>
post_from_last_week:
  title: Pizza
  body: Last night I had pizza.  I really liked that story from AWDWR. :)
  created_at: <%= last_week %>
  updated_at: <%= last_week %>
  user: kelly
post_created_in_future_should_not_display:
  title: Prognostication
  body: I predict that this post will show up next week.
  created_at: <%= next_week %>
  updated_at: <%= next_week %>
  user: kelly
updated_post_displays_based_on_updated_time:
  title: This should show up as posted today.
  body: blah blah blah
  created_at: <%= last_week %>
  updated_at: <%= today %>
  user: barney
```

Not only does this technique save time and reduce the chance for error, but it's also a lot easier to read. The words *next week* carry a lot more semantic significance than a hard-coded date. They tell you not just *what* the data is but a little of *why* it's set the way it is. Other dated-related method names such as month_end_closing_date() or random_date_last_year() could convey significance (or *insignificance*) of a value. And, of course, there's no reason to stop with dates. This is ERb, which means it's Ruby, and anything that's possible with Ruby is possible in these fixtures.

You probably noticed the calls to, for example, 1.week.ago(). These aren't included with Ruby; also not included is the ability to format a Time object for use with a database. These methods ship with Rails. Since your fixtures are loaded in the context of a Rails application, all your model classes, helper libraries, and the Rails framework itself are available for your use.

Though you can generate fixtures at runtime with ERb, sometimes it's easier to pregenerate your fixtures. If you just need a bunch of static data that isn't going to change much, you might consider writing a script that creates static YAML fixtures that you then just check in and manage like usual.

Also See

An increasingly popular approach to fixtures, especially relevant when you need to generate test data dynamically, is the Factory approach. If you find yourself getting too deep in code in your YAML fixture files, strongly consider switching to factories or to using a hybrid of factories and fixtures. For more on factories, see Recipe 47, *Create Test Data with Factories*, on page 176.

Another way to quickly generate fixture data is to generate scaffolding for your models, enter your data via the autogenerated forms, and then dump your live data into fixtures files. For more information about how to dump data into fixtures, see Recipe 44, *Extract Test Fixtures from Live Data*, on page 163.

Measure and Improve Your Test Coverage

Problem

Well-tested code not only is safer to change but is usually better designed. How do you measure your test coverage?

Solution

To improve test coverage, we first need to be able to measure it so we can remedy the parts of our application that are being overlooked. We can measure test coverage using a special tool that inserts itself into our code and keeps track of all branches of execution during a test run, reporting which lines or statements weren't executed as the tests run. There are a number of choices for test coverage tools, but my favorite is SimpleCov.[12] If you haven't already done so, install SimpleCov now, which we'll be using in the rest of this recipe to demonstrate the benefits of a test coverage tool. Once you've installed SimpleCov, you can hook it into the execution of your tests. To do this, add the following lines to your test/test_helper.rb file at the top, before the Rails environment is loaded:

rr2/test_coverage/test/test_helper.rb

```
require 'simplecov'
SimpleCov.start
```

If you require and start SimpleCov after your application code is loaded, it will not work; SimpleCov must always run first. Once it's in place, run your tests as you would without SimpleCov. If all is well, when the test run completes, you should see a line like this:

```
        Coverage report generated for Unit Tests,
Functional Tests to /Users/chad/src/rr2/Book/code/rr2/test_coverage/coverage.
83.33% covered.
```

SimpleCov has now created a series of HTML documents containing our test coverage report. The main file to look at is coverage/index.html. The expected output is shown in Figure 1, *A SimpleCov test coverage report*, on page 174.

---

12. SimpleCov works only with Ruby 1.9 and newer. If you need a test coverage tool for Ruby 1.8, use RCov, which is documented at http://eigenclass.org/hiki.rb?rcov.

Installing SimpleCov

Installing SimpleCov is, well, simple. Just follow these steps to install and run it.

First, add SimpleCov to your application's Gemfile:

```
rr2/test_coverage/Gemfile
gem 'simplecov'
```

Next, run bundle install to download and install SimpleCov into your bundle:

```
$ bundle install
Using rake (0.8.7)
Using abstract (1.0.0)
Using activesupport (3.0.6)
Using builder (2.1.2)
Using i18n (0.5.0)
Using activemodel (3.0.6)
Using erubis (2.6.6)
...
Using simplecov (0.4.0)
Using sqlite3 (1.3.3)
Your bundle is complete! It was installed into /Users/chad/.rvm/gems/ruby-1.9.2-p0
```

Oh! Our test coverage doesn't look very good for the Person model! Clicking the path to any file on the left of this table presents an annotated view of that file's source. The Person model's annotated source looks like Figure 2, *SimpleCov annotation for Person with 67 percent coverage*, on page 174.

That explains it. We haven't yet written a test for the full_name() method. That's easy to fix. Here's a new test in the test/unit/person_test.rb file:

```
rr2/test_coverage/test/unit/person_test.rb
test "can return full name" do
  person = Person.new(:first_name => "Clem", :last_name => "Snide")
  assert_equal "Clem Snide", person.full_name
end
```

Rerunning our tests shows 100 percent coverage for the Person model, as shown in Figure 3, *SimpleCov annotation for Person with 100 percent coverage*, on page 175.

We all try, but sometimes testing can be hard to do. Using a code coverage tool makes it easier to motivate yourself. You can treat it like a game. Enjoy!

File	% covered	Lines	Relevant Lines	Lines covered	Lines missed
All Files (93.06%)					Generated about a minute ago

All Files (93.06%)

15 files in total. 72 relevant lines. 67 lines covered and 5 lines missed

Search:

≎ File	⌃ % covered	≎ Lines	≎ Relevant Lines	≎ Lines covered	≎ Lines missed
🔍 ./app/models/person.rb	66.67 %	5	3	2	1
🔍 ./app/controllers/people_controller.rb	90.0 %	83	40	36	4
🔍 ./app/controllers/application_controller.rb	100.0 %	3	2	2	0
🔍 ./app/helpers/application_helper.rb	100.0 %	2	1	1	0
🔍 ./app/helpers/people_helper.rb	100.0 %	2	1	1	0
🔍 ./config/application.rb	100.0 %	42	7	7	0
🔍 ./config/boot.rb	100.0 %	6	3	3	0
🔍 ./config/environment.rb	100.0 %	5	2	2	0
🔍 ./config/environments/test.rb	100.0 %	35	9	9	0
🔍 ./config/initializers/backtrace_silencers.rb	100.0 %	7	0	0	0
🔍 ./config/initializers/inflections.rb	100.0 %	10	0	0	0
🔍 ./config/initializers/mime_types.rb	100.0 %	5	0	0	0
🔍 ./config/initializers/secret_token.rb	100.0 %	7	1	1	0
🔍 ./config/initializers/session_store.rb	100.0 %	8	1	1	0
🔍 ./config/routes.rb	100.0 %	60	2	2	0

Showing 1 to 15 of 15 entries

Generated by simplecov v0.4.0 and simplecov-html v0.4.3
using Unit Tests, Functional Tests

Figure 1—A SimpleCov test coverage report

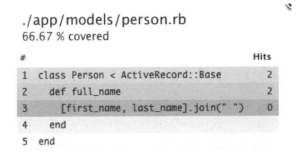

./app/models/person.rb
66.67 % covered

#		Hits
1	class Person < ActiveRecord::Base	2
2	def full_name	2
3	[first_name, last_name].join(" ")	0
4	end	
5	end	

Figure 2—SimpleCov annotation for Person with 67 percent coverage

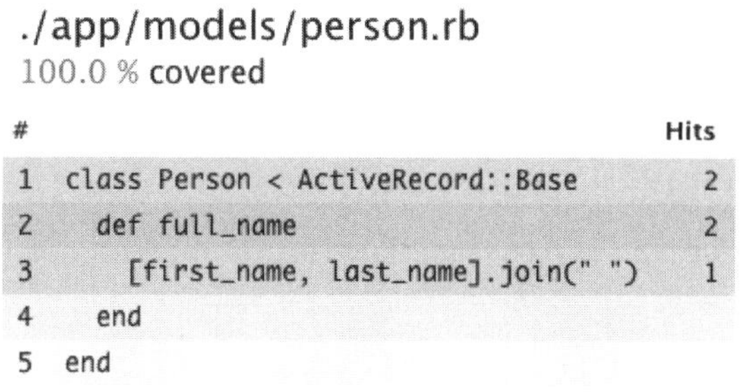

./app/models/person.rb
100.0 % covered

#		Hits
1	class Person < ActiveRecord::Base	2
2	def full_name	2
3	[first_name, last_name].join(" ")	1
4	end	
5	end	

Figure 3—SimpleCov annotation for Person with 100 percent coverage

Create Test Data with Factories

Problem

Rails introduced test fixtures early on as the built-in mechanism for reproducibly creating sample data for unit tests. Although fixtures are a big improvement over the way most people were doing sample test data in 2005, their limitations quickly become apparent. They are inflexible and on a large scale can become difficult to manage.

We need a more flexible, maintainable solution for generating sample data for our tests.

Solution

The Rails community has evolved toward using a technique called *factories* for test data. In the world of object-oriented software design, *factory* refers to a design pattern[13] describing how to create objects in a clean, decoupled manner. In Rails testing, factories generate sample data for tests. The most popular implementation of this technique is a library called "factory_girl," written by the Rails consultancy thoughtbot.[14] With factory_girl, we can create generators for Active Record objects with default data. Additionally, these generators can be overridden on a per-instance basis. Let's give it a try.

First we'll add factory_girl to our application's Gemfile. Since we're only going to use factory_girl in our tests, we can add it to the "test" environment, as discussed in Recipe 58, *Use Bundler Groups to Manage Per-Environment Dependencies*, on page 224:

rr2/factories/Gemfile
```
group :test do
  gem 'factory_girl_rails'
end
```

To use factory_girl in a Rails application, we install the "factory_girl_rails" gem.

---

13. See *Design Patterns* [GHJV95] for a full description of the Factory pattern.

14. http://thoughtbot.com

After updating our application's bundle, we can use factory_girl in our tests. First, we define a factory. We can do this in any code that our tests load. Here's an example definition for a Product model:

rr2/factories/test/unit/product_test.rb
```
Factory.define :product do |product|
  product.name "A product"
  product.price 20
  product.listed_on 3.days.ago
end
```

This defines a generator that we can use to create sample Product objects for our tests. As a simple example, let's say we want to write a new method, free?(), for Product instances. Using our factory, we can test the method like this:

rr2/factories/test/unit/product_test.rb
```
test "A product with a price greater than zero is not free" do
  @product = Factory.build(:product)
  assert !@product.free?,
         "Should not have been free since it has a non-zero price"
end
```

Here, we use the Factory.build() method to generate an instance of the factory we defined earlier. Because we have provided default values for the factory, our new object is created with those values. Specifically, this means that @product has a price of 20, so it is not free. When we use the build() method, factory_girl creates instances in memory but doesn't save them to the database. That's good for tests like this one where a database save isn't necessary (and slows down test performance needlessly). If we wanted to test code that required a database save, we could use Factory.create() instead.

What if we wanted to override one or more of the default values in the factory? Easy! Just pass the overridden values in as a Hash when you generate the object:

rr2/factories/test/unit/product_test.rb
```
test "A product not yet listed is not in stock" do
  @product = Factory.build(:product, :listed_on => 2.days.from_now)
  assert !@product.in_stock?,
       "Should not have been in stock since it's listed in the future"
end
```

This test checks that a Product listed in the future doesn't report itself as being in stock. To do that, we create a new Product instance using the factory but set just the listed_on attribute to have a different value. This makes what we're testing more explicit. We still have the other default values, but we don't care about them for this test.

Sometimes we need to dynamically generate attribute values based on other attributes in our sample data. For example, imagine our products have SKU codes that are manually set by the maintainers of our hypothetical product catalog system. They usually consist of the product name capitalized followed by a unique identifier. To generate this automatically for our tests, we could do something like this:

rr2/factories/test/unit/product_test.rb
```
Factory.define :product do |product|
  product.name "A product"
  product.price 20
  product.listed_on 3.days.ago
  product.sku { |prod| [prod.name.gsub(/ /, '-').upcase, "-", rand(999)].join}
end

test "Demonstrating dynamically generated values" do
  @product = Factory.build(:product)
  assert_match /^A-PRODUCT-[0-9]+$/, @product.sku
end
```

Rather than pass a value directly in for the product's SKU, we pass a block. factory_girl sees the block and runs it, passing in the Product instance with its static values populated. We then return the dynamically generated value for this attribute from the block.

One thing fixtures never did well was associations. Factories make this much easier to follow. Let's add a one-to-many relationship between categories and products. A Product now belongs to a Category. To set up a sample Category for a Product, we can configure the factory like this:

rr2/factories/test/unit/product_test.rb
```
Factory.define :category do |category|
  category.name "Goods"
end

Factory.define :product do |product|
  product.name "A product"
  product.price 20
  product.listed_on 3.days.ago
  product.sku { |prod| [prod.name.gsub(/ /, '-').upcase, "-", rand(999)].join}
  product.category {|prod| prod.association(:category, :name => "Stuff")}
end

test "A product belongs to a category" do
  @product = Factory.build(:product)
  assert_equal "Stuff", @product.category.name
end
```

First we set up the new factory for the Category model. Then we add the category() attribute to our product factory definition. As in the previous example, if a block is passed to the attribute call in the factory, the populated model is returned. From here, we can call factory_girl's association() method, which allows us to instantiate and connect an object from another factory. In this case, we use the :category factory, setting its name to an explicit value via the standard second argument used when calling Factory.build().

Finally, it would be good if we could generate similarly configured objects of the same class reproducibly. For example, we might want to write a series of tests that reference products that are not yet listed. Rather than repeat ourselves in the tests, we can use factory inheritance to get the job done. The following defines a factory for products not yet listed:

rr2/factories/test/unit/product_test.rb
```
Factory.define :not_yet_listed, :parent => :product do |product|
  product.listed_on 1.week.from_now
end
```

We name the factory :not_yet_listed and specify its :parent to be :product. Now, whenever we build or create a :not_yet_listed object, it will create a Product with all of the values from the :product factory and the overridden value for listed_on from our child factory.

Factory definitions are just Ruby code. That makes them very easy to work with. It also makes it tempting to store them in separate files and require() them into your tests. In fact, this is so common that factory_girl automatically loads factories from any Ruby file in the spec/factories/ or test/factories directory.

While this might be a good way to organize code with many factories, try to resist the temptation to move your factories out of view too soon. Err on the side of littering your tests with factory definitions. Why? For the same reason factories were created in the first place. If your sample data definitions are tucked away outside your tests, they become opaque to the reader of the test code. Defining them local to the tests that use them makes it very clear what the tests are actually testing. Getting it right is a balance.

Also See

For information on how to add dependencies to your test environment but not to your development and production environments, see Recipe 58, *Use Bundler Groups to Manage Per-Environment Dependencies*, on page 224.

Part V

Email Recipes

Decades after the invention of the Internet, email for the average user remains its killer application. While Rails is primarily a web application framework, its email capabilities are considerable. In these recipes, we'll look at both how to generate rich outgoing emails as well as how to process incoming email.

Send Gracefully Degrading Rich-Content Emails

Problem

Despite the historic hoopla over the World Wide Web, the real killer app of the Internet has always been email. Even as the Web evolves, email is taking on an ever-increasing role in the dissemination of information. Modern web applications are about making things easier for the user. And with the Web's information fire hose showing no sign of letting up, receiving information by email makes it easier for users to keep up with what's happening in each of many web applications that they may be subscribed to.

That said, the Web has spoiled all of us email users. We're so used to the rich experience of using a well-designed HTML-based application that the plain-text emails that suited us in the past look dull by comparison. It's so much harder to make out what's important in a plain-text message. So, over time, email has become richer. How we build our applications so that it's possible to distribute an email message without having to worry whether the recipient will be a simple text-based mail client or the HTML-friendly Apple Mail client?

Solution

The Internet Engineering Task Force (IETF) has defined a standard MIME type called multipart/alternative that is designed to solve this problem. Messages with the multipart/alternative MIME type are structured exactly like messages of type multipart/mixed, which is the typical MIME type of a mail message with one or more attachments. But, though structurally identical, multipart/alternative messages are *interpreted* differently by their receivers.

Each part of a multipart/alternative-encoded message is assumed to be an alternative rendering of the same information. Upon receiving a message in the multipart/alternative format, a mail client can then choose which format suits it best.

Rails gives us an easy way to send multipart/alternative messages. Let's explore!

Assuming we've already generated an application to work with, we'll generate a new mailer class to hold our code:

```
$ rails g mailer Notifier multipart_alternative_rich
      create  app/mailers/notifier.rb
      invoke  erb
      create    app/views/notifier
      create    app/views/notifier/multipart_alternative_rich.text.erb
      invoke  test_unit
      create    test/functional/notifier_test.rb
```

We also asked the generator to set up multipart_alternative_rich() as a mail method for us. We'll edit this method to add our own logic. The multipart_alternative_rich() method should look like the following:

rr2/gracefully_degrading_rich_text_emails/app/mailers/notifier.rb
```
class Notifier < ActionMailer::Base
  default :from => "from@example.com"

  def multipart_alternative_rich
    @greeting = "Hi"

    mail :to => "chad+rails3recipes@chadfowler.com"
  end

end
```

The Rails 3 mailer API is sleek and simple. In the generated code, the example instance variable @greeting is set to be passed to the view, and we call the mail() to actually generate the mail to a recipient.

The plain-text version of the view looks like this:

rr2/gracefully_degrading_rich_text_emails/app/views/notifier/multipart_alternative_rich.text.erb
```
Notifier#multipart_alternative_rich

<%= @greeting %>,
find me in app/views/app/views/notifier/multipart_alternative_rich.text.erb
```

Now let's turn this mailer into a multipart/alternative mailer! All we have to do is to define additional views under app/views/notifier with the base part of the filename set to notifier and the middle part of the filename set to a reference to a content type. For example, we might create a file called app/views/notifier/multipart_alternative_rich.html.erb to contain our HTML version of the mail:

rr2/gracefully_degrading_rich_text_emails/app/views/notifier/multipart_alternative_rich.html.erb
```
This is the <h1>HTML</h1> version of our mail.

<a href="http://pragprog.com">Visit the Pragmatic Bookshelf</a>.

We can still reference this: <%= @greeting %>
```

That's all there is to it! We can now deliver a message and see how it looks:

```
$ rails runner "Notifier.multipart_alternative_rich.deliver"
```

On my Macbook Pro, this message looks like this:

This is the

HTML

version of our mail. Visit the Pragmatic Bookshelf. We can still reference this: Hi

The same message on the console-based mutt email client (http://www.mutt.org/) looks like this:

```
From: chad@chadfowler.com
To: chad+rails3recipes@chadfowler.com
Subject: Multipart alternative rich

Notifier#multipart_alternative_rich

Hi, find me in app/views/app/views/notifier/multipart_alternative_rich.text.erb
```

How did this work? It's all about the conventions. Rails saw multiple templates matching the name of the mail we were sending and automatically set the MIME type of the message to multipart/alternative and rendered *all* of the templates as parts of the mail. If we wanted to create even more parts to the message, we'd simply need to create more files with names starting with the name of the mailer and using different content types. Simple!

Since Rails makes it so easy to send multipart/alternative-formatted messages, you won't ever again risk sending HTML to a client that might not be able to read it.

Also See

Reader Peter Michaux points out that going beyond the simple HTML example here, you might want to use images and CSS in your HTML-formatted mails. You need to consider a number of issues when you do this. CampaignMonitor has an excellent article available at http://www.campaignmonitor.com/blog/archives/2006/03/a_guide_to_css_1.html.

Send Email with Attachments

Problem

You need to send emails with attachments from your Rails application.

Solution

Action Mailer makes it easy to send rich email with attachments using its attachments[]=() method. Let's walk through a simple example.

First we'll generate a controller to provide an interface to the user. Let's call it SpamController:

```
$ rails generate controller spam
    create  app/controllers/spam_controller.rb
    invoke  erb
    create    app/views/spam
    invoke  test_unit
    create    test/functional/spam_controller_test.rb
    invoke  helper
    create    app/helpers/spam_helper.rb
    invoke    test_unit
    create      test/unit/helpers/spam_helper_test.rb
```

Next we'll generate a mailer. We'll call our mailer Spammer and have the generator create a single mail method called spam_with_attachment():

```
$ rails generate mailer Spammer spam_with_attachment
 create  app/mailers/spammer.rb
 invoke  erb
 create    app/views/spammer
 create    app/views/spammer/spam_with_attachment.text.erb
 invoke  test_unit
 create    test/functional/spammer_test.rb
```

We'll look at the implementation of the mailer shortly. First let's focus on the user interface.

We'll start with a mail form. We'll put it in the file index.html.erb in the app/views/spam/ directory. The form accepts a name, a recipient email address, and a file upload. Notice that the call to form_tag() declares the form to be multipart.

This is necessary in order to submit both the normal form data and the uploaded files. Here's the code for the form:

rr2/SendingEmailsWithAttachments/app/views/spam/index.html.erb
```erb
<%= form_tag send_spam_path, :multipart => true do %>
  <p>
    <%= label_tag :name %>
    <%= text_field_tag :name %>
  </p>

  <p>
    <%= label_tag :email %>
    <%= text_field_tag :email %>
  </p>

  <p>
    <%= label_tag :file %>
    <%= file_field_tag :file %>
  </p>
  <%= submit_tag "Spam!" %>
<% end %>
```

As you can see, the form submits to a route called send_spam(), which we have pointed to the SpamController's send_spam() action. The send_spam() action's primary job is to delegate to an Action Mailer class. We'll do that and just redirect back to the form. After all, we've called this thing Spammer, so it's safe to assume that its users will want to send one mail after another.

Here's the entire SpamController class:

rr2/SendingEmailsWithAttachments/app/controllers/spam_controller.rb
```ruby
class SpamController < ApplicationController
  def send_spam
    Spammer.spam_with_attachment(params[:name],
                                 params[:email],
                                 params[:file]).deliver
    redirect_to spam_form_url, :notice => "Keep 'em coming!"
  end
end
```

We're almost there. All that's left is to implement the actual mailer. The mailer is implemented as a pair of files: the mailer itself and the template it uses to render a message body. The view is a dead-simple ERb template that's named after the send method on the mailer class, which in this case is spam_with_attachment.text.erb.

rr2/SendingEmailsWithAttachments/app/views/spammer/spam_with_attachment.text.erb
```erb
Hello <%= @name %>!  Have some spam!
```

The real work happens in the mailer class. Here's what ours looks like:

```
rr2/SendingEmailsWithAttachments/app/mailers/spammer.rb
class Spammer < ActionMailer::Base
  default :from => "from@example.com"
  def spam_with_attachment(name, email, file)
    @name = name
    attachments[file.original_filename] = file.read
    mail :to => email, :subject => "Have a Can of Spam!"
  end
end
```

The method starts by setting the name to an instance variable called @name. As is the case with actions and their views, setting the instance variable allows us to reference the name argument in the view.

Next is the code for adding the attachment. To add an attachment, we call the attachments[]=() method, passing in the filename for the attachment and the actual attachment data. In this case, both of those pieces of information are pulled from the uploaded file object we passed in from the controller. Had we needed to explicitly set the MIME type for the attachment, instead of passing the file content directly into the attachments[]=(), we could have passed a Hash containing values for :mime_type and :content.

If we needed to, we could have attached multiple files here. Simply call attachments[]=() with a different filename for each attachment.

If you're sending HTML email, you may want to do inline attachments. This allows you to, for example, embed images in the message. ActionMailer makes this trivial. Here's a rewritten version of our mailer and view that embeds an uploaded image in an email message:

```
rr2/SendingEmailsWithAttachments/app/mailers/spammer.rb
class Spammer
  def spam_with_attachment_inline(name, email, file)
    @name = name
    attachments.inline['photo.png'] = file.read
    mail :to => email, :subject => "Have a Can of Spam!"
  end
end
```

```
rr2/SendingEmailsWithAttachments/app/views/spammer/spam_with_attachment_inline.html.erb
<h1>Hurray!</h1>
I hope this is a picture!
<%= image_tag attachments['photo.png'].url %>
```

The only difference in the mailer is that instead of calling attachments[]=(), we call attachments.inline[]=(). In the view, ActionMailer gives us a mechanism to refer to the URL of an attachment, which makes it possible to embed the image in the message using image_tag().

Test Incoming Email

Problem

You are developing an application that processes incoming email messages. Your development process is too slow and complicated if you have to send an email and wait every time you make a change to the email processor. Some of your team's developers don't have the ability to easily start an email server on their development computers, so until now, the development of the email-processing component has been limited to developers whose computers have a working email server. You need a working test harness that will let you test your email-processing code.

Solution

Support for testing incoming email with Action Mailer isn't as explicit as it is with outgoing email. There are test harnesses in place to access all the mail you've sent with Action Mailer, but there are no such explicit clues as to how to test *incoming* mail processing.

Fortunately, though not quite as obvious as testing outgoing email, it's not any more difficult to test incoming email. To test incoming mail, we will simulate mail being piped into our mailer by passing in raw, unprocessed mail messages and allowing our mailer to process them exactly as they'd be processed in a production deployment.

To understand this, let's quickly review how to set up an incoming email processor. For the sake of a brief discussion, we'll assume we're using sendmail and procmail. For detailed information on setting up your system to process mail with Rails, see *Agile Web Development with Rails* [RTH11].

On a typical sendmail system, you can set up a .forward file in your home directory, specifying an email address to which to forward your incoming mail. If, instead of an email address, you specify a pipe symbol (|) followed by the name of a program, incoming email will be *piped* to that program's standard input for processing. A simple example .forward file might look like the following:

```
"|procmail"
```

The procmail program will then look in the user's home directory for a file called .procmailrc, which will tell procmail how to process incoming mail based on a configurable set of rules. We won't go into what those rules mean here, but suffice to say that the following .procmailrc file tells procmail to pipe all incoming email to a Rails application called mail_receiver—specifically to its Receiver class. (We've split the command onto multiple lines to make it fit the page.) Here's the file:

```
:0 c
*
| cd /home/listener/mail_receiver && \
            rails runner 'Receiver.receive(STDIN.read)'
```

This is where it gets interesting from the perspective of writing tests:

```
Receiver.receive(STDIN.read)
```

The Action Mailer mail receiver simply accepts a raw email message, which in this case we've configured to come in via the application's standard input. What this means is that to run the mail receiver in a test, all we have to do is get the raw text of an email message and pass it into our mail receiver's receive() method.

Let's stop talking about it and start cookin'!

If you're like me, your email inbox is flooded with not-to-miss business opportunities every day. Whether it's a sweet deal on a miracle diet pill or the chance to make millions of dollars just by helping someone transfer some money from one bank account to another, I'm constantly worried that I get too many emails from friends and family, and I might not notice one of these gems as a result. So, to demonstrate how to test incoming email processors in Rails, we'll start on a little application to help us sort through all of these incoming opportunities to make sure we don't miss any of them.

First we'll set up a mailer using the rails generate command:

```
chad> rails generate mailer Receiver
      create  app/mailers/receiver.rb
      invoke  erb
      create    app/views/receiver
      invoke  test_unit
      create    test/functional/receiver_test.rb
```

As is typical in Rails for code that sets up a mailer, not only did the generator create a skeleton for our mail receiver implementation, but it set up a test file for us as well. Let's look at the file in its pristine form before we start spicing it up:

```
rr2/testing_incoming_email/test/functional/receiver_test_pristine.rb
require 'test_helper'

class ReceiverTest < ActionMailer::TestCase
  # test "the truth" do
  #   assert true
  # end
end
```

This file is pretty simple. It's a basic-looking unit test; however, you'll notice that the class inherits from ActionMailer::TestCase, which gives us some extra mail-specific functionality. The functionality most applicable to us now is ActionMailer::TestCase's read_fixture() method. It's not magic, but it gives us a clue as to how we should manage the raw email text we're going to be stuffing into our mail receiver. Namely, we can store each message in a text file under our application's test/fixtures/receiver directory. If we do that, we need to call only the generated read_fixture() method and pass the returned data into our Receiver class's receive() method.

Now, all we need is some raw email text. Since it's just text, we could construct it by hand, but we have spam to read, and time is money!

It turns out that though most of us don't need to use it much, most email clients have the ability to show you the raw source of an email message. If you can do this with your email client, you can send yourself test emails with the desired characteristics or pull existing email from your inbox and then just copy and paste their raw source into a text file to save into your fixtures directory.

Since we're going to be writing code to help us sort through the many money-making opportunities in our inboxes, I'll pull out a relevant email. The text of the raw email is as follows:

```
Return-Path: <webmaster@elboniabank.com>
Received: from [192.168.0.100] (c-192-168-0-1.sd.o.nonex.net [192.168.0.100])
  by rasp.chadfowler.com (8.12.10/8.12.10) with ESMTP id jBLUc021232
  for <chad@chadfowler.com>; Wed, 21 Dec 2015 11:19:40 -0500
Mime-Version: 1.0 (Apple Message framework v746.2)
Content-Transfer-Encoding: 7bit
Message-Id: <E75372B2-32AD-402B-B930-5421238557921@chadfowler.com>
Content-Type: text/plain; charset=US-ASCII; format=flowed
To: chad@chadfowler.com
From: N'Dugu Wanaskamya <webmaster@elboniabank.com>
Subject: CONFIDENTIAL OPPORTUNITY
Date: Wed, 21 Dec 2015 04:19:00 -0700

Bulwayo, Republic of Elbonia.
```

MY PLEASURE,

This is a proposal in context but actually an appeal soliciting for your
unreserved assistance in consummating an urgent transaction requiring
maximum confidence. Though this approach appears desperate,I can assure
you that whatever questions you would need to ask or any other thing you
will need to know regarding this proposal, will be adequately answered
to give you a clearer understanding of it so as to arrive at a
successful conclusion.

No doubt this proposal will make you apprehensive, please i employ you
to observe utmost confidentiality and rest assured that this transaction
would be most profitable for both of us. Note also that we shall require
your assistance to invest our share in your country.

Thanks and Regards,
Mr. N'Dugu Wanaskamya
First Bank of Elbonia

We'll save this text in a file called confidential_opportunity in the directory test/fixtures/receiver under our application's root directory. We can now write a simple test to make sure things are working as expected. Add the following to your receiver_test.rb file:

```
rr2/testing_incoming_email/test/functional/receiver_test.rb
test "fixtures are working" do
  email_text = read_fixture("confidential_opportunity").join
  assert_match /opportunity/i, email_text
end
```

This is just a smoke test to make sure we can get to the fixture and that it produces a String that can be fed into our mail receiver. Run the test. It should work. If it doesn't, you probably have a file in the wrong place. If you retrace your steps, you'll find it in a jiffy:

```
chad> ruby -I test test/functional/receiver_test.rb
Loaded suite test/unit/receiver_test
Started

ReceiverTest:
     PASS fixtures are working (0.39s)

     Finished in 0.393521 seconds.

     1 tests, 1 assertions, 0 failures, 0 errors, 0 skips
```

Now that we have the safety net set up, we can start actually writing some code. The goal of our application is to somehow separate the emails we care about from the ones that just clutter up our mailboxes. To that end, we'll create a simple model to store messages and to rate them numerically. The higher the rating, the more "interesting" the message is. We won't look at the details of the data model here, but just keep in mind that we have a model named MailMessage (with a corresponding mail_messages table) that has the expected subject, body, sender, and so on, attributes as well as a numeric rating attribute.

We'll start small and test the simple processing of a message to make sure it gets added to the database. Let's write the test first:

rr2/testing_incoming_email/test/functional/receiver_test.rb

```ruby
test "incoming mail gets added to the database" do
  assert_difference "MailMessage.count" do
    email_text = read_fixture("confidential_opportunity").join
    Receiver.receive(email_text)
    assert_equal "CONFIDENTIAL OPPORTUNITY", MailMessage.last.subject
  end
end
```

This test will fail, since our mail receiver is unimplemented. Go ahead and run it. Watch it fail now, and it'll feel better when it passes.

```
chad> rake test:functionals
Started

ReceiverTest:
    PASS fixtures are working (0.03s)
    ERROR incoming mail gets added to the database (0.17s)
        NoMethodError: undefined method `receive' for #<Receiver:...>
        action_mailer/base.rb:421:in `block in receive'


Finished in 0.208125 seconds.

2 tests, 1 assertions, 0 failures, 1 errors, 0 skips
```

Now we'll make it pass. Let's implement the mail receiver. Edit your app/mailers/receiver.rb, and define a receive() method like this:

rr2/testing_incoming_email/app/mailers/receiver.rb

```ruby
def receive(email)
  MailMessage.create(:subject => email.subject, :body    => email.body.to_s,
             :sender => email.from,     :rating  => 0)
end
```

We simply create a new instance of the MailMessage class and populate it with the contents of the incoming email. But we have the rating() set to 0. Let's put in a simple rule to increase the rating of any email that contains the word *opportunity*. Again, we'll start with the test:

```
rr2/testing_incoming_email/test/functional/receiver_test.rb
test "email containing opportunity rates higher" do
  email_text = read_fixture("confidential_opportunity").join
  Receiver.receive(email_text)
  assert MailMessage.find_by_subject("CONFIDENTIAL OPPORTUNITY").rating > 0
end
```

And the simplest possible implementation would look like some variation of this:

```
rr2/testing_incoming_email/app/mailers/receiver.rb
def receive(email)
  rating = 0
  if([email.subject, email.body].any?{|string| string =~ /opportunity/i})
    rating += 1
  end
  MailMessage.create(:subject => email.subject, :body    => email.body.to_s,
              :sender => email.from,    :rating  => rating)
end
```

It's easy to see how you could continue to iterate this way, decreasing a message's rating if it's from a friend or family member or increasing the rating if the mail's origin is the Republic of Elbonia (known to be a hotbed of high-return financial opportunities for the open-minded entrepreneur). We'll leave you to season to taste in this regard. But what if you need to check a message's attachments? How do you test that?

Mail attachments, though usually made of nontextual materials, are encoded as text for transfer over the Internet. This is lucky for us, because it means we don't have to change our approach at all. The following is what the raw text of an email with an attachment would look like:

```
rr2/testing_incoming_email/test/fixtures/receiver/latest_screensaver
Return-Path: <chad@chadfowler.com>
Received: from [192.168.0.100] (c-24-8-92-53.hsd1.co.comcast.net ..)
Mime-Version: 1.0 (Apple Message framework v746.2)
To: chad@chadfowler.com
Message-Id: <689771CD-862F-49CB-B0E8-94C1517EB5C5@chadfowler.com>
Content-Type: multipart/mixed; boundary=Apple-Mail-1-231420468
From: Chad Fowler <chad@chadfowler.com>
Subject: The latest new screensaver!
Date: Thu, 22 Dec 2015 19:28:46 -0700
X-Mailer: Apple Mail (2.746.2)
X-Spam-Checker-Version: SpamAssassin 2.63 (2004-01-11) on ns1.chadfowler.com
X-Spam-Level: *
X-Spam-Status: No, hits=1.2 required=5.0 ...


--Apple-Mail-1-231420468
```

```
Content-Transfer-Encoding: 7bit
Content-Type: text/plain;
        charset=US-ASCII;
        delsp=yes;
        format=flowed

Hey bro,  I thought you would like to see this.  It's the latest new
screensaver.  Everyone at the office loves it!


--Apple-Mail-1-231420468
Content-Transfer-Encoding: base64
Content-Type: application/zip;
        x-unix-mode=0644;
        name="screensaver.zip"
Content-Disposition: attachment;
        filename=screensaver.zip
```

```
iVBORw0KGgoAAAANSUhEUgAAABAAAAFTCAIAAAC/KhtAAAAB6GlDQ1BJQ0MgUHJvZmlsZQAAeJyV
kbFrE3EUxz+/07UVS9QapEOHHyjSQlJCglC7mJigrUQINWqS7Xo5k4O7y4+7S2vAVaSrQv8BQcS1
QkUHMzroIKIWHV3E0UIXCedwDRlKKD548HlfeLz3vg/0mqGUowGuF/qrN67JWr0hJ74wxUlOs0Ta
...
4Bv4JE4RyYntVaLtouSfBg28b6Dgse+7vFJvL6V/J+g+lnVdl2XZtu2eGIZhmqaU0umGlJLW+ulI
rfWRPj2ptWatvaStta21rzufwHsfY7yAGKP3/jkQkVKKMeZojTGllMuIE+j7fp7no53due/774CI
5JydcyLinMs5y62uQClVa+26rtaqlPoZiEgIYYRzHEML9SEQe//G3AgAAAAAAAAAAAAAAAAAAAAA
AAAAAAAAAAAAAAAAAAAAAAAAAAAAAAAAAAAAAAAAAAAAAAAAAMBfAe8r3B9sCnIPeQAAAABJRU5ErkJg
gg==
```

```
--Apple-Mail-1-231420468--
```

If we were interested in tracking screensavers and other similar attachments
that were sent to us at random, we could add another rule and assert in our
tests that an attached zip file increases the rating() of an email:

rr2/testing_incoming_email/test/functional/receiver_test.rb
```ruby
test "zip file increases rating" do
  email_text = read_fixture("latest_screensaver").join
  Receiver.receive(email_text)
  #assert MailMessage.find_by_subject("The latest new screensaver!").rating > 0
end
```

We could then add the code to our mail receiver to check for zip files, and the
test would run:

rr2/testing_incoming_email/app/mailers/receiver.rb
```ruby
def receive(email)
  rating = 0
  if([email.subject, email.body].any?{|string| string =~ /opportunity/i})
    rating += 1
  end
```

```ruby
  if email.has_attachments?
    email.attachments.each do |attachment|
      rating += 1 if attachment.original_filename =~ /zip$/i
    end
  end
  MailMessage.create(:subject => email.subject, :body => email.body.to_s,
              :sender  => email.from,    :rating  => rating)
end
```

If we expand this application, we'll want to refactor it into a more flexible set of rules, and with our tests in place, we would be in great shape to do just that.

Part VI

Big-Picture Recipes

These recipes are about solving high-level problems that may span multiple layers of the Rails MVC stack. In this section, we present solutions to common configuration, security, and automation needs.

Roll Your Own Authentication

Problem

You're developing an application with some functions whose use you want to limit to users with special privileges. Perhaps the application is an online trivia game with screens for adding questions and their answers. Naturally, you don't want every player to have access to the answers. Instead, you'd like to protect the administrative interface and restrict its use to registered users only.

Solution

A solution to this common problem is best achieved with a scheme for authenticating registered users. Although several Rails authentication libraries are available as plugins and generators, simple authentication is so easy to do with Rails that depending on a third-party add-on to handle authentications is often not worth the extra baggage. Besides, rolling your own simple authentication solution is a great way to understand how those third-party libraries work. A new user model and an Action Controller before_filter can have you up and running with login-protected actions in a matter of minutes.

For the sake of simplicity, it's often convenient to place sensitive functionality of an application in a separate controller. Since we're protecting the answers to trivia questions, we can simply shield the entire AnswersController of our application with our authentication scheme. This is where the CRUD functionality that you need to handle an answers database is likely to exist.

The first step is to create a model to hold the data we need to authenticate our users. We'll name the model User:

```
$ rails g model User username:string password_digest:string
invoke  active_record
create    db/migrate/20110105170941_create_users.rb
create    app/models/user.rb
invoke    test_unit
create      test/unit/user_test.rb
create      test/fixtures/users.yml
```

The schema is simple. Users have a username and a password digest. We'll then apply the generated database migration:

```
$ rake db:migrate
```

Next we'll add some authentication-specific code to the User model. Here's the user.rb file:

rr2/simple_auth/app/models/user.rb
```
class User < ActiveRecord::Base
  has_secure_password
end
```

Since we don't want to store plain-text passwords in the database, we use the Rails 3.1 has_secure_password() method to declare that the User class has a reader and writer for the virtual password() attribute, which will automatically use BCrypt to store a secure representation of that password in the password_digest field. When we want to authenticate users, we can look them up by username and then compare the password digest with the digest of the password they have provided. As we'll see, the has_secure_password() method makes this trivial.

Now that we have a data model to support our User objects, we need to create a user. This is a simple model, so we could easily create a user administration form or even use simple scaffolding. But for now, we'll just create a user at the Rails console:

```
$ rails console
Loading development environment.
>> chad = User.create(:username => "chad")
=> #<User:0x2416350 @errors=#<ActiveRecord::Errors:0x241598c...@new_record=false>
>> chad.password = "secret"
=> "secret"
>> chad.password_digest
=> "fa56838174d3aef09623ea003cb5ee468aa1b0aa68a403bd975be84dd999e76c"
>> chad.save
=> true
```

Now that we have a User with which to sign in, we can modify our AnswersController to require authentication before executing any actions. We can do this using the before_filter macro included with Action Controller. At the top of the AnswersController's class definition, let's add the following:

rr2/simple_auth/app/controllers/answers_controller.rb
```
before_filter :check_authentication
def check_authentication
  unless session[:user_id]
    session[:intended_action] = action_name
    session[:intended_controller] = controller_name
```

```
    redirect_to new_session_url
  end
end
```

This filter tells Rails to always execute the method check_authentication() before executing any actions in this controller. This method checks for a user id in the session object. If the user does not exist (which means the user hasn't yet authenticated), the application redirects to the new_session_url, which will display a login form to collect the user's username and password. As you'll soon see, saving session[:intended_action] and session[:intended_controller] will allow us to keep track of what the user was trying to do before authenticating, so we can place them gently back on their intended paths after checking their credentials. This is especially important when we want to support bookmarks.

Now it's time to actually implement the login page. As we've seen, the page application redirects to new_session_url when a user tries to access AnswersController without first authenticating. new_session_url is the named route pointing to the new form for the session resource. Over the years, it has become conventional for developers of Rails applications to take advantage of the Rails REST conventions when they write authentication code. The clearest mapping of REST to authentication is that of performing CRUD operations on sessions. Therefore, we typically put authentication code in a SessionsController and then implement new(), create(), and destroy() actions to handle logging in and out. Since any given user can access only *one* session (their own), we use the singular form of the resource configuration in config/routes.rb:

rr2/simple_auth/config/routes.rb
```
resource :session
```

This will generate singular URLs, none of which will require an id parameter. When a user logs in (creating a session), the new() action will display the login form, and the create() action will accept the form post and perform the authentication. Here's the form:

rr2/simple_auth/app/views/sessions/new.html.erb
```
<%= form_tag session_path do %>
  <p>
          <%= label_tag :username %>
          <%= text_field_tag :username %>
  </p>
  <p>
          <%= label_tag :password %>
          <%= password_field_tag :password %>
          <%= submit_tag "login" %>
  </p>
<% end %>
```

The user then submits their username and password to the create action, which checks them against our User model in the database:

```
rr2/simple_auth/app/controllers/sessions_controller.rb
def create
  session[:user_id] = User.authenticate(params[:username], params[:password]).id
  flash[:notice] = "Welcome back!"
  redirect_to :action => session[:intended_action],
              :controller => session[:intended_controller]
end
```

To support this action, we add an authenticate() method to the User class that looks up the user and uses ActiveModel's built-in authenticate() instance method to do the password comparison for us. While we're in there, we'll add a validator to ensure that only one User can be created with a given username:

```
rr2/simple_auth/app/models/user.rb
class User < ActiveRecord::Base
  has_secure_password
  validates_uniqueness_of :username

  def self.authenticate(username, password)
    user = User.find_by_username(username)
    unless user && user.authenticate(password)
      raise "Username or password invalid"
    end
    user
  end
end
```

Finally, to top this recipe off with a little icing, we'll add the ability to sign out of the application. The SessionsController's destroy action will simply remove the user id from session and redirect to the application's home page:

```
rr2/simple_auth/app/controllers/sessions_controller.rb
def destroy
  session[:user_id] = nil
  redirect_to root_url, :notice => "Come back soon!"
end
```

Note that root_url() refers to the route configured to be this application's home. See Recipe 31, *Set Your Application's Home Page*, on page 108 to find out how to configure your application's home page.

What would we do if we needed authentication to apply to multiple controllers? Simple: move the authentication-related code, including the filter declarations, to our ApplicationController class. Since all our controllers extend ApplicationController by default, they will all inherit the filters and methods we define there.

If you need to store extra profile information along with a user object, you might be tempted, once it has been authenticated, to put the entire User object in session. It's best to avoid doing this, because you'll invariably find yourself debugging your application, wondering why data changes to your user's profile don't seem to be taking effect, only to realize that you're looking at a stale copy of the data from session.

On the other end of the spectrum, sometimes you don't actually need a user object or model at all. If you don't need to track *who* is signing into your application, sometimes a simple password will do. For example, though some blog systems support multiple authors and can display the author of each post, many do not. Simply protecting the right to post a story would be sufficient for such a system, and for that, a password (even a hard-coded password!) could meet your needs and save you time.

One caveat to note with this approach: even though we're redirecting to the initially requested action, we'll lose any parameters passed during the initial, preauthenticated request. Using the same pattern we used to capture the intended action and controller, how could you save the request parameters and pass them along?

Also See

For all but the simplest of applications, rather than rolling your own authentication, you'll want to use an existing framework. For a look at the currently most popular up-and-coming authentication framework, check out Devise at http://github.com/plataformatec/devise.

Protect Your Application with Basic HTTP Authentication

Problem

In a typical Rails application, authentication is done using the session. As we saw in Recipe 51, *Roll Your Own Authentication*, on page 198, actions are wrapped in filters that check for the existence of a session key and redirect clients to login forms if that key isn't present. This works fine for human visitors, but what if we wanted to authenticate another computer making a web service call? The form- and session-based approaches don't make as much sense. Or what if we wanted to just provide a system-wide single username and password to authorized users, who could access our application over the network while it was still in private beta?

In short, how do you add simple HTTP authentication to your application?

Solution

ActionController provides a couple of convenient methods for enabling HTTP authentication. The simplest is a class-level declaration called http_basic_authentication_with(). This wraps a slightly lower-level pair of methods that are combined using authenticate_or_request_with_http_basic(). We'll look at both of these options.

Let's start with the simple case where we want to protect an entire application or controller with a single username and password. In my own work, this is the sort of thing I do when an application is in private beta. Perhaps we want to deploy the application to the Internet but we're not ready for anyone to even see the login page, which might include elements of the final design. By protecting all of our actions with HTTP basic authentication, we inhibit Rails for rendering any templates unless the client has authenticated.

This kind of authentication is trivial to add in Rails 3.1 or newer. Simply place a declaration like this into your controller at the class level:

```
rr2/http_basic/app/controllers/pages_controller.rb
http_basic_authenticate_with :name => "recipes",
                             :password => "secret",
                             :realm => "Beta"
```

In this example, we call the method http_basic_authentication_with(), passing in a name, password, and realm. The name and password are used as the credentials to check against. In this case, the credentials are hard-coded to a controller-wide pair of values. The realm is used to name the authenticated area of the site. Think of it as a label that explains which protected resource a client might be trying to access. In this case, we've set it to "beta" so an incoming client knows they're trying to access the beta site.

This is as simple as authentication gets. If we put this in our ApplicationController, we can protect our entire application with a single username and password combination. But that's the problem. We're limited to a single set of credentials. There's no way for us to know *who* is visiting the application, and there isn't any way to provide different access levels to different users. To overcome these limitations while still using HTTP authentication, we can implement a before_filter() using authenticate_or_request_with_http_basic().

In the following code, we protect only the edit() and update() actions of a controller, limiting access to authenticated users only.

rr2/http_basic/app/controllers/recipes_controller.rb
```
before_filter :authenticate, only: [:edit, :update]
def authenticate
  authenticate_or_request_with_http_basic("Recipe Admin") do |user, pass|
    @current_user = User.authenticate(user, pass)
  end
end
```

We first declare the filter to call authenticate() before the desired actions. Next we define the authenticate() method. The authenticate() filter calls the authenticate_or_request_with_http_basic() method to do its work. We pass in the name of the authentication realm we're protecting and attach a block. If credentials have been supplied by the client, the block is called with the username and password as parameters. We can then use those parameters to try authenticating our user. In this case, we're delegating to our User model's authenticate() method that would authenticate the user, as described in Recipe 51, *Roll Your Own Authentication*, on page 198. If the block returns a value, the authenticate_or_request_with_http_basic() method considers the authentication successful. Otherwise, Rails responds with a request for the client to provide credentials.

Web service clients can supply credentials with every request, foregoing the need to be presented with a form. However, when a person visits a protected part of our site with a web browser, they will be greeted with the authentication dialog shown in Figure 4, *Basic authentication dialog*, on page 205.

Figure 4—Basic authentication dialog

HTTP Basic Authentication causes credentials to be passed in plain text. Technically, they're base64 encoded; however, that's not enough to protect them from potential evil-doers. If you use HTTP Basic Authentication in your application, you *must* connect to the application via an encrypted connection. See Recipe 54, *Force Your Users to Access Site Functions with SSL*, on page 211 to learn how to force certain controllers or actions to be accessible only via HTTPS.

Alternatively, you can use HTTP Digest Authentication, which sends a hashed version of the password from the client to the server. Rails provides support for HTTP Digest Authentication in the method authenticate_or_request_with_http_digest(). See the Rails API documentation for details on how to use this method.

Authorize Users with Roles

Problem

You want to specify which functions of your application your users can access based on who they are and what roles they play. For example, suppose you have built an online community recipe book to which some contributors have the right to add and edit the recipes in its database. These users are more privileged than those who can simply post comments, but they're less privileged than you and a chosen few to whom you have given administrative rights to the website.

How can you model user roles and use them to restrict access to selected parts of your application?

Solution

In this recipe, we'll do the following:

1. Create two models, one for roles and another for rights
2. Associate those models with the user records we're using for authentication
3. Use controller filters to limit access on a per-action basis

Let's assume you have already set up an authentication system for your application like the one described in Recipe 51, *Roll Your Own Authentication*, on page 198. Even if yours is different, don't worry. Whichever app we use, to implement our solution, we need a user identifier in session and an Active Record model to represent our user object. In our recipe example, we'll use session[:user_id] (which contains the user's id as a number) and User to provide those pieces.

The basic parts of any role-based authorization scheme include users, roles, and rights. A user plays many roles. Each role affords the user zero or more rights. Assuming we have already created a User model, we'll start by generating models to represent roles, rights, and the connections between them:

```
$ rails generate model Role name:string
$ rails generate model Right resource:string operation:string
$ rails generate model Grant right_id:integer role_id:integer
$ rails generate model Assignment user_id:integer role_id:integer
```

Next, we'll set up the relationships between User, Role, and Right:

rr2/role_based_authorization/app/models/user.rb
```ruby
class User < ActiveRecord::Base
  has_many :assignments
  has_many :roles, :through => :assignments
end
```

rr2/role_based_authorization/app/models/assignment.rb
```ruby
class Assignment < ActiveRecord::Base
  belongs_to :user
  belongs_to :role
end
```

rr2/role_based_authorization/app/models/role.rb
```ruby
class Role < ActiveRecord::Base
  has_many :grants
  has_many :assignments
  has_many :users, :through => :assignments
  has_many :rights, :through => :grants
  scope :for, lambda{|action, resource|
                where("rights.operation = ? AND rights.resource = ?",
                      Right::OPERATION_MAPPINGS[action], resource
                )
              }
end
```

rr2/role_based_authorization/app/models/grant.rb
```ruby
class Grant < ActiveRecord::Base
  belongs_to :role
  belongs_to :right
end
```

rr2/role_based_authorization/app/models/right.rb
```ruby
class Right < ActiveRecord::Base
  has_many :grants
  has_many :roles, :through => :grants
  OPERATION_MAPPINGS = {
    "new" => "CREATE",
    "create" => "CREATE",
    "edit" => "UPDATE",
    "update" => "UPDATE",
    "destroy" => "DELETE",
    "show" => "READ",
    "index" => "READ"
  }
end
```

This code doesn't contain anything too unusual so far. Users have Roles, which give them associated Rights. We generated the Active Record migrations when we generated the models, so we simply need to apply those migrations now using rake db:migrate.

The most notable part of our authorization scheme's data model is the rights table. A Right signifies something a user can *do*, and in the world of Rails, things are conventionally *done* via CRUD operations on RESTful resources. So for our model, we're going to express rights in terms of the operations a user can perform on a given type of resource. Using the example of an online recipe book, you might create a Right with the resource set to *Recipe* and the operation set to *CREATE*. This Right would then be granted to one or more Roles that should have access to creating recipes. For example, we might have some users who play the role of *Author*. We'll look at some more specific examples shortly.

After applying migrations to create our database tables, we're ready to put this new model into action. This means setting up our controllers to allow a user access only to the operations they have been *granted* access to. We'll accomplish this using a before_filter. The relevant filter in our ApplicationController will look like the following:

rr2/role_based_authorization/app/controllers/application_controller.rb
```
before_filter :check_authorization

private
def check_authorization
  unless current_user.can?(action_name, controller_name)
    redirect_to :back,
                :error => "You are not authorized to view the page you requested"
  end
```

The new method, check_authorization(), gets the User from session using the current_user() method (which we're assuming is provided by the authentication system in use) and asks the User object if it has the capability to run the currently requested action and controller. We get the current action and controller names using the Rails built-in action_name() and controller_name() methods. To find out whether the user has the currently requested capability, we use the can?() method on the User object. This is a method we've defined:

rr2/role_based_authorization/app/models/user.rb
```
def can?(action, resource)
  roles.includes(:rights).for(action, resource).any?
end
```

The can?() searches the user's roles for any role that grants the right to perform this action and controller. It does this by including the rights in the query and then delegating to a named scope on the Role model. For more information on named scopes, see Recipe 2, *Create Declarative Named Queries*, on page 7. The for() scope looks like this:

```
rr2/role_based_authorization/app/models/role.rb
scope :for, lambda{|action, resource|
              where("rights.operation = ? AND rights.resource = ?",
                   Right::OPERATION_MAPPINGS[action], resource
                   )
          }
```

This filter queries for roles whose matching rights have a matching operation and resource. Since we're basing our Rights on CRUD operations, we have a Hash in the Right class that maps action names to their CRUD counterparts:

```
rr2/role_based_authorization/app/models/right.rb
OPERATION_MAPPINGS = {
  "new" => "CREATE",
  "create" => "CREATE",
  "edit" => "UPDATE",
  "update" => "UPDATE",
  "destroy" => "DELETE",
  "show" => "READ",
  "index" => "READ"
}
```

If the user determines that it does not have the right to perform this action, a message is put into flash, and the browser is redirected to the page from which it came. We could display such error messages by decorating our application's standard layout with a snippet like the following:

```
<% if flash[:error] %>
  <div class="errors">
    <%=  flash[:error] %>
  </div>
<% end %>
```

Notice that our filter method redirects if authorization fails. This is necessary to stop additional processing down the filter chain. For example, if we left out the redirect, we would need to return false in check_authorization(), or the requested action would still be executed. Either returning false or performing a rendering action (an explicit render() or a redirect) causes the filter chain to stop.

Finally, with this filter set up, we are ready to try our new authorization scheme! So far, we haven't added any roles or rights to the system, so our once-omnipotent users will now have access to nothing but the application's home page and sign-in forms. For a real application, you'll want to build an administrative interface for managing rights and roles. For our recipe application, we'll add them in the db/seeds.rb file and load them in using rake db:seed.

```ruby
user = User.create!(:name => "Bill")
user.roles << viewers = Role.create!(:name => "Viewer")

author = User.create!(:name => "Chad")
user.roles << authors = Role.create!(:name => "Author")

create = Right.create!(:resource => "recipes", :operation => "CREATE")
read = Right.create!(:resource => "recipes", :operation => "READ")
update = Right.create!(:resource => "recipes", :operation => "UPDATE")
delete = Right.create!(:resource => "recipes", :operation => "DELETE")

viewers.rights << read

authors.rights << create
authors.rights << read
authors.rights << update
authors.rights << delete
```

We have created a role called *Author* and assigned it to the user named *Chad*. We then created a right with the operation *CREATE* and added it to the list of rights afforded to our freshly created Role. Since the *CREATE* right grants access to the create and new actions of the recipes controller, the user *Chad* will now be able to access those actions.

This recipe shows a simple starting point from which you could build more complex authorization schemes. Basing rights on controllers and actions doesn't allow you to, for example, protect access to specific instances of models in your database. For more complex needs, this recipe will provide a solid building point, or you can explore the many third-party options available as RubyGems.

Force Your Users to Access Site Functions with SSL

Problem

How do you ensure that sensitive data on your site is always transferred through an encrypted connection?

Solution

With Rails 3.1, you can use new controller macro called force_ssl(). The force_ssl() macro is configurable on a per-controller or per-action basis, allowing you to specify which controllers or actions *must* be accessed via HTTPS.

The force_ssl() macro is implemented as a simple filter wrapper. Therefore, force_ssl() accepts the same :only and :except options that before_filter() uses to include or exclude actions from its configuration.

Imagine you were developing a site that allowed electronic payments. Any payment-related data such as credit card or bank information should be treated very carefully for obvious reasons. If you wanted to require that all actions from a controller are accessibly exclusively via SSL, you could do this:

```
class PaymentsController < ApplicationController
  force_ssl
end
```

Often, you'll want to apply this requirement to only a subset of actions. In that case, you can do this:

```
force_ssl :only => [:edit, :update, :new, :create]
```

If a client makes a non-SSL request for any restricted action, Rails will automatically redirect the client to the same URL using the HTTPS protocol.

Whenever you use filters to enforce security, think carefully about whether to use the :only or :except option. When possible, use :except with the force_ssl() macro. This makes it less likely that you will accidentally allow sensitive data to be passed via an unencrypted channel.

Create Secret URLs

Problem

Sometimes, you need to restrict access to a resource—be it a URL, an email address, or an instant messaging destination—and it's inconvenient or impractical to use a normal username/password authentication mechanism. A commonly occurring example of this is RSS or Atom feeds. You don't want to require a username and password, because your aggregator may not support that kind of authentication. Or you may be using a public RSS aggregation service such as Google Reader and be (understandably) unwilling to type in your username and password.

Another common example is that of an account activation link. A user signs up for your site, and you send them an email confirmation to ensure that they can at least be traced back to that email address. You want to give them an easy way to get back from the email to the site, so you give them an easy activation link.

How do you protect parts of your Rails site without requiring registration with a username and password?

Solution

A common solution to this problem is to generate an obfuscated URL that will sign someone directly into an account or allow them to gain access to a protected resource.

Let's walk through a simple example. Imagine we are developing a simple messaging module for a larger application. The application gives each user an inbox. Application users can then send and receive simple messages within the context of our larger application.

It's a nice feature that our users have been asking for, but in practice, it's yet another place (in addition to their email and other websites) that users have to go to keep up with the flow of information. To counteract this problem, we decide to set up a simple RSS feed to allow each user to track his or her inbox.

We can easily create a feed for each inbox using the instructions found in Recipe 30, *Syndicate Your Site with RSS*, on page 100. The problem now is that these messages are private, so they need to be protected. But we may not be able to get our RSS aggregator to work with a username and password. So, we'll generate an obfuscated URL through which to access these feeds.

First let's look at the schema describing users, their inboxes, and the messages in those inboxes. Here's the migration file that defines it:

rr2/secret_urls/db/migrate/20101202135612_add_users_inboxes_migrations.rb

```
Line 1  class AddUsersInboxesMigrations < ActiveRecord::Migration
   -      def self.up
   -        create_table :users do |t|
   -          t.string :name
   5          t.string :password
   -        end
   -        create_table :inboxes do |t|
   -          t.integer :user_id
   -          t.string :access_key
   10       end
   -        create_table :messages do |t|
   -          t.integer :inbox_id
   -          t.integer :sender_id
   -          t.string :title
   15         t.text :body
   -          t.datetime :created_at
   -        end
   -      end
   -
   20     def self.down
   -        drop_table :users
   -        drop_table :inboxes
   -        drop_table :messages
   -      end
   25  end
```

This is a simple model. Users have inboxes, and inboxes have messages. The only unusual part of the model is on line 9 where the access_key column is defined for the inboxes table. This is the magic key we'll use to let our users into select parts of the application without a username and password.

Next we'll use the standard Rails model generators to create User, Inbox, and Message models. Here are the models and their associations:

rr2/secret_urls/app/models/user.rb

```
class User < ActiveRecord::Base
  has_one :inbox
end
```

rr2/secret_urls/app/models/inbox.rb
```ruby
class Inbox < ActiveRecord::Base
  has_many :messages
  belongs_to :user
end
```

rr2/secret_urls/app/models/message.rb
```ruby
class Message < ActiveRecord::Base
  belongs_to :inbox
  belongs_to :sender, :class_name => "User"
end
```

Now, how do we populate the inbox's access_key? Since every inbox is going to need one, we can populate it at the time of the inbox's creation. The most reliable way to make sure this happens is to define it in the model's before_create() method. This way, we can set the access_key whenever an Inbox is created without having to remember to set it in our calling code. Here's the new inbox.rb:

rr2/secret_urls/app/models/inbox.rb
```ruby
class Inbox < ActiveRecord::Base
  has_many :messages
  belongs_to :user
  before_create :generate_access_key

  def generate_access_key
    self.access_key = [id.to_s, ActiveSupport::SecureRandom.hex(10)].join
  end
end
```

In Inbox's before_create() callback, we create a random access key and assign the attribute. Then Active Record's instance creation life cycle runs its course, and the Inbox is saved—access key and all.

For this example, we've created a random access key combining the Active Record–assigned id and a random hex value. The access key is not guaranteed to be unique, which could theoretically be a problem. For a more reliably unique id, see Bob Aman's UUIDTools library.[15]

Now each Inbox has its own obfuscated access key. All that's left is to set up access control for the Inbox's RSS feed, allowing passage to those with the proper key.

We'll assume that the feed is set up in a separate FeedsController with no authentication or authorization applied (those should be applied to, for example, the InboxesController, which is one good reason for putting RSS feeds

---

15. http://rubygems.org/gems/uuidtools/

in their own controller even though it's slightly unconventional). We can secure the Inbox feed by simply looking up the Inbox by the provided access_key. Here's the (abbreviated) FeedsController:

rr2/secret_urls/app/controllers/feeds_controller.rb
```
class FeedsController < ApplicationController
  def show
    @inbox = Inbox.find_by_access_key(params[:id])
    if @inbox.blank?
      head 401
    end
  end
end
```

The show() action looks up the Inbox using the provided access_key (which is passed in as the id parameter). If the Inbox query is successful, the action exits, and the show.rss.builder template is rendered. If the requested access_key does not match an Inbox, the application responds with a 401 HTTP response code, telling the client it made an unauthorized access attempt.

The URL for the feed for inbox 5 would look something like this: http://local-host/feeds/b6da56...92f98287b12c04d47.rss. In the URL, we set the id parameter to the value of our access_key, and we request that the Rails controller send us RSS data in response. The routing configuration is a standard RESTful setup:

rr2/secret_urls/config/routes.rb
```
resources :feeds
```

We can generate the URL for this feed (so our users can subscribe) in our views with the following code (assuming we have an @inbox instance variable available):

rr2/secret_urls/app/views/pages/index.html.erb
```
<%= link_to "Feed", feed_url(@inbox.access_key, "rss") %>
```

This technique is simple to implement, but the decision to do so should not be taken lightly. Since anyone who sees such a URL can gain privileged access to your site, extra logging and expiration logic should be added around this functionality. The URLs themselves also need to be treated as sensitive data. Used with the right amount of caution, obfuscated URLs are a nice addition to your Rails toolbox.

Use Rails Without a Database

Problem

As "opinionated" as the framework is, Rails assumes you want to develop with a database. This is *usually* the case, which is the reason for the assumption. But what if you're developing an application with a file-based backend? Or perhaps you're simply frontending an external service-based API. Rails is a little less friendly to you in this case—particularly when testing your application. How can you use Rails to build applications that don't require a database?

Solution

The secret to using Rails without a database is to selectively load pieces of the Rails framework at startup time and to modify the default generated unit test helper to remove Active Record dependencies.

By default, Rails assumes you want to connect to and initialize a database whenever you run your tests. This means that if you don't have a database, testing is difficult to do. Of course, you could just create a database for nothing, but that would mean you'd have extra infrastructure to support for no reason. A little hacking on a generated Rails application will get it into testable shape without a database.

To keep things simple and repeatable, we'll start with a fresh application. You'll be able to easily apply what we do here to your own application. Let's generate an application now. You can call it whatever you like. Mine is named DatabaselessApplication.

Next we'll create a simple class in app/models for which to write some tests. Let's be really simple and create a class called Adder that adds numbers together:

rr2/databaseless_application/app/models/adder.rb
```ruby
class Adder
  def initialize(first, second)
    @first = first
    @second = second
  end
```

```
  def sum
    @first + @second
  end
end
```

Now we'll create a simple test case subclasses ActiveSupport::TestCase for it in test/unit/adder_test.rb:

```
require 'test_helper'
require 'adder'
class AdderTest < ActiveSupport::TestCase
  def test_simple_addition
    assert_equal(4, Adder.new(3,1).sum)
  end
end
```

Let's try to run the test:

```
    $ rake
(in /Users/chad/src/rr2/Book/code/rr2/databaseless_application)
Errors running test:units!
```

It seems that the Rails Rake task test:units() does some database initialization. In fact, rake -P confirms this:

```
chad> rake -P
  ...
rake test:prepare
    db:test:prepare
rake test:profile
    test:prepare
rake test:recent
    test:prepare
rake test:uncommitted
    test:prepare
rake test:units
    test:prepare
  ...
```

Sure enough, test:units() depends on the test:prepare() task, which in turn depends on db:test:prepare(). What if we tried to run the tests directly, not using our Rake task?

```
$ ruby -I test test/unit/adder_test.rb
Loaded suite test/unit/adder_test
Started
.
Finished in 0.255508 seconds.

1 tests, 1 assertions, 0 failures, 0 errors, 0 skips
```

So far, it seems that the problems are limited to running tests within Rake. To be sure, let's try creating and running a functional test:

```
$ rails g controller Addition add
    create  app/controllers/addition_controller.rb
     route  get "addition/add"
    invoke  erb
    create    app/views/addition
    create    app/views/addition/add.html.erb
    invoke  test_unit
    create    test/functional/addition_controller_test.rb
    invoke  helper
    create    app/helpers/addition_helper.rb
    invoke    test_unit
    create      test/unit/helpers/addition_helper_test.rb
```

Generating a controller with an action stubs in a presumably working test for that action:

```
rr2/databaseless_application/test/functional/addition_controller_test.rb
require 'test_helper'

class AdditionControllerTest < ActionController::TestCase
  test "should get add" do
    get :add
    assert_response :success
  end
end
```

Let's just try to run this test as is. Maybe it'll work:

```
$ ruby -I test test/functional/addition_controller_test.rb
Loaded suite test/functional/addition_controller_test
Started
.
Finished in 0.362094 seconds.

1 tests, 1 assertions, 0 failures, 0 errors, 0 skips

Test run options: --seed 61995
```

Sure enough, it worked! All that's missing is to get these tests working with Rake. Having to manually invoke our test files one at a time is a real step backward from the default Rails way of testing. The Rails built-in testing tasks work really well, so we'd rather not lose any functionality as we implement our own tasks. We also don't want to have to copy and paste their code into our own Rake tasks. If we did that, we wouldn't receive the benefits of bug fixes and upgrades to the built-in tasks. If only the built-in tasks didn't have that db:test:prepare() prerequisite!

Fortunately, as of Rails 3, this problem is very easily solved. Rails 3 introduces a concept of a *Rail tie*, which each subframework of Rails uses to load and configure itself. Whereas in the past, the Rails gem itself loaded all of the default Rake tasks, now they happen on a framework-by-framework basis as that framework is loaded.

So, the real task here isn't to fix our tests. It's to stop Rails from loading Active Record on startup. To do that, we'll edit the application's config/application.rb file. Near the top of that file, by default, you'll see a line that loads the entire Rails framework. It should look like this:

```
require 'rails/all'
```

Innocent-looking as it is, this is the line that's causing us problems. If we were to crack open the Rails source code, we'd see that this file is defined as such:

```
require "rails"
%w(
  active_record
  action_controller
  action_mailer
  active_resource
  rails/test_unit
).each do |framework|
  begin
    require "#{framework}/railtie"
  rescue LoadError
  end
end
```

So, you see that for each subframework, Rails loads a file called railtie from that framework, which, as I mentioned earlier, is where the subframework gets a chance to hook itself into the Rails initialization process. So, the solution is simple if a little more manual that you might expect: replace the require 'rails/all' line with a list of the railtie files you need:

```
rr2/databaseless_application/config/application.rb
require "action_controller/railtie"
require "action_mailer/railtie"
require "active_resource/railtie"
require "rails/test_unit/railtie"
```

Now we have control over what subframeworks Rails loads. This would be a good time to remove ActionMailer if you don't plan to use mail in your application or ActiveResource if you're not planning to use its functional to create REST clients. By removing frameworks from the list, we gain the benefit of saving memory for each running Rails process when we deploy our applications.

Let's try to run all of our tests again:

```
$ rake
(in /Users/chad/src/rr2/Book/code/rr2/databaseless_application)
test/test_helper.rb:10:in `<class:TestCase>':
    undefined method `fixtures' for ActiveSupport::TestCase:Class (NoMethodError)
        from databaseless_application/test/test_helper.rb:5:in `<top (required)>'
...
```

This may seem like a setback, but this time we have a stack trace. Stack traces make everything better! If we look at test_helper.rb on line 10 as referenced in the stack trace, we'll see the following code: fixtures :all. That code tells the test framework to load all of the database fixtures for each test. Not surprisingly, the fixtures() method is defined in the ActiveRecord framework, which we have just removed from our application. So, all we need to do is remove this line from test_helper.rb. Now our tests run successfully without a database!

Create Your Own Ruby Gem

Problem

The Ruby ecosystem is a patchwork of libraries all glued together by the RubyGems package management system. Gems allow you to share and reuse code between applications with automatic dependency resolution. How do you create your own Ruby gem?

Solution

We can use the generator that Bundler provides to create the structure for our own gem. First we use the bundle command to generate a skeleton for the gem. We're going to create both a library and a command-line program, so we'll use the -b option to the bundle gem command:

```
$ bundle gem scrape_title -b
    create  scrape_title/Gemfile
    create  scrape_title/Rakefile
    create  scrape_title/.gitignore
    create  scrape_title/scrape_title.gemspec
    create  scrape_title/lib/scrape_title.rb
    create  scrape_title/lib/scrape_title/version.rb
    create  scrape_title/bin/scrape_title
```

Just as rails new does, bundle gem sets up a conventional directory structure for developing and packaging a gem. The key pieces are scrape_title.gemspec and the Rakefile. If we were to move into the freshly created directory and list all of the Rake tasks, we would see this:

```
$ cd scrape_title/
$ rake -D
(in /Users/chad/src/rr2/Book/code/rr2/scrape_title)
rake build
    Build scrape_title-0.0.1.gem into the pkg directory

rake install
    Build and install scrape_title-0.0.1.gem into system gems

rake release
    Create tag v0.0.1 and build and push scrape_title-0.0.1.gem to Rubygems
```

We have everything we need to build, install, and even release our new featureless gem to the waiting world of Ruby developers! Let's add some functionality and then build a release.

This example gem will download a given web page, parse out the page's title, and print it to the console. We'll start by writing code in the bin/scrape_title file:

rr2/scrape_title/bin/scrape_title
```
#!/usr/bin/env ruby
require "scrape_title"

puts ScrapeTitle.new(ARGV.first).scrape
```

The command-line aspect of the program is trivial. The real work happens in lib/scrape_title.rb:

rr2/scrape_title/lib/scrape_title.rb
```
require 'httparty'
class ScrapeTitle
  include HTTParty
  def initialize(url)
    @url = url
  end

  def scrape
    html_content = ScrapeTitle.get(@url)
    html_content.match(%r{<title>(.*)</title>}m).captures.first
  end
end
```

Now the code gets a little fancier. We are relying on the HTTParty library to do the HTTP work. That library is installable as a gem. How do we ensure we have the gem installed? How do we run the bin/scrape_title script such that it will include the proper libraries?

After making the bin/scrape_title script executable, we can run it with our Bundler environment like this:

```
$ bundle exec bin/scrape_title http://chadfowler.com
The Passionate Programmer
```

Nice! bundle exec sets up our library's environment for us, including any dependencies specified in the Gemfile. But, now that our little tool works well enough for an early release, how do we tell RubyGems that in order to install our new gem, we need to have HTTParty installed?

That's where the gem specification comes in. Here's the scrape_title.gemspec file that Bundler generated for us, edited to taste:

rr2/scrape_title/scrape_title.gemspec

```
# -*- encoding: utf-8 -*-
$:.push File.expand_path("../lib", __FILE__)
require "scrape_title/version"

Gem::Specification.new do |s|
  s.name        = "scrape_title"
  s.version     = ScrapeTitle::VERSION
  s.platform    = Gem::Platform::RUBY
  s.authors     = ["Chad Fowler"]
  s.email       = ["chad@chadfowler.com"]
  s.homepage    = "http://chadfowler.com"
  s.summary     = %q{Scrapes and prints the title of a given web page}
  s.description = %q{Scrapes and prints the title of a given web page.
                  Used as an example for the book, Rails Recipes}
  s.add_dependency "httparty", "~> 0.6"
  s.files       = `git ls-files`.split("\n")
  s.test_files  = `git ls-files -- {test,spec,features}/*`.split("\n")
  s.executables = `git ls-files -- bin/*`.split("\n").map{ |f| File.basename(f) }
  s.require_paths = ["lib"]
end
```

The gemspec allows us to name and describe our code as well as listing who
its authors are. We set the version by including lib/scrape_title/version.rb (a common
convention in Ruby libraries). We tell RubyGems about our HTTParty dependency by using the gemspec's add_dependency() method. In this case, we've told
RubyGems that our library requires a version of HTTParty in the 1.6 family
to be compatible.

We can now build our gem:

```
$ rake build
(in /Users/chad/src/rr2/Book/code/rr2/scrape_title)
scrape_title 0.0.1 built to pkg/scrape_title-0.0.1.gem
```

Now, in the pkg directory, we have a gem file that contains the code we just
created along with the metadata specified in scrape_title.gemspec. We could now
distribute this gem file to friends or colleagues, or we could push it up to the
central RubyGems service (or a private, company-operated RubyGems service)
for distribution to the world at large.

Also See

For a thorough explanation of the many features of the gemspec, see the Ruby-
Gems documentation site at http://docs.rubygems.org/.

Use Bundler Groups to Manage Per-Environment Dependencies

Problem

Some gems are useful only during development. Some are applicable only for testing. How do you configure your application to install and load gems only where and when you need them?

Solution

The best way to install and load environment-specific gems is to use a helpful feature that ships with Bundler called *groups*. With Bundler groups, you can specify per-environment dependencies for your application that allow you to control both which gems get installed when you do a bundle install and, more important, which gems get loaded at runtime. Setting it up is simple. In a Gemfile, gems specified at the top level are set up in a Bundler group called :default. To configure gems to be environment-specific, we can create a new group like this:

```
rr2/bundler_environments/Gemfile
group :test do
  gem 'mocha'
end
```

This sets up a Bundler group called :test and tells Bundler that in the :test group our application depends on the "mocha" mock objects gem. That's all there is to setting up a Bundler group. Now how do we take advantage of the group?

First we'll want to avoid installing gems in environments that won't use them. If we were installing in production, we wouldn't want mocha, so we would run the install like this:

```
$ bundle install --without=test
```

If we wanted to exclude installing gems from several groups, we could list them all as a space-separated list.

Now we tell Bundler which groups we want to load. By default, when Bundler is injected into your application's environment, it loads the top-level :default group. You can control this in the call to Bundler.require() by listing the groups you want loaded. It's common in Rails applications to create per-Rails-environment Bundler groups (development, test, and production), so the default generated invocation of Bundler in a Rails 3 config/application.rb file requires both the :default group and the group (if any) whose name matches the current Rails environment. Here's that line from a fresh Rails application's config/application.rb file:

rr2/bundler_environments/config/application.rb
```
Bundler.require(:default, Rails.env) if defined?(Bundler)
```

This line calls Bundler.require(), referencing :default and whatever the current Rails environment is set to. So, by default, it will load the :default and :development environments. If we wanted to load more or fewer groups, we'd simply modify this line to reference the groups we're interested in.

As you can see, Bundler groups give us a great amount of flexibility. There's no reason to avoid an environment-specific gem again. For testing and development, we can include all of our debugging and diagnostic tools without cluttering our production environments.

Package Rake Tasks for Reuse with a Gem

Problem

In Recipe 61, *Automate Work with Your Own Rake Tasks*, on page 230, we
learned how to make our own Rake tasks. Adding custom Rake tasks to an
existing application is trivial and ideally something we are all taking advantage
of regularly. Sometimes, the things we automate for our applications are
reusable. For example, suppose you had written a Rake task to check the
http://rubygems.org gem repository for gem versions that are newer than those
locked into your application with Bundler. That's something any Rails application could use. How do you package Rake tasks in a gem so they're reusable
from other Rails applications?

Solution

The solution is to create your own gem that defines a subclass of Rails::Railtie,
the Rails-defined class that provides extension hooks into the Rails framework.
Inside the Railtie, you can define Rake tasks.

Step 1 is to create a new gem. For this task, we'll use Bundler as outlined in
Recipe 57, *Create Your Own Ruby Gem*, on page 221. We're going to call our
gem "version_checker." We'll eventually reference this gem in our application's
Gemfile. Since we want the gem's (not yet created) Railtie to be loaded by our
application on startup, we need to edit the library Bundler will load with the
gem, which by default is named after the gem: lib/version_checker.rb. From here,
we'll require our Railtie:

rr2/version_checker/lib/version_checker.rb
```
require "version_checker/version"
require 'version_checker/railtie' if defined?(:Rails)

module VersionChecker
end
```

This is the file Bundler generated for us when we created the gem. The only
new code is the second line, which requires the file containing our Railtie if the
Rails environment is loaded (which we check by testing to see whether the
constant Rails is defined).

The next step is to define the Railtie:

rr2/version_checker/lib/version_checker/railtie.rb
```ruby
module VersionChecker
  class Railtie < Rails::Railtie
    rake_tasks do
      extend Rake::DSL
      namespace :version_checker do
        desc "Reports outdated rubygems from Gemfile"
        task :report_outdated do
          # ... do logic here
        end
      end
    end
  end
end
```

In this file, we create our own subclass of Rails::Railtie nested under our own gem's module, VersionChecker. The Railtie class then uses the built-in rake_tasks(), which accepts a block and executes the block in the context of the Rake scope under which tasks are declared. We first extend Rake::DSL, which makes the Rake domain-specific language available to us. We then call namespace() and task() as outlined in Recipe 61, *Automate Work with Your Own Rake Tasks*, on page 230 to define our tasks. From here on, the code is identical to what we would do in a .rake file.

Finally, after building and installing the version_checker gem, we can reference it in our Rails application's Gemfile. We reference it like this:

```ruby
gem 'version_checker'
```

Because the Railtie is loaded, its tasks are automatically loaded when we execute Rake. We can see this by asking Rake to list its defined tasks:

```
$ rake -T
rake about                              # List versions of all Rails ...
rake db:migrate                         # Migrate the database ...
...
rake version_checker:report_outdated  # Reports outdated rubygems from Gemfile
```

That's all there is to it! Now we can define and package up our reusable Rake tasks and distribute them to our teammates or to a world of appreciative Rubyists!

Also See

- Recipe 61, *Automate Work with Your Own Rake Tasks*, on page 230
- Recipe 57, *Create Your Own Ruby Gem*, on page 221
- The Rails documentation on Rails::Railtie at http://api.rubyonrails.org.

Explore Your Rails Application with the Console

Problem

How do you interactively explore your application's data and functionality?

Solution

The rails console command provides a powerful tool for diving into the data and behavior of your application. It's one of the best things about switching to Rails from another platform. It's good to quickly develop the habit of always leaving a console window open when you're working on a Rails application. It's a great tool for both exploration during development and administration in production.

```
$ rails console
Loading development environment.
>>
```

Instead of going directly to your database when you need to query for application data, use your models directly from the console instead of typing SQL into your database server's monitor console. The behavior you experience in the Rails console is a closer match to what your end users will experience, since you're using the same code:

```
>> Person.find_by_first_name("Chad").email
=> "chad@chadfowler.com"
```

Always forgetting the column names for your tables? Just ask for them:

```
>> Calendar.column_names
=> ["id", "creator_id", "description", "org_id"]
```

Or for a verbose view of a model's columns and their types, simply type the model name and let the built-in ActiveRecord::Base to_s() class-level method do its magic:

```
>> Calendar
=> Calendar(id: integer, creator_id: integer, description: text,
            org_id: integer, created_at: datetime, updated_at: datetime)
```

If your Ruby is compiled with readline support,[16] you can autocomplete class and method names using the Tab key. Type part of a method name, press Tab, and you'll see a list of all matching method names. Who needs an IDE?

If you're working repeatedly on the same class or object, you can change your session's scope to that object so all method calls are sent to it:

```
>> me = Person.find_by_first_name("Chad")
...
>> irb me
>> name
=> "Chad Fowler"
>> email
=> "chad@chadfowler.com"
```

Just type exit to shift to the original context.

If you make changes to your models or supporting classes and want those changes to be reflected in your running console, you don't have to exit and restart it. Simply type reload!() into the console, and you'll cause Rails to load the latest versions of your application code.

The console gives you a couple of implicit variables to make life easier. The first is app, which is an instance of ActionController::Integration::Session. You can directly call methods on it as if you were inside a live integration test.[17]

```
>> app.get "/"
=> 302
>> app.follow_redirect!
=> 200
```

The second implicit variable available in the console is helper, which sets up just enough environment for you to run view helper methods in the console:

```
>> helper.pluralize 2, "Mouse"
 => "2 Mice"
>> helper.greeting_helper # custom helpers work too!
 => "HELLO!"
```

As you can see, the Rails console is a critically handy tool. Leave it open in a separate window and use it all day. You'll be a happier and more productive Rails developer.

---

16. To find out, type ruby -rreadline -e 'p Readline'. If Ruby echoes Readline back to you, you have it!
17. See Recipe 42, *Test Across Multiple Controllers*, on page 151.

Automate Work with Your Own Rake Tasks

Problem

Software development is full of repetitive, boring, and therefore error-prone tasks. Even in the ultraproductive Rails environment, any complex application development will result in at least *some* work that would be better automated. And if you're after automation, the "Rails way" to do it is with Jim Weirich's Rake.

Rails comes with its own set of helpful Rake tasks. How do you add your own?

Solution

To create your own Rake tasks, you'll add new files with the extension .rake to the lib/tasks of your Rails application. Rake, like make before it, is a tool whose primary purpose is to automate software builds. Unlike make, Rake is written in Ruby, and its command language is also pure Ruby. As a brief introduction to Rake, we'll start by looking at a couple of simple, non-Rails-dependent Rake tasks that will demonstrate the basics of how Rake works.

Imagine you're maintaining a website that keeps a catalog of jazz musicians, categorized by musical instrument and genre, so users of the site can browse through and discover musicians that they might not know. You accept submissions to the site as comma-separated text files that you review, then convert to XML, and upload to your web server for further processing. This is a perfect candidate for automation.

Commands for Rake should be specified in a Rakefile. By convention, Rake will automatically look in the current directory for a file called Rakefile if you don't specify a filename when invoking the rake command. Otherwise, you can tell rake which file to load by passing the filename to its -f parameter. Here's what a simple Rakefile for processing our musician list would look like:

rr2/creating_your_own_rake_tasks/SimpleRakefile
```
Line 1  desc "Convert musicians.csv to musicians.xml if the CSV file has changed."
   -    file 'musicians.xml' => 'musicians.csv' do |t|
   -      convert_to_xml(t.prerequisites.first, t.name)
   -    end
```

```
 -  require 'rake/contrib/sshpublisher'
 -  desc "Upload Musicians list XML file to web server for processing."
 -  task :upload => 'musicians.xml' do |t|
 -    puts "Transferring #{t.prerequisites.last}..."
10    publisher = Rake::SshFilePublisher.new(
 -                        "chadfowler.com",
 -                        "/var/www/html/jazz_people",
 -                        File.dirname(__FILE__),
 -                        t.prerequisites.first)
15    publisher.upload
 -  end
 -  task :default => :upload
```

In a nutshell, this Rakefile will look for changes to the file musicians.csv and, if it's changed, will convert that file into XML. Then it will transfer the new musicians.xml file to a server. Assuming you've saved this in a file named Rakefile, you can invoke all this logic by typing rake.

And now for how it works. On line 8, we define a Rake task called upload. This name is what we use to tell the rake command what to do when it runs. When defining a Rake task, after the name you can optionally define one or more dependencies. In this case, we've declared a dependency on the file musicians.xml. This is the file that our program will upload to the web server. On line 9, we see a reference to the task's prerequisites() method. Not surprisingly, this is a list of the prerequisites specified in the task's definition—in this case, the musicians.xml file.

Tasks and dependencies are what makes Rake tick. The dependency on line 8 is more than just a static reference to a filename. Because we declared a file task on line 2, our musicians.xml file now depends on another file named musicians.csv. In English, what we've declared in our Rakefile is that before we perform the upload, we need to make sure musicians.xml is up-to-date. musicians.xml is up-to-date only if it was last processed *after* musicians.csv's last update. Rake's file() method handles the automatic creation of a task that checks these timestamps for us. If musicians.csv is more recent than its XML sibling, line 3 will cause a new musicians.xml file to be created from its contents. (The convert_to_xml() method is defined elsewhere in the Rakefile but left out of the example for the sake of brevity.)

The last line declares the upload() task to be the default task, meaning a bare invocation of the rake command will execute the upload() task. The calls to desc, such as the one on line 1, describe the purpose of each task. They have two functions: they're a static code comment for when you're reading the Rakefile, and they provide a description when the rake command needs to list its available tasks:

```
chad> rake -T
rake musicians.xml  # Convert musicians.csv to musicians.xml ...
rake upload         # Upload Musicians list XML file to web ...
```

If we were to create a musicians.csv file that looks like this:

rr2/creating_your_own_rake_tasks/musicians.csv
```
Albert, Ayler, Saxophone
Dave, Douglas, Trumpet
Bill, Frisell, Guitar
Matthew, Shipp, Piano
Rashid, Ali, Drums
William, Parker, Bass
```

invoking our upload task would result in the following output:

```
chad>  rake
Converting musicians.csv to musicians.xml
Transferring musicians.xml...
scp -q ./musicians.xml www.chadfowler.com:/var/www/html/jazz_people
```

But if we immediately run it again, we see this:

```
chad>  rake
Transferring musicians.xml...
scp -q ./musicians.xml www.chadfowler.com:/var/www/html/jazz_people
```

Since musicians.xml was already up-to-date, Rake skipped its generation and continued with the upload.

So, now we know how to define Rake tasks that depend on other Rake tasks and how to set up file generation that depends on other files. Though we obviously haven't touched every detail of Rake, since its command language is Ruby, we know enough to be productive immediately.

Suppose we decide to rewrite our jazz musician database using Rails, and instead of generating and transferring an XML file, we want to simply insert the records from our CSV files into a database. We have a Musician model with string attributes for given_name, surname, and instrument. Let's take our previous example and make it work with Rails.

The first thought you might have is to edit the Rails-generated Rakefile in your application's root directory and add your tasks there. However, to avoid code duplication, the Rails developers have separated their Rake tasks into external files that are distributed with the Rails framework. On opening the generated Rakefile, you'll see that it's all but empty with a friendly comment at the top instructing you to put your own tasks in the lib/tasks directory under your application root. When you invoke the Rails-generated Rakefile, the Rails framework will automatically load any files in that directory with the file extension .rake. This way, upgrading the core Rails Rake tasks is easier and less likely to result in a file conflict.

So, let's create our own tasks in a file called lib/tasks/load_musicians.rake under our application's root directory:

rr2/creating_your_own_rake_tasks/lib/tasks/load_musicians.rake.first_attempt
```
desc "Load musicians and the instruments they play into the database."
task :load_musicians => 'musicians.csv' do |t|
  before_count = Musician.count
  File.read(t.prerequisites.first).each do |line|
    given_name, surname, instrument = line.split(/,/)
    Musician.create(:given_name => given_name,
                    :surname => surname,
                    :instrument => instrument)
  end
  puts "Loaded #{Musician.count - before_count} musicians."
end
```

This task is relatively simple. It depends on the existence of the musicians.csv file, which it naively reads, creating a new Musician entry for each line read (even if an entry already exists for a given musician). It concludes with an announcement of how many records were loaded. Unfortunately, running this task as is doesn't result in the desired behavior:

```
chad> rake load_musicians
rake aborted!
ActiveRecord::ConnectionNotEstablished
```

Hmm. We're apparently not connected to our database. And, come to think of it, we haven't told the Rake task which of our databases to connect to. In a typical Rails application, this is all handled for us implicitly via the environment. Fortunately, the developers of Rails have provided a way for us to write Rake tasks that are dependent on the Rails environment. Intuitively, this is implemented via a Rake dependency called :environment. Let's add :environment to our task's dependency list:

rr2/creating_your_own_rake_tasks/lib/tasks/load_musicians.rake
```
desc "Load musicians and the instruments they play into the database."
task :load_musicians => ['musicians.csv', :environment] do |t|
  before_count = Musician.count
  IO.readlines(t.prerequisites.first).each do |line|
    given_name, surname, instrument = line.split(/,/)
    Musician.create(:given_name => given_name,
                    :surname => surname,
                    :instrument => instrument)
  end
  puts "Loaded #{Musician.count - before_count} musicians."
end
```

With a musicians.csv file in place, the task now works as expected:

```
chad> rake load_musicians
Loaded 6 musicians.
```

Lovely. But our application is really simple right now, and we're planning to evolve it. What do we do if our data model changes fairly often? First, we can make our parsing and loading logic a little smarter. Here's an enhanced version of the task that will adapt to change a little better. It assumes that the first line of the file contains the column names for the data values in the rest of the file.

CreatingYourOwnRakeTasks/lib/tasks/load_musicians.rake
```
desc "Load musicians and the instruments they play into the database."
task :load_musicians_enhanced =>
        ['musicians_with_column_names.csv', :migrate] do |t|
  before_count = Musician.count
  lines = File.read(t.prerequisites.first).split("\n")
  # Strip white space
  attributes = lines.shift.split(/,/).collect{|name| name.strip}
  lines.each do |line|
    values = line.split(/,/)
    data = attributes.inject({}) do |hash,attribute|
      hash[attribute] = values.shift
      hash
    end
    Musician.create(data)
  end
  puts "Loaded #{Musician.count - before_count} musicians."
end
```

Now, we can lay the files out more flexibly and even add columns to the files. Of course, if we add columns to the file, we'll need to add them to the database as well. If we're managing our data model via Active Record migrations, we can save ourselves the trouble of trying to remember to keep it updated by adding the db:migrate task to the dependency list for our task. Since the db:migrate task already initializes the Rails environment, we can replace the :environment dependency with db:migrate. Now whenever we run the :load_musicians_enhanced task, our database schema will be automatically updated first!

Also See

Martin Fowler has written an excellent introduction to Rake, which is freely available from his website at http://www.martinfowler.com/articles/rake.html.

Generate Documentation for Your Application

Problem

Ruby comes with a powerful documentation system called RDoc. How do you use RDoc to generate and browse documentation for your application and its dependencies?

Problem

The first thing you'll probably want to have documentation for is Rails itself. If you've installed Rails using RubyGems, you can always get to the documentation for all your installed Rails versions (and every other gem on your system!) using the gem server command.

Just run gem server, and direct your web browser to http://localhost:8808. If you need to run it on a different port, you can set the port with the -p option: gem server -p 2600. You'll see a list of all your installed gems, and you can click the gem to browse its documentation.

You can use the built-in Rake task doc:rails to generate locally accessible documentation for the exact version of Rails that your application is using. The generated HTML will go into doc/api. This is especially helpful since the main documentation site doesn't maintain current documentation for the evolving world of the Rails trunk or previous versions. If you like, you can change the RDoc template used by setting the template environment variable to the name of the template in question.

The Rails team also maintains a helpful set of guides to the framework that are usually accessible via http://guides.rubyonrails.org. If you'd like a local copy, you can generate the guides using rake docs:guides. This will generate and place the guides into the doc/guides directory of your Rails application.

Finally, you can generate documentation for your *own* application with rake doc:app. This will, predictably, store its generated documents in doc/app.

Render Application Data as Comma-Separated Values

Problem

Sometimes the easiest and most satisfying (for you *and* your users) way to implement a reporting requirement is to simply provide your application's data in a format your users can import into their favorite reporting and analytical tools. The most common format for such a thing is comma-separated values (CSV). How do you render CSV from a Rails action?

Problem

To render CSV, we'll use the respond_to() in our action to allow the browser to specify CSV as the format it expects. We'll then use Ruby's standard CSV library and the Rails send_data() method to send the CSV data down to the client.

Imagine you have an Order model that tracks product orders. Here's a simple controller action that will export your orders to a CSV file:

rr2/render_csv/app/controllers/orders_controller.rb
```
require 'csv'
class OrdersController < ApplicationController

  def index
    @orders = Order.all
    respond_to do |format|
      format.html
      format.csv do
        send_data(csv_for(@orders),
                  :type => csv_content_type,
                  :filename => "orders.csv")
      end
    end
  end
```

This is a standard, scaffold-generated RESTful index() action. The CSV-related code all happens inside the respond_to() block. If an incoming HTTP client requests CSV data, the format.csv() block will be invoked to render the action's response.

Here we use send_data() to stream raw data back to the client. The first parameter to send_data() is the actual data to send. We generate this data by passing the @orders Array into our csv_for() method. Here's the definition of csv_for():

```ruby
def csv_for(orders)
  (output = "").tap do
    CSV.generate(output) do |csv|
      orders.each do |order|
        csv << [order.id, order.price, order.purchaser, order.created_at]
      end
    end
  end
end
```

csv_for() uses the standard Ruby "csv" library to generate comma-separated values. We set up a String to collect the CSV data in the output variable. We use Object's tap() method to allow the code to operate on the output variable without having to remember to explicitly return the value at the end of the method. Inside the tap() block, the real CSV magic happens. We use the generate() method on the CSV class to create a CVS generator (yielded to the block as csv) onto which we can append CSV rows using the <<() method.

Note that between Ruby 1.8 and Ruby 1.9, the API for the "csv" library has changed. Specifically, the call to CSV.generate would need to be changed to CSV::Writer.generate to work in Ruby 1.8.

Back in the index() action, we'll see a reference to a fun hack. Rather than hard-code the MIME type of the CSV response, we delegate to our own csv_content_type() method:

```ruby
def csv_content_type
  case request.user_agent
  when /windows/i
    'application/vnd.ms-excel'
  else
    'text/csv'
  end
end
```

If the browser's USER_AGENT contains the string windows, we set the content type of the response to one that will cause Microsoft Excel to pop open if it's installed. Otherwise, the content type is set to the standard text/csv.

This action renders something like the following:

```
1,123.22,Kilgore Trout,Sun Apr 02 17:14:58 MDT 2006
2,44.12,John Barth,Sun Apr 02 17:14:58 MDT 2006
3,42.44,Josef K,Sun Apr 02 17:14:58 MDT 2006
```

Here we use Ruby's CSV library in its most basic incarnation. If you need more customizable output, consult the documentation for the CSV library.

Credit

Thanks to Mike Clark for his ideas on this recipe.

Debug and Explore Your Application with the ruby-debug Gem

Problem

Ruby on Rails applications are less complex and easier to troubleshoot than many of the technologies and frameworks that came before them. In my own experience, things usually *just work*, and when applications break, it's pretty obvious what's wrong.

Every once in a while, though, an obscure bug pops up. It might be a mis-named instance variable or a concurrency issue. But when these sorts of hard-to-find problems arise, you need something more than print statements and log files. How do you debug, trace, and explore the inner workings of your Ruby and Rails applications?

Solution

The best tool for debugging Ruby applications is the ruby-debug gem. This gem provides command-line access to the internals of a running Ruby application. To use the gem, first add it to your application's Gemfile:

rr2/ruby-debug/Gemfile
```
gem "ruby-debug19", :groups => [:development, :test]
```

In the Gemfile, notice that we invoked the gem named ruby-debug19, not the one named ruby-debug. This is because we're using Ruby version 1.9 to run the code for this book, and Ruby's internals changed enough between version 1.8 and 1.9 for the ruby-debug gem to be forked into two versions. If you're still running Ruby 1.8, use ruby-debug instead of ruby-debug19 in your Gemfile.

We also chose to require this gem for only the test and development environments. There's no need to load the debugger in production, so we can set up our deployment scripts to skip ruby-debug when we deploy our application. For more information on Bundler environments, see Recipe 58, *Use Bundler Groups to Manage Per-Environment Dependencies*, on page 224.

Now let's take the debugger for a spin. Our sample code is a simple reminders application. We have a model representing reminders and a simple CRUD controller for managing them. The index() action of the controller contains logic to filter out expired reminders. Since the logic is complex, it requires both database filtering and in-Ruby application logic. Here's the action:

rr2/ruby-debug/app/controllers/reminders_controller.rb
```
def index
  @reminders = Reminder.all.select do |reminder|
    reminder.expired?
  end
end
```

We can use ruby-debug to explore this action. Traditional debuggers use metadata to set breakpoints at various lines or conditions in code. The approach ruby-debug takes is simpler. To set a breakpoint from which you'd like to explore, simply insert a call to the debugger() method. You also need to make sure the ruby-debug library is loaded. I usually just require() the library and call the debugger() on the same line, making it easier to remove when I'm finished:

rr2/ruby-debug/app/controllers/reminders_controller.rb
```
def index
  require 'ruby-debug';debugger
  @reminders = Reminder.all.select do |reminder|
    reminder.expired?
  end
end
```

Now if we start our Rails server and execute the action via the web browser, we'll see a command-line prompt in the console from which we started the server. From here, we can inspect the current state of the application. Here's a short sample session:

rr2/ruby-debug/session_output.txt
```
/app/controllers/reminders_controller.rb:12
@reminders = Reminder.all.select do |reminder|
(rdb:1) p params
{"action"=>"index", "controller"=>"reminders"}
(rdb:1) n
/app/controllers/reminders_controller.rb:13
reminder.expired?
(rdb:1) list
[8, 17] in /app/controllers/reminders_controller.rb
   8
   9
   10    def index
   11      require 'ruby-debug';debugger
```

```
    12         @reminders = Reminder.all.select do |reminder|
=>  13           reminder.expired?
    14         end
    15       end
    16
    17
(rdb:1) p reminder
#<Reminder id: 1,
           title: "Give the dog his medicine",
           starts_on: "2011-11-28",
           expires_on: "2011-11-30",
           created_at: "2011-11-27 15:00:31",
           updated_at: "2011-11-27 15:00:31">
(rdb:1) n
/app/controllers/reminders_controller.rb:13
reminder.expired?
(rdb:1) p reminder
#<Reminder id: 2,
           title: "Walk the dogs",
           starts_on: "2011-11-27",
           expires_on: "2012-04-15",
           created_at: "2011-11-27 15:00:31",
           updated_at: "2011-11-27 15:00:31">
(rdb:1)
```

When we loaded the reminders page in our browser, ruby-debug opened a prompt when the debugger() method was executed. This prompt gives us access to the current state and scope at the time debugger() was called. We can use the p command to inspect the value of any Ruby expression, as demonstrated by the call to p params.

We then used the n (or next) command to execute the next call in this scope of the program. In this case, the program advanced to the inside of the select block, giving us access to the block-local reminder object. At any time, we can use list to see the current and surrounding code, which is helpful to keep mental track of the context while we are debugging.

What if we wanted to follow Ruby into the expired?() method in the Reminder class? No problem. From the point where we left off, we can use the step command to step into the next method:

```
(rdb:1) step
/Users/chad/src/rr2/Book/code/rr2/ruby-debug/app/models/reminder.rb:5
!holiday? &&
(rdb:1) list
[0, 9] in /Users/chad/src/rr2/Book/code/rr2/ruby-debug/app/models/reminder.rb
   1
   2  class Reminder < ActiveRecord::Base
   3    def expired?
```

```
   4        expires_on < Date.today &&
=> 5          !holiday? &&
   6          price_of_oil < 40
   7     end
   8     # ...
   9  end
(rdb:1) p holiday?
false
```

Cool! From here, as you can see, we can use the same commands we used before to list, inspect, and control the flow of the program. To stop your debugging session and allow the program to continue from this point, use the continue (or cont) command. Continuing a Rails request allows the request to finish, so you should see the action's response render in your browser.

What if you weren't sure which part of the code was causing a problem? How do you insert multiple breakpoints? Easy: just use the debugger() method multiple times. Since it's just a Ruby method, you can call it as often as you like. Continuing from one debugger() call allows the code to execute until the next one.

Since we're dealing with Ruby methods, we can also use the debugger() conditionally. If you know you want to start the debugger only when an expired Reminder is encountered, simply call it with a condition like this:

```
debugger if reminder.expired?
```

A number of commands are available in ruby-debug. To see the full list, use the help command. When all else fails, ruby-debug includes a remarkable feature: the ability to jump into a pure Ruby prompt at any point! Here's a quick demonstration:

```
@reminders = Reminder.all.select do |reminder|
(rdb:10) irb
> Reminder.count
=> 3
> params[:action]
=> "index"
> session.keys
=> ["session_id", "_csrf_token"]
```

At the breakpoint, we use the irb command from ruby-debug to open an interactive Ruby prompt at this point in the code. From here we can use Ruby to explore the application's current state. The irb prompt is scoped such that any code entered is executed as if it were in line at the point where the debugger() method were invoked. So, in this case, we have access to all of the local variables, instance variables, and methods available to controller actions!

To exit the irb prompt, type "exit" or press Ctrl+D to be returned to the ruby-debug prompt.

The ruby-debug gem is useful for more than debugging. Learn it well, and you'll find it gets you out of tough jams when troubleshooting but also gives you an easy way to explore how the code you have written (or inherited!) behaves.

Render Complex Documents as PDFs

Problem

Most of the time we as web developers can get away with generating HTML, CSS, and the occasional JavaScript. But sometimes we need to render complex reports, prefilled forms, coupons, or receipts. And in those cases, HTML isn't always the best choice.

When you *really* need control of how something is going to look on your end user's computer, PDF is an excellent choice. How do you generate and serve PDF files from Rails?

Solution

This is a problem whose solution is divided into two parts. The first part is to actually generate a PDF. The second part is to deliver that in an idiomatic way from a Rails action to a client. We'll start with PDF generation.

The best way to generate PDF files from Ruby is to use Gregory Brown's Prawn gem. To use Prawn in your Rails application, the first step is to add it to your project's Gemfile:

rr2/generate_pdfs/Gemfile
```
gem 'ttfunk'
gem 'prawn'
```

After running bundle install, we're ready to write our first PDF generation program. To learn about Prawn, let's just create a Ruby script in the root of our Rails application that generates a PDF. We'll call it shopping_list.rb:

rr2/generate_pdfs/shopping_list.rb
```
shopping_list = [
  ["Carton of Goat Milk", 1],
  ["Head of Garlic", 2],
  ["Chocolate Bar", 9]
]
Prawn::Document.generate("shopping_list.pdf") do
  table([[ "Item", "Quantity" ], *shopping_list]) do  |t|
    t.header = true
    t.row_colors = [ "aaaaff", "aaffaa", "ffaaaa" ]
    t.row(0).style :background_color => '448844', :text_color => 'ffffff'
```

```
    t.columns(1).align = :right
  end
end
```

An easy way to run this script would be to use rails runner like this:

```
$ rails runner shopping_list.rb
```

You'll find a PDF file called shopping_list.pdf in the directory from which you ran the program. The PDF displays a table of items and quantities with alternative row colors. Fancy!

Looking back at the code, we see an Array of shopping list items and quantities that will serve as the data for our PDF table. When we move this into our Rails application, that data will come from the application's database. The important part comes next. We use the Prawn::Document class to generate a PDF by calling its generate() method, passing in the desired path to the new PDF file. The generate() method takes a block in which we can call methods to draw into the PDF. Here, we use the table() method, passing in header label values and our data. We can then configure the table by passing a block, into which Prawn passes an instance of, unsurprisingly, Prawn::Table.

Prawn is a rich and powerful PDF generation library capable of rendering many types of layouts, text, and graphics. For a fuller understanding of its capabilities, see the Prawn website at http://prawn.majesticseacreature.com/ and take a look at the examples supplied with the Prawn distribution.

Now that we know how to interact with the Prawn library, let's move our shopping list PDF code into our Rails application. First, we'll create a model-level method on our Recipe class called shopping_list_pdf(), which will return raw PDF data. This is where we'll copy and modify our existing PDF generation code:

rr2/generate_pdfs/app/models/recipe.rb
```
def shopping_list_pdf
  shopping_list = ingredients.map do |ingredient|
    [ingredient.name, ingredient.quantity]
  end

  pdf = Prawn::Document.new
  pdf.table([[ "Item", "Quantity" ], *shopping_list]) do |t|
    t.header = true
    t.row_colors = [ "aaaaff", "aaffaa", "ffaaaa" ]
    t.row(0).style :background_color => '448844', :text_color => 'ffffff'
    t.columns(1).align = :right
  end
  pdf.render
end
```

Unpack the Prawn Gem

An easy way to see the Prawn examples is to unpack the Prawn gem. You can unpack the gem by changing to the directory of your choice and running this:

```
$ gem unpack prawn
```

This will extract the gem file into a new subdirectory, under which you'll find a directory called examples.

This code is the same as our previous code with two exceptions. The first difference is that it retrieves the shopping list data from the database. The other difference is that instead of using the generate() method, we instantiate a Prawn::Document, assign it to a local variable pdf, and explicitly call methods on that object. This enables us to call render() at the end of the method to return the rendered PDF data.

The next step is to register a MIME type for PDF documents so Rails will know who to recognize and honor requests for PDF data. To register this MIME type, edit config/initializers/mime_types.rb to add the following:

rr2/generate_pdfs/config/initializers/mime_types.rb
```
Mime::Type.register "application/pdf", :pdf
```

Finally, we'll add a controller action and route to serve the PDF shopping list. In our RecipesController, we'll define a new action called shopping_list() to look like this:

rr2/generate_pdfs/app/controllers/recipes_controller.rb
```
def shopping_list
  @recipe = Recipe.find(params[:id])
  respond_to do |format|
    format.html
    format.pdf do
      send_data @recipe.shopping_list_pdf,
                content_type: Mime::PDF
    end
  end
end
```

This action looks up a Recipe by id and, if the client requests PDF data, sends the rendered PDF shopping list to the client with the appropriate MIME type set. Since this action isn't one of the seven standard Rails CRUD actions, we'll need to configure the route. This custom action expects to be operating on a specific Recipe, so we'll configure it as a member route. Here's our route configuration:

rr2/generate_pdfs/config/routes.rb
```ruby
GeneratePdfs::Application.routes.draw do
  resources :recipes do
    member do
      get "shopping_list"
    end
    resources :ingredients
  end
end
```

Now we can visit, for example, http://localhost:3000/recipes/1/shopping_list.pdf in our browser, and the Rails application will send a PDF file down.

Part VII

Extending Rails

With the release of Rails 3, the framework became much more pluggable and extensible than it had previously been. Rails 3.1 makes it even more extensible than before. Experienced Rails developers take advantage of this extensibility to make their applications cleaner and more expressive as well as to save themselves time. These recipes walk through some of the most powerful techniques for extending the Rails framework.

Support Additional Content Types with a Custom Renderer

Problem

As Rails programmers, we get spoiled by the ability to easily render XML or JSON from our controllers. There's no need to call special methods or set content types. To render XML for a collection of Meeting objects, for example, we only need to do this:

```
render :xml => @meetings
```

How can we enable this succinct, declarative syntax for content types not supported by Rails out of the box?

Solution

In this recipe, we'll learn how to hook into the Rails framework to make a customer renderer. We'll define a block of code that knows how to render ICAL files and will register it with ActionController.

If we had a Meeting model and corresponding controller, rendering an ICAL calendar file from the controller would require some ugly, explicit code in the controller. For this example, we'll use the icalendar gem, which we can add to our application's Gemfile with this line:

```
gem "icalendar"
```

Given a table of meetings, our index() action to render those meetings as a calendar might look something like this:

```ruby
rr2/renderer/app/controllers/meetings_controller.rb
def index
  @meetings = Meeting.all

  respond_to do |format|
    format.html # index.html.erb
    format.json { render json: @meetings }
    format.ics do
      render text: ical_for_meetings, content_type: "text/calendar"
    end
  end
end
```

```
def ical_for_meetings
  calendar = Icalendar::Calendar.new
  @meetings.each do |meeting|
    meeting.add_to_calendar(calendar)
  end
  calendar.to_ical
end
```

This code creates an Icalendar::Calendar instance and then loops through each Meeting asking the meeting to add itself to the calendar using the add_to_calendar() method. Here's that method:

rr2/renderer/app/models/meeting.rb
```
require 'icalendar'
class Meeting < ActiveRecord::Base
  def add_to_calendar(calendar)
    meeting = self
    calendar.event do
      dtstart meeting.starts_at.to_datetime
      dtend meeting.ends_at.to_datetime
      description meeting.description
    end
  end
end
```

To make Rails recognize the ICAL MIME type, add the following to your confg/initializers/mime_types.rb file:

rr2/renderer/config/initializers/mime_types.rb
```
Mime::Type.register "text/calendar", :ics
```

If we wanted this code to be more declarative and we wanted to remove all of the Icalendar-specific code from the controller, we could add a customer renderer. If we created a custom renderer, we could refactor our index() action to look like this:

rr2/renderer/app/controllers/meetings_controller.rb
```
def index
  @meetings = Meeting.all

  respond_to do |format|
    format.html # index.html.erb
    format.json { render json: @meetings }
    format.ics {render ical: @meetings }
  end
end
```

Much better! Now all we have to do is ask Rails to render iCal for requests to the .ics format, and we let our custom renderer do the work. To actually create the custom renderer, create a new file called config/initializers/ical_renderer.rb (the actual filename is arbitrary, because Rails will pick up all Ruby files in config/initializers on startup) with the following contents:

rr2/renderer/config/initializers/ical_renderer.rb
```
ActionController::Renderers.add :ical do |obj, options|
  filename = options[:filename] || 'events.ics'
  calendar = Icalendar::Calendar.new
  obj.each do |event|
    event.add_to_calendar(calendar)
  end
  send_data calendar.to_ical, :type => Mime::ICS,
                              :disposition => "attachment; filename=#{filename}"
end
```

This code does essentially the same thing the controller code did before. We first register the renderer named :ical with ActionController and then define a block that accepts the object to be rendered and any options passed into the call to render(). Our code allows the caller to optionally specify the filename Rails should report with the streamed ICAL file, which it defaults to events.ics. At the end of the block, we use the built-in send_data() method to send the rendered ICAL data down to the browser with the correct registered MIME type.

For use in a single action like this, adding a custom renderer may seem like overkill. But, what if we wanted to render more objects in ICAL format? All we would need to do is to implement the add_to_calendar() method for any new class that might generate calendar events, and our renderer works with no modifications!

Even if we wanted to use it in only one place, a custom renderer makes our controller more readable. Controllers shouldn't know low-level details of how object graphs are traversed and how content is specifically rendered. The custom renderer keeps our controller code at a consistent level of abstraction, making it easier to understand and therefore easier to maintain.

Accept Additional Content Types with a Custom Parameter Parser

Problem

Through the power of convention over configuration, standard form-based Rails actions need no enhancements to process incoming XML, JSON, or YAML data. As long as the client sets the proper content type for the request, Rails automatically parses the incoming request body into a Hash.

That's great if your application needs only to support incoming form posts or XML, JSON, and YAML data. But what if you have more specific needs? How could you implement your own parameter parser to get the same succinct, convention-driven controller code for custom data formats?

Solution

To insert your own custom parser for the content type of your choice, you simply need to replace the default parameter parser middleware with a parser middleware that is configured with your own parser. Here's how.

First we'll register the MIME type for our custom content type. For this recipe, we'll accept base64-encoded serialized Ruby objects. There isn't a standard MIME type for this, so we'll make one up. Here's the entry that could go in your config/initializers/mime_types.rb file:

rr2/param_parser/config/initializers/marshal_parser.rb
```
Mime::Type.register "application/rubymarshal", :marshal
```

Here's an example Ruby client, demonstrating what we'd like the server to be able to accept. The goal is for the payload Hash to be deserialized and reconstituted on the server as the params Hash.

rr2/param_parser/client.rb
```
require 'net/http'
require 'base64'
payload = Base64.encode64(Marshal.dump({:x => 123, :y => 456}))
Net::HTTP.start("localhost", 3000) do |http|
  http.post "/check/index", payload, {"Content-Type" => "application/rubymarshal"}
end
```

This client dumps a Hash and base64 encodes it and then makes an HTTP POST to the server running locally with that serialized data as its payload.

The last step to make this all work is to reconfigure the Rails parameter parser. This gets a little trickier. Since the parameter parser is set up as part of the Rails middleware stack, we should start by understanding how that works.

The architecture of ActionPack rests on a simple HTTP application framework called Rack. Rack abstracts the specifics of the web server from any application or framework built on it, making frameworks such as Rails, Sinatra, and others portable across Ruby web servers. Rack accomplishes this abstraction by specifying a very simple API for Rack applications.

A Rack application is any object that supports a method called call() that takes one parameter and returns an Array. The parameter to the call() is the Rack HTTP environment and will be provided by the framework. The return value of a Rack application is an Array of three elements. The first element is the HTTP response code to return, the second element is a Hash of response headers, and the third element is the response body. That's all there is to it.

These simple applications can also be stacked together and used as "middleware." When a Rack application acts as middleware, it must provide an initialize() method that accepts an argument that tells it which Rack application is next in the chain. The Rack middleware can then store this argument as an instance variable and, when it is called, delegate to the next application in the chain. This creates a filtering or chaining effect.

Rails applications configure their Rack middleware using the config object during initialization. Specifically, the middleware stack is accessible using config.middleware.

Now that we have the necessary context for Rack and middleware, here's how we remove the default parameter parser and add our own configured one:

```
rr2/param_parser/config/initializers/marshal_parser.rb
parser = lambda do |raw_body|
  Marshal.load(
    Base64.decode64(raw_body)
  )
end
ParamParser::Application.config.middleware.delete ActionDispatch::ParamsParser
ParamParser::Application.config.middleware.use ActionDispatch::ParamsParser,
                                  {Mime::MARSHAL => parser}
```

The first thing we do here is define our actual parameter parser. It's defined as a Proc, which we create with the lambda() method. This is effectively an anonymous function that takes one argument, the raw body of the incoming request, and returns the base64-decoded, deserialized Ruby object contained within. We assign that Proc to a local variable called parser, which we'll use next.

We then delete the default parameter parser from the middleware and replace it with another instance of itself but with our parser included for the Mime::MARSHAL type. The config.middleware.use() method takes a class and a list of arguments to pass to that class when instantiated. In the case of ActionDispatch::ParamsParser, the argument is an optional Hash of parsers with the key in the Hash being a MIME type and the value being the Proc to use to parse the incoming request body.

Templatize Your Generated Rails Applications

Problem

If you're like me, every time you create a new Rails application you go through the same setup steps. You remove the public/index.html file. You route the root of your application to a more desirable location. You install various gems and plugins that make your life easier as a developer. You check your code into a source repository.

How can you automate all of these changes so they're done for every new application you generate?

Solution

The Rails application generator makes it possible to script application generation through a mechanism called *Rails templates*. A Rails template is a separate Ruby script that you can store on a local file system or on a web server to be referenced by URL. When generating a new application, you tell Rails to invoke the template by using the -m switch:

```
$ rails new myapplication -m always_do_this.rb
```

The file always_do_this.rb is a simple Ruby script containing calls to Rails template API methods. Let's walk through an example section by section. We'll put it together in its entirety at the end of the recipe.

First, our example template uses the run() method to run an arbitrary system command. In this case, it uses rm to remove the Rails welcome page from the application.

rr2/new_app_template/always_do_this.rb
```
run "rm public/index.html"
```

Second, we use the generate() to generate both a model and a controller. The generate() method takes the name of the generator followed by a string containing the rest of the command-line arguments to pass to the generator. The syntax is just what you'd expect having used the Rails generators.

```
rr2/new_app_template/always_do_this.rb
generate :model, "Page title:string body:text"
generate :controller, "Pages index"
```

Since we generated a model with an associated migration, we use the rake()
method to run the "db:migrate" task.

```
rr2/new_app_template/always_do_this.rb
rake "db:migrate"
```

Also, having removed the standard welcome page, we should route the root
URL for our application to something useful. For this, we use the route() to
modify the generated config/routes.rb file.

```
rr2/new_app_template/always_do_this.rb
route 'root :to => "pages#index"'
```

I always like to have the ruby-debug gem handy, so we'll use the gem() method
to add it to our Gemfile. If we're running Rails 3.1 or newer, this gem will be
installed immediately after the application is generated, since Rails 3.1 runs
bundle install as the last step of application generation.

```
rr2/new_app_template/always_do_this.rb
gem "ruby-debug"
```

It's even possible to generate initializer files with arbitrary code in them. Here,
we generate an initializer called enumerable_ar.rb, which adds the each() to
ActiveRecord::Base and makes the class and its children Enumerable (I always make
this mistake at the Rails console, and I've never understood why it doesn't
just work.)

```
rr2/new_app_template/always_do_this.rb
initializer "enumerable_ar.rb", <<-INIT
module ActiveRecord
  def Base.each(&block)
    all.each &block
  end
  Base.extend Enumerable
end
INIT
```

I always use Capistrano to deploy my Rails applications, so we might as well
add a basic Capistrano configuration to every application as it's generated:

```
rr2/new_app_template/always_do_this.rb
capify!
```

Finally, any project worth generating should be stored and versioned in a version control system. I usually use git. This part of the template initializes a new git repository and commits the generated application:

rr2/new_app_template/always_do_this.rb
```
git :init
git :add => "."
git :commit => "-m 'Generated initial application'"
```

To wrap it all up, here's the entire template file:

rr2/new_app_template/always_do_this.rb
```
run "rm public/index.html"
generate :model, "Page title:string body:text"
generate :controller, "Pages index"
rake "db:migrate"
route 'root :to => "pages#index"'
gem "ruby-debug"
initializer "enumerable_ar.rb", <<-INIT
module ActiveRecord
  def Base.each(&block)
    all.each &block
  end
  Base.extend Enumerable
end
INIT

capify!
git :init
git :add => "."
git :commit => "-m 'Generated initial application'"
```

The template file contains very little code, but it both saves times and makes new applications more consistent. If you work with a team of developers in a company or other organization, consider standardizing a template for all applications and sharing it using a web server. Automate common setup tasks and provide a common base that developers can count on as they move from application to application.

Automate Recurring Code Patterns with Custom Generators

Problem

You find yourself repeating the same set of steps to create pieces of an application. Perhaps you've created a framework or a pattern that you use consistently throughout your code. As a result, every time you create a new application or a new widget within your application, you find yourself robotically applying the pattern.

How can you automate the repetitive creation of the similar application components?

Solution

Rails generators: if you're using Rails, you've seen them. You at least use them to create the initial structure of your application in order to create new controllers and views, to add new models, and to generate new migrations. And, of course, the most infamous Rails generator is the scaffold generator, which creates code to implement the CRUD elements of a given model. Thankfully, instead of creating a one-off hack to implement these generators, the Rails developers came up with a reusable framework for template-driven code generation. In this recipe, we'll use that framework to first generate a generator and to then customize it with our own templates.

This makes it easy to create your own generators and install them so that they're first-class citizens in the eyes of the rails generate command.

Working with Generators

Generators can come in handy either for repeating a pattern across multiple applications or for creating a similar structure for multiple elements in a single application. For a concrete example, imagine you've created a Tumblelog,[18] which is like a blog but with many small posts of different types. You may, for example, post pictures, quotes, links, or sound clips, and each type of post would have its own input form and its own specialized view. A picture

---

18. For an example, see http://tumblr.com.

might need a form with a title and a URL, while a quote would require fields for a body and an attribution. For every type, you would also need to create model files, and you've decided it would be easiest to separate specialized behavior into one controller per post type. With just a few post types implemented, you end up with a structure that looks something like this:

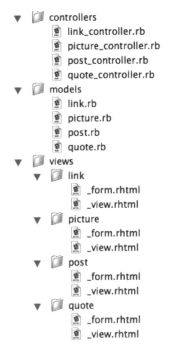

In this structure, each model class inherits from Post to take advantage of Rails' single-table inheritance model. All the controllers inherit from PostsController to get access to functionality that is common to all types of posts. And to get up and running quickly when you add a new type of post, it's convenient to have _view.html.erb and _form.html.erb partials that include every possible field for a Post so you can immediately add posts of the new type and then incrementally modify the views to be appropriate to that type.

If you had an active imagination, you could concoct an unending list of post types to add to your new Tumblelog system. Even using the built-in generators for models and controllers that come with Rails, adding new post types would quickly become a burden. This is a perfect opportunity to whip up your very own generator.

The first step in creating your generator is to set up the generator's directory structure in one of the places the Rails framework is expecting it. Rails looks for user-defined generators in the following locations when the rails generate command is invoked (where *RAILS_ROOT* is the root directory of your application and ~ is your home directory):

- *RAILS_ROOT*/lib/generators
- *RAILS_ROOT*/vendor/generators
- *RAILS_ROOT*/vendor/plugins/*any subdirectory*/generators
- ~/.rails/generators

In addition to these paths, the rails generate command will look for installed gems whose names end in *_generator*.

Appropriately, Rails provides a generator to help get us started:

```
$ rails generate generator tumblepost
      create  lib/generators/tumblepost
      create  lib/generators/tumblepost/tumblepost_generator.rb
      create  lib/generators/tumblepost/USAGE
      create  lib/generators/tumblepost/templates
```

By convention, a generator is laid out as shown in the output of the generate command here. The generator's directory matches the name of the generator. In the example here, the generator would be called tumblepost and would be invoked by calling this:

```
rails generate tumblepost
```

The file tumblepost_generator.rb in the tumblepost directory holds our generator's main logic. USAGE is a text file containing usage instructions that will be displayed when invoking our generator without any arguments, and templates is a directory where we'll put the source templates from which our code will be generated. For our Tumblelog Post generator, we'll create one template for every file the generator should create.

The heart of the generator is the Manifest, which is defined in tumblepost_generator.rb. Let's look at that file:

```
rr2/generators/lib/generators/tumblepost/tumblepost_generator.rb
class TumblepostGenerator < Rails::Generators::NamedBase
  source_root File.expand_path('../templates', __FILE__)
  check_class_collision
  desc "Generator tumblelog post types and supporting files"

  def manifest
    template "app/controllers/controller_template.rb",
             "app/controllers/#{file_name}_controller.rb"
    template "app/models/model_template.rb",
             "app/models/#{file_name}.rb"
    template "app/views/form_template.html.erb",
             "app/views/#{file_name}/_form.html.erb"
```

```
    template "app/views/view_template.html.erb",
            "app/views/#{file_name}/_view.html.erb"
    readme "POST_GENERATION_REMINDER"
  end
end
```

Rails ships with two classes from which you can extend your generators: Rails::Generator::Base and Rails::Generator::NamedBase. NamedBase is an extension of the bare-bones Base generator, providing a lot of helpful functionality for dealing with a single named argument on the command line (for example, the name of a controller or model you want to create). Unless you're doing something *extremely* simple with generators, you probably want to use NamedBase.

Defining a Manifest

A generator's primary job is to create a Manifest, which Rails expects to be accessible via a method called manifest(). The record() method provides an easy way to create a new manifest, which it yields (as the variable m in this case) to the block it is called with. The manifest's job is to hold the information about what a generator should do. This includes actions such as copying files, creating directories, and checking for naming collisions. When you make a generator, you write a list of actions into a manifest that will then be executed by the rails generate command. Because the manifest doesn't actually *do* the requested actions, Rails can do helpful things by using them as the list of files to remove via the rails destroy command.

Our manifest for Tumblepost is pretty simple. First it checks, using the class_name() method of class NamedBase, to make sure that the requested class name isn't yet taken by Ruby or Rails. This prevents you from doing something like this:

chad> **rails generate tumblepost File**

A *File* Post type in a Tumblelog might seem like a good idea for creating a post that consists of nothing but an attached file, but naming the class File might result in some unexpected behavior since it overlaps with Ruby's core File class. class_name will help you catch oddities like that before they occur.

Next in the manifest, we have two calls to template(). Each tells the generator to use the first argument as a template from which to generate the second argument. By convention, your template files should live in a directory called templates, while the generated files will be placed in the relative path from the root of your application's directory. Here, we use NamedBase's file_name() method to generate the properly inflected version of the generated object's name for a filename. Because we've used the `template()` method, the source file will be run through ERb before being written to the destination. This allows us to programmatically construct the contents of the generated files. For example, the beginning of our `controller_template.rb` might look like this:

```
class <%= class_name %>Controller < TumblepostsController
  def new
    @thing = <%= class_name %>.new
  end
end
```

If we had instead used NamedBase's `file()` method, the generator would have done a simple copy from the source to the destination. `file()` and `template()` both support options for setting file permissions on the generated files as well as autocreating the generated file's *shebang* line (the magic first line of a UNIX shell script, which tells the operating system which program to execute the script with). So, for a script that is meant to be executable, you might do something like this:

```
m.file "bin/source_script",
       "scripts/generated_script",
        :chmod => 0755,
        :shebang => '/some/weird/path/to/ruby'
```

This would set the script's permissions to be readable and executable by everyone and would set its first line to look like this:

```
#!/some/weird/path/to/ruby
```

In addition to these options, the `template()` method can accept a hash of local *assigns*, just like regular Action View ERb templates. So, for example, the following binds the local variable `name_for_class` to the value `"HelloWorld"` for use within the template file:

```
m.template "source_file.rb",
           "destination_file.rb",
            :assigns => {:name_for_class => "HelloWorld"}
```

Since templates are evaluated by ERb, we could run into problems if our source files are ERb templates that have dynamic snippets to be called at runtime by our application. For example, the inclusion of `<%= flash[:notice] %>` in a source .erb file would cause the generator to substitute the value in `flash[:notice]` while it generates the destination files, which is obviously not what we want. To prevent that from happening, .erb templates can escape these tags by using two percent signs, such as `<%%= flash[:notice] %>`. These tags will be replaced by their single percent-sign equivalents in the generated .erb files.

Finishing our walk through the manifest, we see a call to readme(). The readme() method allows generator creators to specify one or more text files to be displayed during code generation. If, for example, there are postgeneration steps that should be taken manually to create a post in the Tumblelog of the new type, we could display a message (stored in templates/POST_GENERATION_REMINDER) that would be displayed at the end of our generator's run.

Putting Generators to Work

Now that we have our generator set up, we can call it from our application's root directory. If we wanted to create a new Post type that would allow us to upload sound files, we could generate the structure for that type with the following:

```
chad> rails generate tumblepost SoundClip
      create  app/controllers/sound_clip_controller.rb
      create  app/models/sound_clip.rb
      create  app/views/sound_clip
      create  app/views/sound_clip/_form.rhtml
      create  app/views/sound_clip/_view.rhtml
      readme  POST_GENERATION_REMINDER
Don't forget to customize the auto-generated views!
```

Code generation is a contentious topic. If a code generator is buggy, it will propagate bugs in such a way that they are hard to fix when they're discovered. You may think you've fixed a bug to find that you have fixed only one of many occurrences of the bug. There is a fine line between when it's the right choice to use a code generator and when the same thing could be accomplished more cleanly with runtime framework code.

What if your generator needs to create database tables? Rails generators support the creation of Active Record migrations. If you use the migration_template() method, the generator is smart enough to find the last migration number available and to name the new file appropriately. The call looks like this:

```
m.migration_template "db/migrations/migration_template.rb", "db/migrate"
```

Unlike template(), with migration_template() you don't specify the full destination file's path in the second parameter. You specify only the destination directory, and migration_template() will create the filename for you.

Also See

Try running the following command from your shell:

```
gem search -r generator
```

You'll see a listing of many Rails generators that have been created and deployed as gems. Not only is this a great source of examples from which to learn more about how to implement your own generators, but you may even find that the generator you thought you needed to create already exists in some shape or form. Install a few and play around with them. Some great stuff has already been done for you.

Create a Mountable Application as a Rails Engine Plugin

Problem

As another recipe (Recipe 57, *Create Your Own Ruby Gem*, on page 221) in this book demonstrates, reusing Ruby code is pretty straightforward. This is nothing specific to Ruby or Rails. How to package classes and functions and distribute them for reuse is a well-understood problem.

Sometimes, though, we want to reuse more than just library code. How do we create entirely embeddable, reusable applications? How could we create full-stack Rails applications that could be mounted and deployed inside other applications?

Solution

To create mountable Rails applications, we'll use the Rails generator to create a plugin skeleton for the application and designate it as mountable. We'll then install and add that gem to our application's Gemfile and map incoming URLs to the gem in our application's route configuration.

The first step is to generate the skeleton for our mountable application. We do that with the Rails plugin generator:

```
$ rails plugin new db_viewer --mountable
  create
  create  README.rdoc
  create  Rakefile
  create  db_viewer.gemspec
  create  MIT-LICENSE
  create  .gitignore
  create  Gemfile
  create  app
  create  app/controllers/db_viewer/application_controller.rb
  create  app/helpers/db_viewer/application_helper.rb
  create  app/mailers
  create  app/models
  create  app/views/layouts/db_viewer/application.html.erb
  create  app/assets/images/db_viewer
  create  app/assets/images/db_viewer/.gitkeep
  create  config/routes.rb
```

```
create  lib/db_viewer.rb
create  lib/tasks/db_viewer_tasks.rake
create  lib/db_viewer/version.rb
create  lib/db_viewer/engine.rb
create  app/assets/stylesheets/db_viewer/application.css
create  app/assets/javascripts/db_viewer/application.js
create  script
create  script/rails
create  test/test_helper.rb
create  test/db_viewer_test.rb
append  Rakefile
create  test/integration/navigation_test.rb
vendor_app  test/dummy
run  bundle install
```

Here we've asked the Rails generator framework to create the skeleton for a plugin that will act as a mountable database table viewer. To do this, we used the rails plugin new command, passing in the name of the plugin and the extra option --mountable.

The generator has created a directory structure resembling a full Rails application. We have places to put our models, JavaScript, style sheets, controllers, views, mailers, and routes. One notable difference is the addition of the lib/db_viewer.rb file and lib/db_viewer directory. The file lib/db_viewer/engine.rb defines the Rails Engine, which is the primary configuration and entry point in a mountable Rails application:

rr2/db_viewer/lib/db_viewer/engine.rb
```
module DbViewer
  class Engine < Rails::Engine
    isolate_namespace DbViewer
  end
end
```

You'll notice the call to isolate_engine(). This method causes Rails to protect the mountable application from the classes, helpers, and routes of the parent application. Since mountable applications are meant to be reusable, it's important for their classes and methods to be isolated from the applications into which they're included. Otherwise, mountable applications would result in a clashing, unmaintainable mess of name collisions. We'll see this Engine class again when we install our mountable application.

Next, we'll write some code for the mountable application. The functionality we're after is simple. We're just going to list the tables in the default database and allow users to click the table names to see all of the columns and types of those tables. We'll start by generating a controller. To do this, we can use the rails command as if we were inside a full Rails application:

```
$ rails g controller Tables
  create  app/controllers/db_viewer/tables_controller.rb
  invoke  erb
  create    app/views/db_viewer/tables
  invoke  test_unit
  create    test/functional/db_viewer/tables_controller_test.rb
  invoke  helper
  create    app/helpers/db_viewer/tables_helper.rb
  invoke    test_unit
  create      test/unit/helpers/db_viewer/tables_helper_test.rb
  invoke  assets
  invoke    js
  create      app/assets/javascripts/db_viewer/tables.js
  invoke    css
  create      app/assets/stylesheets/db_viewer/tables.css
```

Here are the filled-in controller and views, which use standard Active Record APIs to inspect the database. First, here's the controller:

rr2/db_viewer/app/controllers/db_viewer/tables_controller.rb
```ruby
module DbViewer
  class TablesController < ApplicationController
    def index
      @tables = ActiveRecord::Base.connection.tables.sort
    end

    def show
      @table = ActiveRecord::Base.connection.columns params[:id]
    end
  end
end
```

Next, here's the view for the index() action:

rr2/db_viewer/app/views/db_viewer/tables/index.html.erb
```erb
<h1>Database Tables</h1>
<ul>
  <% @tables.each do |table| %>
    <li><%= link_to table, table_path(table) %></li>
  <% end %>
</ul>
```

Here's the view for the show() action:

rr2/db_viewer/app/views/db_viewer/tables/show.html.erb
```erb
<h1><%= params[:id] %></h1>
<ul>
<% @table.each do |column| %>
  <li>
  <strong><%= column.name %></strong>: <%= column.sql_type %>
  </li>
<% end %>
```

```
</ul>
<p>
  <%= link_to "all tables", tables_path %>
</p>
```

Now that we have a controller and views, just as we would have to do for a full application, we need to add them to the plugin's routing configuration. Here's the route file for our mountable application:

rr2/db_viewer/config/routes.rb
```
DbViewer::Engine.routes.draw do
  resources :tables
end
```

Now we're ready to install our new plugin into a Rails application! To install our plugin into a Rails application, we need to first add it to the application's Gemfile and then create a routing rule in the application's config/routes.rb. For the Gemfile change, we have two options. The first is to package and install the plugin as a gem and then reference the gem as usual. This is a good idea for production use, but it can be a hassle while developing the plugin. While we develop the plugin, we'll reference it in the host application's Gemfile like this:

rr2/engine/Gemfile
```
gem 'db_viewer', :path => "../db_viewer"
```

Here we're using the Gemfile to point to the path on disk for our plugin. This way, we can make changes to our plugin and see them in our host application by simply restarting the Rails server. This is much more convenient than having to package and install the gem every time we change something during development.

Finally, we need to tell the host application where we'd like to mount the new plugin. We do this in the host application's routing configuration like this:

rr2/engine/config/routes.rb
```
mount DbViewer::Engine => "db_viewer"
```

This tells Rails to mount the plugin under the path db_viewer. To access the TablesController in development with this routing configuration, we could access the URL http://localhost:3000/db_viewer/tables.

That's all there is to it.

Also See

Recipe 57, *Create Your Own Ruby Gem*, on page 221

Bibliography

[Bur11]   Trevor Burnham. *CoffeeScript: Accelerated JavaScript Development*. The Pragmatic Bookshelf, Raleigh, NC and Dallas, TX, 2011.

[GHJV95]   Erich Gamma, Richard Helm, Ralph Johnson, and John Vlissides. *Design Patterns: Elements of Reusable Object-Oriented Software*. Addison-Wesley, Reading, MA, 1995.

[HT00]   Andrew Hunt and David Thomas. *The Pragmatic Programmer: From Journeyman to Master*. Addison-Wesley, Reading, MA, 2000.

[Hog10]   Brian P. Hogan. *HTML5 and CSS3: Develop with Tomorrow's Standards Today*. The Pragmatic Bookshelf, Raleigh, NC and Dallas, TX, 2010.

[RTH11]   Sam Ruby, Dave Thomas, and David Heinemeier Hansson. *Agile Web Development with Rails, 4th Edition*. The Pragmatic Bookshelf, Raleigh, NC and Dallas, TX, 2011.

.

Index

Advanced Ruby and Rails

What used to be the realm of experts is fast becoming the stuff of day-to-day development. Jump to the head of the class in Ruby and Rails.

Rails 3 is a huge step forward. You can now easily extend the framework, change its behavior, and replace whole components to bend it to your will, all without messy hacks. This pioneering book is the first resource that deep dives into the new Rails 3 APIs and shows you how to use them to write better web applications and make your day-to-day work with Rails more productive.

José Valim
(184 pages) ISBN: 9781934356739. $33
http://pragprog.com/titles/jvrails

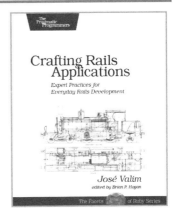

As a Ruby programmer, you already know how much fun it is. Now see how to unleash its power, digging under the surface and exploring the language's most advanced features: a collection of techniques and tricks known as *metaprogramming*. Once the domain of expert Rubyists, metaprogramming is now accessible to programmers of all levels—from beginner to expert. *Metaprogramming Ruby* explains metaprogramming concepts in a down-to-earth style and arms you with a practical toolbox that will help you write great Ruby code.

Paolo Perrotta
(296 pages) ISBN: 9781934356470. $32.95
http://pragprog.com/titles/ppmetr

What you Need to Know

Each new version of the Web brings its own gold rush. Here are your tools.

HTML5 and CSS3 are the future of web development, but you don't have to wait to start using them. Even though the specification is still in development, many modern browsers and mobile devices already support HTML5 and CSS3. This book gets you up to speed on the new HTML5 elements and CSS3 features you can use right now, and backwards compatible solutions ensure that you don't leave users of older browsers behind.

Brian P. Hogan
(280 pages) ISBN: 9781934356685. $33
http://pragprog.com/titles/bhh5

Modern web development takes more than just HTML and CSS with a little JavaScript mixed in. Clients want more responsive sites with faster interfaces that work on multiple devices, and you need the latest tools and techniques to make that happen. This book gives you more than 40 concise, tried-and-true solutions to today's web development problems, and introduces new workflows that will expand your skillset.

Brian P. Hogan, Chris Warren, Mike Weber, Chris Johnson, Aaron Godin
(344 pages) ISBN: 9781934356838. $35
http://pragprog.com/titles/wbdev

Testing is only the beginning

Start with Test Driven Development, Domain Driven Design, and Acceptance Test Driven Planning in Ruby. Then add Shoulda, Cucumber, Factory Girl, and Rcov for the ultimate in Ruby and Rails development.

Behaviour-Driven Development (BDD) gives you the best of Test Driven Development, Domain Driven Design, and Acceptance Test Driven Planning techniques, so you can create better software with self-documenting, executable tests that bring users and developers together with a common language.

Get the most out of BDD in Ruby with *The RSpec Book*, written by the lead developer of RSpec, David Chelimsky.

David Chelimsky, Dave Astels, Zach Dennis, Aslak Hellesøy, Bryan Helmkamp, Dan North
(448 pages) ISBN: 9781934356371. $38.95
http://pragprog.com/titles/achbd

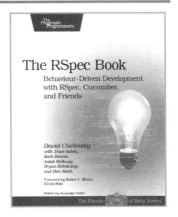

Rails Test Prescriptions is a comprehensive guide to testing Rails applications, covering Test-Driven Development from both a theoretical perspective (why to test) and from a practical perspective (how to test effectively). It covers the core Rails testing tools and procedures for Rails 2 and Rails 3, and introduces popular add-ons, including RSpec, Shoulda, Cucumber, Factory Girl, and Rcov.

Noel Rappin
(368 pages) ISBN: 9781934356647. $34.95
http://pragprog.com/titles/nrtest

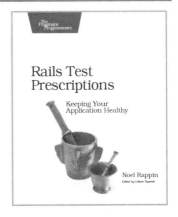

The Pragmatic Bookshelf

The Pragmatic Bookshelf features books written by developers for developers. The titles continue the well-known Pragmatic Programmer style and continue to garner awards and rave reviews. As development gets more and more difficult, the Pragmatic Programmers will be there with more titles and products to help you stay on top of your game.

Visit Us Online

This Book's Home Page
http://pragprog.com/titles/rr2
Source code from this book, errata, and other resources. Come give us feedback, too!

Register for Updates
http://pragprog.com/updates
Be notified when updates and new books become available.

Join the Community
http://pragprog.com/community
Read our weblogs, join our online discussions, participate in our mailing list, interact with our wiki, and benefit from the experience of other Pragmatic Programmers.

New and Noteworthy
http://pragprog.com/news
Check out the latest pragmatic developments, new titles and other offerings.

Save on the eBook

Save on the eBook versions of this title. Owning the paper version of this book entitles you to purchase the electronic versions at a terrific discount.

PDFs are great for carrying around on your laptop—they are hyperlinked, have color, and are fully searchable. Most titles are also available for the iPhone and iPod touch, Amazon Kindle, and other popular e-book readers.

Buy now at *http://pragprog.com/coupon*

Contact Us

Online Orders:	*http://pragprog.com/catalog*
Customer Service:	*support@pragprog.com*
International Rights:	*translations@pragprog.com*
Academic Use:	*academic@pragprog.com*
Write for Us:	*http://pragprog.com/write-for-us*
Or Call:	+1 800-699-7764